RELOCATING AUTHORITY

THE GEORGE AND SAKAYE ARATANI

NIKKEI IN THE AMERICAS SERIES

SERIES EDITOR **LANE RYO HIRABAYASHI**

This series endeavors to capture the best scholarship available illustrating the evolving nature of contemporary Japanese American culture and community. By stretching the boundaries of the field to the limit (whether at a substantive, theoretical, or comparative level) these books aspire to influence future scholarship in this area specifically, and Asian American studies, more generally.

The House on Lemon Street, Mark Howland Rawitsch

Relocating Authority: Japanese Americans Writing to Redress Mass Incarceration, Mira Shimabukuro

Starting from Loomis and Other Stories, Hiroshi Kashiwagi, edited and with an introduction by Tim Yamamura

Taken from the Paradise Isle: The Hoshida Family Story, edited by Heidi Kim and with a foreword by Franklin Odo

Relocating Authority

JAPANESE AMERICANS WRITING TO REDRESS MASS INCARCERATION

Mira Shimabukuro

UNIVERSITY PRESS OF COLORADO
Boulder

Published by University Press of Colorado
5589 Arapahoe Avenue, Suite 206C
Boulder, Colorado 80303

The University Press of Colorado is a proud member of
Association of American University Presses.

The University Press of Colorado is a cooperative publishing enterprise supported, in part, by Adams State University, Colorado State University, Fort Lewis College, Metropolitan State University of Denver, Regis University, University of Colorado, University of Northern Colorado, Utah State University, and Western State Colorado University.

∞ The paper used in this publication meets the minimum requirements of the American National Standard for Information Sciences—Permanence of Paper for Printed Library Materials. ANSI Z39.48-1992

ISBN: 978-1-60732-400-3 (paperback)
ISBN: 978-1-60732-401-0 (ebook)

Library of Congress Cataloging-in-Publication Data

Shimabukuro, Mira.
Relocating authority : Japanese Americans writing to redress mass incarceration / Mira Shimabukuro.
pages cm
Includes bibliographical references.
ISBN 978-1-60732-400-3 (paperback : alkaline paper) — ISBN 978-1-60732-401-0 (ebook)
1. Japanese Americans—Evacuation and relocation, 1942-1945—Historiography. 2. Japanese Americans—Reparations—History—20th century. 3. Authority—Social aspects—United States—History—20th century. 4. Creative writing—Social aspects—United States—History—20th century. 5. Literacy—Social aspects—United States—History—20th century. 6. Japanese Americans—Intellectual life—20th century. 7. Japanese Americans—Social conditions—20th century. 8. Community life—United States—History—20th century. 9. Social change—United States—History—20th century. 10. Social justice—United States—History—20th century. I. Title.
D769.8.A6S54 2015
940.53'1773072—dc23

2015012280

The publisher gratefully acknowledges the generous support of UCLA's Aratani Endowed Chair as well as Wallace T. Kido, Joel B. Klein, Elizabeth A. Uno, and Rosalind K. Uno toward the publication of this book.

Cover image: Japanese Americans taking citizenship classes (public domain photograph from the Densho Digital Repository).

CONTENTS

FOREWORD: VALORIZING THE VERNACULAR

Putting Everyday People's Writing in the Camps Front and Center

Why consider the vernacular? In *Relocating Authority* Mira Shimabukuro asserts that ordinary Japanese Americans wrote critically about the American-style concentration camps where they were imprisoned during World War II. The larger significance of her book, however, goes well beyond the substantive topics that she covers in proving her thesis. It lies in demonstrating that the tools that allow this re-reading must often be constructed *sui generis* and only after one has moved beyond conventional assumptions.

We can more fully appreciate *Relocating Authority* after noting that the lion's share of scholarly research on mass removal and the subsequent incarceration of Japanese Americans was generated by persons ensconced in the very agencies responsible for planning, constructing, and then managing the camps. As a result, many of the so-called standard accounts of the War Relocation Authority—and the US Department of Justice—camps are based on "official" tallies and documents. First and foremost are the WRA's own records, as well as those generated by the US Army and its branches, such as the Wartime Civil Control Administration, which coordinated the initial roundup and removal of Japanese Americans. Still other institutional projects—such as the Japanese American Evacuation and Resettlement Study at the University of California, Berkeley, and the BIA's Bureau of Sociological

Research at Poston, both of which collected massive amounts of data—have been tapped. More recently, scholars have utilized declassified DOJ files, the ultimate federal records. These official sources have been deeply mined and are the primary basis for a sustained historiography that emerged during the war and continues today. This is a blessing of sorts—but also a curse. These sources are useful because the government invested copious funds to collect, analyze, and publish demographic and statistical information on the incarcerated. But as Pierre Bourdieu, among others, has pointed out, data collected under the auspices of "colonial science" can be subtly marred by a host of deleterious assumptions and biases if deployed without the proper context.

Such has certainly been the fate of those trying to study popular resistance in the camps. The mainstream interpretation has been that the bulk of Japanese Americans cooperated or stoically put up with that which "could not be helped," and resistance was minimal and came only from Quixotic individuals such as Gordon Hirabayashi, rabid Issei and Kibei who were ardent Axis nationalists, and unpatriotic draft resisters who were unwilling to defend their country. Significantly, these negative characterizations of resistance were embraced by the wartime iteration of the Japanese American Citizens League, the second-generation Nisei organization. (That the JACL's national leadership went into hyper-patriotic mode, to assure itself and others of the Nisei's true-blue Americanism, generated bad feelings in the 1940s, and many in the ethnic community haven't forgotten or fully forgiven the JACL, even today.)

So what has changed?

For one, the Redress movement of the 1970s and 1980s undermined the WRA's and JACL's stereotypical image of quiet, loyal Japanese Americans, who, for the most part, cooperated with the government. The community's effort to garner an official apology, as well as a token monetary payment for rights violated and injuries sustained, from the federal government resulted in a new climate where ordinary people could openly testify about what had happened to them and their families, neighbors, and ethnic communities, many of which were broken economically and demographically by mass removal and postwar dispersal.

The other recent development has to do with the rise of the Internet and the many possibilities of digitized information. Anyone who has perused WRA files in the National Archives or the massive JERS files at the University of California, Berkeley, appreciates how much time and effort that process once entailed. Those who went through this routine will remember the steps: one had to request the material through the use of "finder's guides," submit the relevant call numbers and pull slips, and then wait for hours, or perhaps a day or more, for the material to be retrieved and brought to a special reading room. At Cal, you had to check in your bag and possessions and could only take notes with a pencil and paper—and, a bit later, a laptop. Copies of the original material could be requested, but they were expensive, had to be made by special order, and often took two or three weeks to be mailed. Now more and more of these materials are available online. Experts, professors, students, community-based researchers, and members of the public have access to these online resources, such as the JERS collection, "24-7," as they say, and this easy access allows more people to see these materials than ever before.

As more of these resources are digitized, the Internet will further expand and democratize access to information about the camps and their impact. The Densho project, in Seattle, provides an excellent example of this recent trend. Originally specializing in videotaped oral histories—primarily of second-generation Nisei respondents—Densho branched out and started digitizing thousands of documents from the 1940s, including letters, diaries, newspapers, photographs, and related primary source materials. The Japanese American National Museum has done this as well. New initiatives along these same lines also hold great promise, including a recent project, coordinated at California State University, Dominguez Hills, that aspires to put key archival holdings of a number of CSU campuses online. What stands out about the holdings of the CSU libraries that I've seen are the many personal documents and memorabilia by and about ordinary men and women who, with foresight and vision, donated their papers to their local university libraries. Once digitized, material that might have taken months, if not years, to assess, plus money/time/travel in the pre-Internet age, has become readily available online, and anyone with Internet access has the ability to download documents and print them out. This accessibility has greatly enhanced our ability to see and mine personal documents, and I fully expect that the expanded access to data sets of all kinds will likewise transform our interpretations of the camps, what happened in the camps, and how living through Executive Order 9066 transformed the individuals, families, networks, and communities subject to incarceration.

Note that my claims here are not to argue that the official data about mass removal and the incarceration are useless. Accounts based on such data have certain strengths as well as limitations, as do any data sets that one chooses to utilize, but it is important to remember that the official data were generated by the jailors and thus represent only one perspective. These everyday vernacular accounts, generated by ordinary men and women, present a different perspective and are invaluable resources that students, scholars, and interested community members can peruse to gain a more comprehensive view of what happened to more than 120,000 persons of Japanese ancestry during the 1940s and, more importantly, how it felt to go through this particular experience as a Japanese American.

Beyond this, Mira Shimabukuro shows us that to effectively read the vernacular—especially since it was produced during times of stress and travail—we need to question "official" accounts and the corresponding interpretations, terms, and conditions based on those accounts. To cite one example, the standard literature covers and to some extent highlights Japanese words and phrases such as *gaman* and *shikata-ga-nai*. Here, stoically putting up with adversity and a fatalistic stance toward that which cannot be helped are referenced as if Japanese values alone are enough to account fully for the supposed passivity that enabled Japanese Americans to endure the injustices and indignities of the wartime incarceration. To read past—or, perhaps, *beyond*—these received notions we need to approach vernacular expression with new kinds of theoretical tools. Without new conceptual tools, we will not be able to fully render the implications of everyday popular resistance. So, in effect, what Mira Shimabukuro presents in *Relocating Authority* is a whole new *episteme*—that is, new perspectives and new sets of tools—for reading resistance in vernacular accounts. In this sense, Shimabukuro's narrative on "writing to gaman," as mysterious as that phrase might sound at first, is one of the carefully wrought tools she offers us.

In sum, I believe that anyone interested in the use of the vernacular, broadly speaking, to generate new kinds of critical cultural analysis will find *Relocating Authority* to be an invaluable resource.

Lane Ryo Hirabayashi
George and Sakaye Aratani Professor in Japanese American Incarceration, Redress, and Community, Asian American Studies, University of California, Los Angeles

ACKNOWLEDGMENTS

Most of us in writing studies take as a given that writing is an inherently social, collective act. From my perspective, it begins with the collective efforts of an entire community authorizing a given writer to "break into print."

For me personally that community begins with my father, Robert Sadamu Shimabukuro, who was my first and most personal Writing-to-Redress teacher. In addition, my mother, Cathie DeWeese-Parkinson, heavily sponsored a number of literacy activities that brought this study into being. And throughout my life, both of my stepparents, Alice Ito and Lynn DeWeese-Parkinson, have served as additional support and inspiration through their very different approaches to social change and their very similar commitments to social justice.

Beyond my parents, I have to thank the following friends, family, teachers, and *compas* who both directly and indirectly have helped me "relocate authority" and come to public voice: Kendal, J. C., and Adisa; Vero, Chiloe, and Yume; Wil and Kathleen Au; Priscilla Welles; the entire Shimabukuro *'ohana*; the DeWeeses; Kendra Parkinson; Linda Christensen, Bill Bigelow, Betsy Shally-Jensen, Kimiko Hahn, Eugene Fujimoto, Gary Wessels-Galbreath, Ratna Roy, Gail Tremblay, Anne Fischel, Angela Gilliam, Colleen McElroy, and Shawn Wong; Ken Matsudaira, Jeanie Hirokane, Tomoko Burke Yokooji, the Women of Color Coalition at The Evergreen State College and Asian Americans In Alliance, the Young Women's Editorial Collective at CALYX Press, Haunani-Kay Trask, Alan Lau, Mayumi Tsutakawa, Wadiyah Nelson, Melissa Ponder, the Kumasakas, Mariellen Cardella, Rogelio Rigor, Allison Green, Arline Garcia, Wendy Swyt, Lonny Kaneko, Susan Landgraf, Angi Caster, Matt Schwisow, Tarisa Matsumoto-Maxfield, Ken and Isabel Garcia-Gonzales, Jody Sokolower, Sharon Doubiago, and Lyle Daggett; Corey Mead, Keita and Mayumi Takeyama, Kate Viera, Matthew Pearson, Nga-Wing Anjela Wong, Minerva Chavez, Eric Pritchard, Rasha Diab, Rhea Lathan, Heidi Hallman, the *Rethinking Schools* editorial board, the CCCC Asian/Asian American Caucus, including LuMing Mao, Terese Guinsatao Monberg, Haivan Haong, Gail Okura, Asao Inoue, Bo Wang, and Amy Wan; David Fleming, Marty Nystrand, Brad Hughes, Melissa Tedrowe, Michael Olneck, James Paul Gee, Mike Bernard-Donals, Stacey Lee, Michael and Rima Apple, Meiko Shimura, Mark Ellis, Pablo and Rosie Jasis, Sarah Wilhelm, Jesse Hagopian, Kory and Therese Kumasaka; the entire staff, faculty, and administration of Highline Community College (now Highline College), who generously granted me a sabbatical to finish writing this book, and my new colleagues in the School of Interdisciplinary Arts and Sciences at University of Washington Bothell, who widely model, embrace, and encourage an ethos of scholarship committed to social justice.

Special thanks is owed to the community and academic scholars who directly sponsored my work. Over the course of my research, the support, scholarship, and time offered to me by Arthur Hansen, Thomas Fujita-Rony, Susan Ginoza Fukushima, Frank Abe, Frank Chin, Frank Emi, Tom Ikeda, and Aiko Herzig-Yoshinaga were immeasurable. In addition, I'm forever indebted to the cochairs of my dissertation committee, upon which this book is based, Morris Young and Deborah Brandt.

Beyond everyone above, let me extend much gratitude to my editor, Michael Spooner, who encouraged me to finish the manuscript long before he officially took on the project. In addition, a deep thank you to Nikkei in the Americas Series Editor Lane Ryo Hirabayashi, whose work I have long admired. It is an honor to have had this work encouraged and authorized by both of you.

Finally, *mil, mil, mil gracias* to the home team: to my son, Mako, whose presence reminds me each and every day that redress matters, not just for the past but for the future, and to my partner-in-crime, Wayne Wah Kwai Au. This book, as everything: *circles moving outward in an open lake . . .*

NOTE ON USAGE AND FORMATTING

Throughout this text, many words of Japanese origin that typically require the use of italics have been employed in Roman type. Following Asian American literary scholar Stephen Sumida (1991), I would argue that "these terms are . . . integral to the lexicon of the whole American language of the peoples whose cultures are my subjects" (xxiii). For this reason, there is nothing "foreign" about words like *gaman* or *shikataganai* to many US-based Nikkei communities. However, given the potential diverse readership of this study, I follow Sumida's lead by "generally italiciz[ing]" such terms when they are first used in the text but presume that "[o]nce incorporated," they are "no longer foreign to the discussion," meaning that they should not be set off by any further marks of difference (xxiii).

In addition to the employed words of Japanese origin, I have also used terms of Spanish and Hawaiian origin. In most places within this text, Spanish is employed during narratives that relate personal memories from my childhood. During this time of my life, Spanish came to me as a "foreign" language; as such, italics are employed for these terms, even though the realities of growing up in multicultural environments—as I and many others have—mean multiple terms from multiple languages often feel "native" to our ears and tongue. For Hawaiian words and terms, I follow a similar pattern to the one employed for Japanese terms, as the ones used in this text are ones with which I grew up as a child (e.g., *hapa haole*). But I also follow both Morris Young (2004) and Sumida with regard to spelling such terms. As both scholars note, among other standardized conventions, "[n]ecessary to the spelling of Hawaiian words [is] the *'okina*, or glottal stop, which appears thus as a single inverted comma (')" seen in such terms as *Hawai'i*. However, "[w]hen Hawaiian words are Anglicized, the [okina is] generally not used," as "in the word 'Hawaiian,' or in the possessive, 'Hawaii's,' both derived in English from 'Hawai'i' " (Sumida 1991, xxiii).

In addition, given that my focus is on specific uses of writing, I wanted to keep most of the original spellings, capitalizations, and notations incarceree writers had used. As such, in block quotations from original documents, both within the main body of the text and in the appendices, these copyediting "mistakes" have been left intact without the more common [*sic*] notation. However, if the quote is indirect or the original document had a [*sic*] in its text, then I kept whatever [*sic*] marking was used in the quotation. Finally, this text relies on unconventional spacing employed for visual, poetic effect. As such, readers should assume that any and all spacing—such as double-tab indentations—is completely intentional on my part.

References

Sumida, Stephen H. 1991. *And the View from the Shore: Literary Traditions of Hawai'i*. Seattle: University of Washington Press.

Young, Morris. 2004. Minor Re/Visions: Asian American Literacy Narratives as a Rhetoric of Citizenship. Carbondale: Southern Illinois University Press.

RELOCATING AUTHORITY

1
WRITING-TO-REDRESS
Attending to Nikkei Literacies of Survivance

Much of the past is, of course, irrevocably silenced: gestures, conversations, and original manuscripts can never be recaptured. Silence and silencing still greet us in every library, every archive, every text, every newscast—at every turn . . . Still, while most of the female and male tradition has been regrettably lost, enormous amounts of material survive.

—*Glenn (2004)*

As we suspected, contrary to the stereotype, Chinese and Japanese immigrants were a literate people from literate civilizations whose presses, theaters, opera houses, and artistic enterprises rose as quickly as their social and political institutions. They are not few. They are not gone. They are not stupid. They were only waiting to be asked.

—*Chan (1991)*

[T]he more he questioned her, the more he was her accuser and murderer. The more he killed her, the deeper her silence became. What the Grand

DOI: 10.5876/9781607324010.c001

> Inquisitor has never learned is that the avenues of speech are the avenues of silence. To hear my mother, to attend to her speech, to attend the sound of stone, he must first become silent. Only when he enters her abandonment, will he be released from his own.
>
> —*Kogawa (1981)*

Two years into my PhD program, a bunch of us TAs are sitting around our six crammed-in desks in the windowless office we share talking about dissertation ideas. When I say I've been thinking about the political writing in the World War II incarceration camps, about the loud and quiet ways literacy helped Japanese Americans perform rhetorical activity, Adam asks if I've read *Unspoken*, Cheryl Glenn's (2004) new book on the "rhetoric of silence." I'm intrigued, having read Glenn's (1997) *Rhetoric Retold* and her efforts to "regender" the rhetorical tradition. But I also know that work has now been done in Asian American studies on the issue of silence for several years, as poets, artists, activists, and scholars have long complicated quiet, orientalist model minority–type representations of people racialized as Asian.[1] The litany of titles speak, yell even: *Breaking Silence, Breaking the Silence, Shedding Silence, YELL-oh Girls!, Aiiieeeee!, The Big Aiiieeeee!, Tell This Silence.*[2] I ask Adam if Glenn cites *Articulate Silences* by King-Kok Cheung (1993), one of those lit theorists I read back in the day, not for any class or paper but because I was trying to understand patterns I saw in my life. A highly influential Asian American feminist literary critic, Cheung is the kind of author I would expect to see in a feminist rhetorician's account of silence's rhetorical possibilities. Adam hands me a library copy off of his shelf. I search the index. I flip through the text. No Cheung. No Asians. No Asian Americans. A rhetoric of silence.

> From Unit 5
> *Japanese American Internment and the Problem of Cultural Identity: Testimony of the Interned*
> Writing Analytically
> 2. Write a paper in which you discuss the options open to people who suffer injustice because of their membership in a particular group . . . You should also consider which Nikkei responses (if any) might be useful to other oppressed groups. Alternative: Write a dialogue between X and Y concerning what people ought to do in response to an injustice . . . Write

yourself into the dialogue if you wish.
(Bizzell and Herzberg 1996, 748)

This absence. This presence. Perhaps I shouldn't be surprised by Glenn's negligence. It's just that, as Elaine Richardson so perfectly recalled Fannie Lou Hamer, I'm "sick and tired of being sick and tired" (Richardson 2003, ch. 1). I didn't enter the PhD program with plans to focus on Asian American writing, didn't enter with great concern that the first voice I heard wasn't "my own." Tired of the navel-gazing expected of so many US-trained poets, I wanted the right to reach beyond myself, wanted to recognize myself in others, wanted to come back to writing through the ways I had come in—through that felt identification with the lives of other people. Not lives of the *Other*, just lives beyond my own skin: *El otro soy yo, el otro soy yo* . . . rhetorics of solidarity integral to the political life in which I had been raised, I wanted them back . . . *el pueblo unido*, panethnicity, common ground, *International Examiner*, coalition politics, *internacionalismo* . . .

But I had thought, perhaps too naively, that by now, by the twenty-first century, by the time I entered the doctoral program in composition and rhetoric, the voices I would hear, at the very least, would *include* my own. I assumed, by now, in this day and age, when Asian Americans have supposedly made it, supposedly surpassed any gap that exists, supposedly need no affirmative action to ensure that their bodily and historical presence is accounted for in all institutions of higher education, that the voices, the rhetorics, the literacies, and the composition struggles of "my" people (read: *our* people) would be attended to, would not be relegated to independent study, final seminar papers, individually tailored reading lists for prelims—in short, restricted roads of individual inquiry, special interest topics, segregated study.

Fill in the gap.

This is ~~a text about~~ literacy practice.

This is ~~a text about~~ Japanese American writing.

This is ~~a text about~~ symbolic-meaning making and exchange.

This is ~~a text about~~ yearning for more than what we have now.

This is ~~a text about~~ standpoint.

This is ~~a text about~~ struggle.

This is ~~a text about~~ history.

And this is consciously performative,
strategically essential,
romantically engaged,
and strongly objective.[3]

Mira Chieko Shimabukuro
Dissertation Proposal
Relocating Authority: Japanese Americans Writing to Redress Mass Incarceration

> In spring 1942, a few months after the United States officially joined World War II, the US government rounded up 110,000 of its residents of Japanese ancestry—two-thirds of them legal citizens—and sent them to what has been called, at different times by different people, internment, concentration, or incarceration camps. These incarcerated immigrants and their US-born children have often been culturally and politically constructed as the "Quiet Americans" (Hosokawa 1969), implicitly and explicitly suggesting that they not only passively consented to the institutionalized racism embodied by the camps but fully succumbed to the cultural oppression brought about by the racist hysteria during the so-called good war. However, many incarcerated Nikkei (those of Japanese heritage) resisted the racist logic of internment and often did so in writing. Even as the US government's War Relocation Authority (WRA) controlled the location of Nikkei bodies, the composition of diaries, poetry, short fiction, petitions, letters, manifestos, and political demands all served as means by which Nikkei writers sought to redress the circumstances of camp and regain the authority to determine the course of their lives. As one body of rhetoric yet to be analyzed in comp/rhet or literacy studies, such camp-generated writing will serve as the focus for this dissertation.

I'm not exactly sure why, within the field of composition and rhetoric, our understanding of the uses of writing by US-based writers racially constructed as Asian has been so under-theorized. Even as some Asian American compositionists began to publicly reflect on their personal teaching and literacy histories (Chiang 1998, Lu 1987, Okawa 1998), for the most part, Catherine Prendergast (1998, 51) was correct when she noted in the late 1990s that "Asian-Americans don't exist in composition studies." Nor did we seem to exist in "the rhetorical tradition" (Bizzell and Herzberg 2001), "the legacies of literacy" (Graff 1987a), or "the nineteenth-century origins of our times" (Graff 1987b) despite the fact that people of Asian ancestry have been composing English-language texts in what is now called the United States since at least 1878, when Chinese merchants petitioned the state of California for the establishment of schools their children would be allowed to attend (Odo 2002, 33). As Jamie Candeleria Greene (1994) pointed out, these kinds of Anglocentric biases in and "misperspectives" of US literacy distort perceptions that serve as foundations for current and future policies, practices, and theories related to the teaching and history of writing.

Fortunately, over the past ten or so years, a few comp/rhet scholars have started to account for the "ways with words" (Heath 1983) generated within and out of Asian American communities by examining Asian American writing and rhetoric, as well as their sociocultural histories and contexts, through the lenses of specific genres, contrastive cultural rhetorics, and community-based literacy practices (Mao 2006; Duffy 2007; Young 2004). Subsequent dissertations have continued in this vein, using ethnography, oral history, close readings of literature composition studies, and other cultural texts to highlight the "solidarity" rhetoric of Asian American student activists (Hoang 2004), the multimodal cultural rhetorics of a Filipino American community organization (Monberg 2002), Asian American literary performances of literacy (Hiramine 2004) and "hyperliteracy" (Hasegawa 2004), and subject positions available to Asian American composition teachers (Yoon 2003). And in 2008, LuMing Mao and Morris Young brought us the first anthology on Asian American rhetoric, subsequently honored with an honorable mention for the MLA 2009 Mina P. Shaughnessy Prize. The first anthology to showcase the multiple ways that "Asian Americans use language to perform discursive acts and . . . develop persuasive and other rhetorical strategies to create knowledge and to effect social, political and cultural transformations," *Representations: Doing Asian American Rhetoric* also "illuminat[ed] . . . those conflicting, ambivalent moments . . . central to Asian American discursive experiences" (Mao and Young 2008, 3).

All of the work described above attends to the ways race/racism, ever-evolving cultural concepts, and material historical processes shape the contemporary rhetorical choices US-based Asians have made with their writing. But despite the fact that both academic and independent scholars working in Asian American communities have long argued that early Asian American history (pre-1965) is rife with written activity,[4] as a field we still have little theoretical understanding of the literacy practices and/or rhetorical interventions of US-based Asians during this period. This historical gap is important to address for a couple of reasons, the least of which is simply a matter of historical accuracy. But the other reason has to do more with a tenacious stereotype—that of the "perpetual foreigner."

Aside from the model minority, this stereotype has probably been the most redressed representation in the history of pan-ethnic Asian American consciousness. This redressing took place, for example, in the capitalized proclamation "WE ARE NOT NEW HERE," serving as the kickoff to the first section of *Aiiieeeee!*, the first anthology of pan-ethnic Asian American literature (Chin et al. 1974). With this proclamation, the editors explicitly and implicitly called attention to the fact that some of our communities (mainly Chinese, Japanese, and Filipino but also some Korean) have been in the United States for over a hundred years and are four, five, six generations deep, more than many white families. In terms of literacy and rhetoric, this kind of historical depth means, whether we know it or not, our contemporary discursive experiences reflect the century-long legacies of sugar cane plantations, Gold Mountain, Chinese-built American railroads, Japanese-cultivated farmlands, Pinoy (Filipino) labor struggles, anti-Asian exclusion acts, the prisons of Angel Island and World War II "internment" camps, Americanization initiatives between the two world wars, and the rise of urban Chinatowns and Little Tokyos. Amidst these legacies, depending on the complex trajectories our lives have taken, our heritage language might come to us as foreign—that is, our Spanish might be better than our Cantonese or we might be more naturally versed in African American "talkin and testifyin" than the compressed images of Japanese haiku. But no matter how long "our" people have been in the United States, many of us will be asked, at one time or another, "where are you from?," meaning not what state, what city, what 'hood, but what *country*. In other words, despite the fact that people of Asian ancestry have taken part in this nation-state since before it even was a nation-state,[5] many folks of Asian ancestry continue to be complimented on the use of their own first language (English) or asked how long they've been in their country of birth (the United States).

This perpetual state of foreignness in which US-based Asians often find themselves can even be detected in comp/rhet where, aside from the studies mentioned earlier, Asians have tended to attain visible subjectivity only as international or ESL/ELL students. While the dynamically complex and heterogeneous, transnational, translingual (Lu and Horner 2013), code-switching, and code-meshing (Young 2007) realities of international and/or immigrant students are vital for all composition teachers to understand, if people racialized as Asian are only understood through the prism of national/cultural difference, we risk perpetuating the myth that Asian/American experience is a new phenomenon.

Which is why writing about early Asian American discursive practices can be a performance of Asian American rhetoric itself, a way to "bring about material and symbolic consequences" (Mao and Young 2008, 3). In order to do so, though, I have had to rely heavily on the interdisciplinary efforts of those working in Asian American studies, which, like comp/rhet, is a relatively young discipline born out of the civil rights and liberation struggles of the 1960s and 1970s. The recovery of early Asian American writing began in the 1970s when Frank Chin, Jeffrey Paul Chan, Lawson Fusao Inada, and Shawn Wong, four writers and the soon-to-be editors of *Aiiieeeee!* (Chin et al. 1974), began searching for literary ancestors who might prove to be part of a hidden tradition of Asian Americans writing about being Asian American (Partridge 2004). The poetry and prose that they found convinced them, as well as scholars in the newly emerging field of Asian American studies, that "Asian Americans have been writing seriously since the nineteenth century" (Chin et al. 1974, xxi). Literary recovery work since this initial declaration has only bolstered their claim as more and more English- and Asian-language prose and poetry authored by US-based Asians have been retrieved from the "spectre of lost history" (Chang 1996, xiv) to be anthologized, summarized, and analyzed by both academic and independent scholars (Chang 1996; Lawrence and Cheung 2005; Yogi 1997; Chan et al. 1991).

The clustered concept of "Asian American," though, is relatively recent, coined during the pan-ethnic Asian American movement beginning in the late 1960s as part of the mass social movements of the time (Espiritu 1992). As such, conceiving of Asian American writing composed before that movement as a composite body of work means one must imagine a rhetorically collected and conceived community (Anderson 1991) of writers that did not necessarily imagine themselves as belonging to that particular community as they put their words onto the page. Instead, even as pan-ethnic Asian American writers/rhetoricians may have dealt with similar topoi of anti-"yellow" racism, bicultural tensions/celebrations, embraced/rejected orientalism, or cultural/political "rhetorics of citizenship," they were just as often responding to ethnic-specific cultural, political, and historical exigencies. And as far as the continental Nikkei community is concerned, there has been no greater ethnic-specific exigency than their mass incarceration during World War II.

My choice of language here, *mass incarceration*, over the more popularized term of *internment* is twofold. As a number of camp scholars have pointed out, a wide variety of euphemisms have been used throughout history to mask the reality of Nikkei imprisonment during World War II. While terms like *evacuation* and *relocation* are particularly problematic for their harmless tone, the inaccuracy of the word *internment* significantly hampers our understanding of the injustice. As Densho explains, "The commonly used term 'internment' is misleading when describing the concentration camps that held 120,000 people of Japanese descent during the war. 'Internment' refers to the legally permissible detention of enemy aliens in [a] time of war. . . . [Y]et two-thirds of the Japanese Americans incarcerated were U.S. citizens." Tetsuden Kashima and others have pointed out that, technically, these "imprisonment centers" were *concentration camps*, or "barbed wire enclosure[s] where people are interned or incarcerated under armed guard" (8), and many activists over the years have taken this framing up, simultaneously arguing that the Nazi-run camps should be referred to as *slave* or *death camps*. But to avoid initial confusion, I have followed both Densho and Kashima's lead here and chosen *incarceration camps* to refer to the imprisonment centers that held both immigrant Japanese nationals ("enemy aliens") and their US-born descendants (US citizens).

Initially, I chose *mass incarceration* to emphasize the ways in which the community was rounded up *en masse*. That is, all persons of Japanese ancestry who lived on the West Coast in 1942 were subject to this experience. It was not, even on the surface or for public show, the imprisonment of "crime"-committing individuals. But conversations about terminology are, of course, important, and they are ongoing. Had my first writing of the book taken place alongside the rise of the Black Lives Matter movement, current discussions of the school-to-prison pipeline, growing awareness of the Immigration and Customs Enforcement (ICE) "family detention centers" (Ina 2015), and the mainstream appeal of Michelle Alexander's (2011) *The New Jim Crow: Mass Incarceration in the Age of Colorblindness*, I might have chosen a different term or addressed the connection between Nikkei and African American and Latino experiences of incarceration more head-on throughout my entire manuscript. But I am also swayed by more recent arguments that *mass incarceration* masks both the severity of prison conditions and the "triply selective" manner in which race, class, and place shape who is more likely to be locked up under the contemporary carceral state (Wacquant 2010; Cooper 2011; Forman 2012; Gottschalk 2015). In this way, I believe Loïc Wacquant's term *hyper-incarceration* better addresses the *targeted intensity* of current imprisonment practices in black and brown communities, while the term *mass incarceration* better addresses the World War II imprisonment of Nikkei persons *en masse*.[6]

Regardless, my project is not a comparative study on the rhetorics of terminology and euphemisms—though this would indeed make an excellent focus for another book. Instead, the focus of this book is on how Nikkei incarcerees *redressed* the conditions of their imprisonment and how they used literacy to do so.

To understand Nikkei rhetorical uses of literacy, however, one needs to begin before the period of mass incarceration. More than one social historian of Japanese American communities have reminded their audiences that starting with camp means starting with victimhood, eliding a rich and complex prewar history where Issei (first or immigrant generation) forefathers and foremothers engaged in both domestic and transnational struggles to carve out material, cultural, and ideological space to improve both their lives and those of their children (Ichioka 1988; Azuma 2005). Literacy and rhetoric played a large role in such struggles, as historians such as Yuji Ichioka (1988), David Yoo (2000), and Eiichiro Azuma (2005) all reference an active Nikkei vernacular press dating back to at least the 1880s, when an ideologically heterogeneous collection of both Japanese-language and bilingual newspapers began to circulate. In addition, Nisei literary writers found a public stage in *Current Life*, a San Franscisco–based magazine published and edited by writer James Omura, who dedicated himself to showcasing Nisei literary writing in English (Chin 1991). Meanwhile, haiku and senryu writing clubs also developed in at least California and Washington, where Issei and Nisei writers met regularly to write, read, and workshop their poems and then vote on the evening's best (De Cristoforo 1997a; J. Kobayashi 2005; Honda 1989; Yamada, Yasutake, and Yasutake 2002). These vibrant glimpses of bilingual rhetorics left by both literary and social historians of Asian and Japanese America suggest that Nikkei communities up and down the West Coast were teeming with the written word.

Regardless of this prewar history, interdisciplinary studies of Nikkei experiences during World War II have dominated the landscape of Japanese American history and Asian American studies, with over a thousand books published on the subject (Hayashi 2004, xiv). Despite this abundance of material, relatively few scholars have focused their analyses on the ways written words were broadly used by incarcerees in camp, even though "writing flourished" within this key period and location of Japanese American history (Chin et al. 1974, xxi). While independent writer-scholars Chin et al. (1974, xxliii) provided us with initial assertions that uniquely Japanese American symbolic structures were codified in such print genres as "camp newspapers, literary magazines, diaries and journals" by writers who would later help make up the literary canon of Asian America, their only close reading and/or analysis of camp-generated texts is in their second book, where Chin (1991) contrasts the written perspective of the Heart Mountain Fair Play Committee (FPC) with that of the Japanese American Citizens League in his rhetorically polemic discussion of "real" and "fake" Asian American writing.

Other valuable work dealing with camp writing has come in the form of anthologies and memoirs. While some anthologies have collected and translated Japanese-language poetry by Issei writers (De Cristoforo 1997a; Soga et al. 1983), others have included English-language poems, letters, and diary excerpts as part of general collections of pre- and post-camp writing on the experience (Inada 2000; Harth 2001). In addition, two books—a more recently published poet's memoir and a collection of camp-era writings by a former Stanford professor—provide self-portraits of established Nikkei writers during World War II (Chang 1997; Suyemoto 2007). As helpful as all of these texts are in illuminating several subjective perspectives on incarceration, none of them offer an analysis of camp writing as forms of literacy or rhetoric.

In terms of work that involves more scholarly analysis, several literary, cultural, and historical scholars have included camp-generated texts as part of discussions of non-camp specific themes (Arakawa 2005; Schweik 1991; Yamamoto 1999; Lawrence 2005; Yoo 2000). Three studies have explored the ways incarceration impacted, shaped, and framed various types of Japanese American discourse (Suzuki 1976; Ono 1992; Lain 2005), but only one part of one of those examines writing composed behind the barbed wire of the camp. Aside from this brief discussion on the Heart Mountain draft resistance bulletins, scholarly studies dealing with nonliterary writing in camp are limited. Two studies by Louis Fiset (1997, 2001) look at the censorship of mail going in and out of the camps. Articles written by history of journalism scholars examine the level of censorship at play in camp newspapers (Mizuno 2001, 2003; Kessler 1988; Omura 1989), but as these studies argue, the Nikkei community never had complete control over these War Relocation Authority–sponsored newspapers, even though, as communication studies scholar Danny Toshio Molden (1998) argues, the papers still served as a significant rhetorical site for the shaping of "internee identity."

Other scholarly studies that focus on writing in camp examine the work of more literary writers. In their work on the well-published Nisei poet Toyo Suyemoto, Susan Schweik (1989) and John Streamas (2005) focus on cultural and historical contexts for understanding the poet's political intentions in her body of camp-written work. Two dissertations also employ discussions of cultural, historical, and political contexts to their close readings of writing in camp. The first examines literary texts written in Japanese as evidence of the maintenance of bicultural identity through the internment era (J. Kobayashi 2005) and the second employs "critical rhetorical analysis" to analyze the "ethos of trustworthiness" strategically developed by the Nikkei writers and the publisher of *TREK*, a literary magazine published and distributed out of the Topaz camp (Card 2005). Work by Schweik, Streamas, Kobayashi, and Card is extremely valuable to our sense of incarcerees as rhetorical actors, but because they focus only on those who already identified and would have been recognized as Writers, these studies do not offer a broad enough picture of the multiple ways the Nikkei community as a whole may have regularly used writing in order to redress the conditions of mass incarceration.

Over the past ten years, work on mass incarceration by comp/rhet-identified scholars in our own field of interdisciplinary affiliations has started to emerge. Hui Wu (2007) published an article in *College Composition and Communication* on "Writing and Teaching behind Barbed Wire," focusing more on the agency of the white instructor than her students, as she speculated on the political intent behind the teacher's pedagogy. More personally grounded,

Gail Okawa has published several pieces from her ongoing research project that began with looking into government records on her Hawai'i-based grandfather's World War II arrest and imprisonment (Okawa 2003, no. 269; Okawa 2008, no. 270; Okawa 2011, no. 584).

While all of this work is extremely valuable to our sense of Nikkei literacy under mass incarceration, even in Asian American studies we are still left without a clear picture or theoretical framework for how incarcerated Nikkei, as a collectively disenfranchised and mass imprisoned group, actively *used* writing on their own terms, as somewhat separate from government agents, in order to survive and/or resist the conditions in which they had forcibly been placed. Trying to determine this use, trying to trace the shape of what literacy meant to the recovery of Nikkei authority and what it still means, has not been easy. At least, not easy to explain.

Sure, there are the archives, the discourse analysis, the interviews, the oral history collections, the books upon books upon books. And like any good researcher, I have used these, as you will see in what follows. But James Paul Gee once told us grad students in a Discourse Analysis class that a good deal of good research comes down to *taste*. But how does one lay *taste* bare? Sure, there's Pierre Bourdieu's (1991) distinction and habitus and all that great class-based analysis. But what does *taste* feel like? How does Jacqueline Jones Royster "recognize an important story when [she] see[s] it" (Royster 2000, ix)? With what is she trying "to make better sense?" (Royster 2000, 9)? Aside from the library catalogs and book reviews and advisors' directives and archives' stamp of authority, what tells us *something is missing*? How do any of us know *it's more complicated than that*?

FROM LISTENING TO ATTENDANCE: STRETCHING TOWARD RELEVANCE

> A preliminary step in making sense is learning to look, listen and look again, to think well, and to speak as though knowledge is now and has always been in the making.
>
> —*Royster (2000)*

How do any of us know? Krista Ratcliffe (2005) tells us we must "rhetorically listen," must "assume a stance of openness" in the interest of "cross-cultural exchange" (1), must "listen . . . with the intent to understand" (33). And Ratcliffe does listen, does self-reflect, does carefully consider the experience of the women of color to whom she attempts to rhetorically listen in the interest of cross-cultural dialogue. However, while Ratcliffe's framework does seem to be inherently feminist, her *rhetorical listening* seems to be better suited for those with more privilege, for those who can use it to "foster *conscious* identifications with gender and whiteness in ways that may, in turn, facilitate cross-cultural communication" (Ratcliffe 2005, 2, emphasis in original). It also seems highly individualized, between one author/speaker and one reader/listener in one moment of exchange. As Terese Guinsatao Monberg recently pointed out, Ratcliffe's listening is somewhat dependent upon "women of color being audibly or visibly present" (Monberg 2008, 86). In other words, the one moment of exchange is contingent upon work being recorded and published (in print or on video or online) and/or people being in the vicinity of each other. There's no way of knowing how representative this voice being rhetorically listened to is, no way of gauging the collectivity that surrounds its articulation, the jostling sponsorship that made it possible, the particular ideologies it embraces or eschews.

When Ratcliffe reads Jeanne Wakatsuki Houston's autobiography of mass incarceration, for example, she "listens" for the "competing cultural logics of the Manzanar camp culture and the dominant white culture," which allows her to "not only question the fairness and legality" of Houston's "situations" but to "ask [her]self, once again, if and how [she] ever participate[s] in white discourses in ways that might unknowingly erase the desires and material existence of others" (Ratcliffe 2005, 40). While Ratcliffe displays an admirable self-reflectivity about the "competing . . . logics" represented in the book, what's missing is a discussion of the ways such logics are complicated by the text's own rhetorical context. Explicitly composed for a mass US audience, Houston's "autobiography" was coauthored by her white husband, James Houston, whose name appears on the cover and who has been quoted as saying that when the couple was writing, they purposely de-emphasized "the political" in lieu of "the personal" since "everyone can relate to that" (Friedson 1984, 53). As the couple purposely composed their text to be the first on incarceration with broad, mainstream appeal, their strategic move to only emphasize the personal certainly had its own rhetorical underpinnings, but it also raises questions regarding the *range* and *depth* of "cultural logics" one may be able to "hear" in Houston and Houston's text. As Traise Yamamoto (1999, 106) has argued, many Nisei autobiographers like Jeanne Houston have often been, understandably, quite "selective in their use of personal detail and guarded in their criticisms of white America" given their anticipation of "a potentially defensive and hostile white American audience." When Ratcliffe points us toward this text, we do not "hear" it amidst a chorus of other incarcerated voices; we do not see where the microphone is plugged in; we do not know who has "spoken" before.[7] We also do not know how expensive or cheap or easily found this memoir is over others, like those penned by the Issei, whose adult lives were more dramatically impacted by the imposition of camp. Houston's autobiography is only one individual expression of the "competing cultural logics" written from the perspective of one adult remembering one seven-year-old's experience of camp.

This is not to say there is nothing to learn from these reconstructed memories, or to denigrate in any way the epistemological or rhetorical potential of memory and memoir. It is not even to argue over the degree of representativeness of Houston's (and Houston's) (auto)biography. It is only to note the epistemological limitations, the embedded yet somewhat unacknowledged, individualist leanings of Ratcliffe's approach. While Ratcliffe's model of rhetorical listening certainly holds value for the classroom, it still seems predicated on an assumption that a plethora of voices that should be rhetorically listened to will have the access they need to that shared rhetorical space, that microcosm of the public sphere. As far as I can tell from the past ten years of teaching, access (both in terms of the bodies of students and teachers of color *and* of materials in multicultural-ized curriculum) continues to override the good intent behind Ratcliffe's model.

Yet, to be clear, I fully appreciate Ratcliffe's (2005, 28) desire for a deeper form of "intersubjective receptivity" in the face of mass injustice. My discussion here simply reflects a quest for a methodology to find a more relevant model. Monberg finds feminist rhetoricians of color, like Royster and Malea Powell, to be of more assistance in coming to more culturally and politically relevant models of "listening" but also observes that this trope of receptivity, as put forth by feminist historiographers of rhetoric, often conflates *what can be heard* with *what can be seen*: "[M]ost forms of listening have largely rested in seeing—seeing women at the podium, seeing women's texts, seeing women's words in print before they can be heard. But seeing is only one part of the dynamic equation when listening for/to women's voices . . . beyond what is immediately visible and documented" (Monberg 2008, 86–7). Monberg then moves to pull listening and seeing apart to argue for the value of oral history as a method in rhetorical recovery projects and the critical importance of listening-with-intent as one becomes immersed in the tapes and transcripts of one's living historical subject/s. For Monberg, oral history becomes a particularly rich "rhetorical site" for those working in Filipina/o American communities. Careful to avoid inscribing orality as inherently Pinay/Pinoy (Filipina/o), Monberg nonetheless calls attention to the "traditions of orality" and how they have been "put to *different uses* . . . in order to carry history, cultural memory, and tradition" in the face of both transnational and US-domestic colonization (92). Through this politically historicized discussion, Monberg formulates what she earlier foreshadows as a "culturally contingent context" of listening (86), a more specific form of "intersubjective receptivity" than has yet to be theorized by other feminist rhetorical theories of listening.

Following Monberg, I too want to call attention to the conflation of listening and seeing in order to theorize a more culturally and politically relevant model of intersubjective receptivity. However, unlike Monberg's important move of pulling apart sight and sound in order to foreground the recovery potential of oral history, I want to keep these modes of reception together but give their symbiosis a new name.

RHETORICAL ATTENDANCE: A CULTURALLY RELEVANT MODEL OF NIKKEI INTERSUBJECTIVE RECEPTIVITY

> I have learned to engage in a painstaking process of recovery and reconstruction; to use multidisciplinary sources; to count experience variously, especially when the people whose experience it was are no longer alive and when did not always leave clear records of themselves. I have learned to cross-reference tidbits of information in making sense of evidence; to recognize an important story when I see it; to develop strategies for retelling it respectfully despite the inevitable missing pieces. What I have learned best, however is the value of two virtues: the importance of caring about "the subject" and the importance of patience.
>
> —*Royster (2000)*

> To travel with confidence down this route the most reliable map I am given is the example of my mother's and Grandmother's alert and accurate knowing. When I am hungry, and before I can ask, there is food. If I am weary, every place is a bed . . . A sweater covers me before there is any chill and if there is pain there is care simultaneously. If grandma shifts uncomfortable, I bring her a cushion.
>
> "Yoku ki ga tsuku ne." (Fujita 1985; You really notice / are aware / are attentive, aren't you?) Grandma responds. It is a statement in appreciation of sensitivity and appropriate gestures."
>
> —*Kogawa (1981)*

> From working in the Japanese American community, I have learned to listen just as much to what is not said.
>
> —*A. Ito*

Through her concept of "culturally relevant pedagogy," education theorist Gloria Ladson-Billings argues for a vision of teaching that facilitates academic prowess as well as "cultural competence" and a "sociopolitical or critical consciousness" (Ladson-Billings 1995b, 483) that students can use to "challenge the status quo of the current social order" in the interest of "collective . . . empowerment" (Ladson-Billings 1995a, 160). Following one of my many reads of Ladson-Billings, I realized that I had been searching for a relevant method and methodology not just of teaching but of inquiry. As a *hapa haole* (mixed blood, Asian / Pacific Islander, and white) Yonsei (fourth generation) partially raised by a father who grew up in Hawaiʻi but went on to become an activist and community historian of the Japanese American redress movement, I have spent a lot of time living both within and on the margins of West Coast Nikkei communities, reconstructed and re"imagined" (Anderson 1991) after World War II. My living "within" identification has meant a constant embodiment of what Nancy Hartsock (1998) refers to as "outrage and observation" over racist acts and representations, including those motivated by what Frank Chin and Jeffrey Chan (1971) have called a "racist love" of orientalist others and model minorities. My on-the-margins-of-the-Nikkei-community identification (margins are relational, not inherent) has, however, meant a constant anxiety over whether I really have anything to say or any right to say it. But as in all good contradictions, it is my marginal position that makes me struggle, fuels the drive for a better way, a better method. It is the anxiety, coupled with knowledge, that willing listeners await, that makes me know *this had better be good.*

My search has meant a degree of ongoing, extracurricular attention to Asian American and Japanese American culture and history. Never one to major in Asian American studies or focus my schooling in such a way that I would be graded on such a search—really, the threat of a low grade over something so intimate, I think, was too much to bear—I tried to keep up for many years but in a low-profile manner. You won't find Japanese American subjects on my transcripts, won't see them if you rifle through my old papers. But that doesn't mean that I was not constantly reflecting on Japanese Americanness, doesn't mean I was not *in attendance* at the rhetorical sites of its meaning continuously and contestedly being made.

Dictionary.com:

ATTEND

–verb (used with object)

1. to be present at: to attend a lecture; to attend church.
2. to go with as a concomitant or result; accompany: Fever may attend a cold. Success attended her hard work.
3. to take care of; minister to; devote one's services to: The nurse attended the patient daily.
4. to wait upon; accompany as a companion or servant: The retainers attended their lord.
5. to take charge of; watch over; look after; tend; guard: to attend one's health.
6. to listen to; give heed to.
7. Archaic. to wait for; expect.

–verb (used without object)

8. to take care or charge: to attend to a sick person.
9. to apply oneself: to attend to one's work.
10. to pay attention; listen or watch attentively; direct one's thought; pay heed: to attend to a speaker.

11. to be present: She is a member but does not attend regularly.
12. to be present and ready to give service; wait (usually fol. by on or upon): to attend upon the Queen.
13. to follow; be consequent (usually fol. by on or upon).
14. Obsolete. to wait.

Etymology:

a. c. 1300, "to direct one's mind or energies," from O.Fr. atendre "to expect, wait for, pay attention," from L. attendere "give heed to," lit. "to stretch toward," from ad- "to" + tendere "stretch" (see tenet). The notion is of "stretching" one's mind toward something.

In two separate works of Asian American literary criticism, both Gayle Fujita and King-Kok Cheung highlight the trope of attendance in *Obasan*, Joy Kogawa's (1981) novel about the complex array of silences carried in the memories of mass incarceration by Canada's Nikkei community. For Fujita, "the essence of Kogawa's 'brilliant artistic tour de force,' as one of many impressed reviews put it, is Naomi's [the protagonist] nonverbal mode of apprehension summarized by the term 'attendance.' This sensibility, rooted in Naomi's *nikkei* inheritance and her before-the-war Vancouver home, is therefore not simply the novel's stylistic achievement but a form of Japanese Canadian and American culture" (Fujita 1985, 34). Following Fujita, Cheung devotes a chapter in *Articulate Silences* to Kogawa's use of "attentive silence," which, she writes, seems to be

> related to the Japanese notions of *sassi*, "a mental function of catching a sign from a speaker" . . . and *ishin-denshin*, "telepathy" or "sympathy, quiet understanding." . . . As a noun *sassi* can be translated as "conjecture, surmise, guess, judgment and understanding what a person means and what a sign means"; in its verb form, *sassuru*, "its usage is expanded to mean 'imagine, suppose, and even sympathize with, feel for, and make allowances for' . . . The phrase *ishin-denshin*—literally "by means of heart to heart"—has Chinese roots . . . it describes an "immediate communication (of truth) from one mind to another, or "a tacit understanding." (Cheung 1993, 146)

As Cheung (1993, 146) further explains, "Attentive silence in *Obasan* incorporates the visual sensitivity and the anticipatory responsiveness implied in *sassi*, the intuitive understanding implied in *ishin-denshin*, and the empathy implied in both," which is all to say that "[v]isual attendance . . . is inseparable from thoughtfulness and [a] poised hand. Far from suggesting passivity, this form of silence entails both mental vigilance and physical readiness" (147).[8]

In this way, I offer up *attendance* or *attending (to)* as another rhetorical model of the deeper forms of intersubjectivity reception that Ratcliffe and Monberg (following Royster and Powell) seem to be calling for. From a methods perspective, I cannot abandon the visual (or conflate it with the aural/ oral) because my focus is print literacy and the ways in which its material forms allowed for the rhetorical processes of social justice under discussion. From a methodological perspective, however, I find myself reaching for the most relevant framework I can muster, one that allows for the development of both cultural competence and political consciousness that can serve the interests of collective empowerment and social change. If Fujita (1985, 39) is right, if "attendance [is] the *nikkei* legacy," then perhaps it can "support" me, as it did for the central character of *Obasan*, "in [my] moment of . . . need."

Listening also assumes someone has spoken, and this is not always the case when it comes to literacy. For many folks in comp/rhet, and perhaps Western intellectual traditions in general, not speaking is quickly equated with silence, which is then seen as the exact and only converse of speech. That is, the word *silence* becomes a stand-in signifier for an absence of words or verbal activity. While Glenn's (2004, 4) claim that "silence is absence with a function" helps continue the recovery of silence as a valid rhetorical art, my point is that the verbal activity of literacy can be both full of words and silent at the exact same time. As Cheung noted within her larger discussion of silence's "articulate" possibilities, the character for *silence* in Chinese and Japanese is not so much the opposite of *speech* than it is the opposite of "'noise,' 'motion' and 'commotion'" (Cheung 1993, 8n11). We are reminded, via Cheung, that silence is not simply the *absence of verbal action* but the *absence of noise*. This distinction is important as we remember that writing signals an activity and a body of work where its participants can, if they choose, both "speak" and remain silent at the exact same time. That is, with writing, words can verbalize feeling and thought all the while never making any outward noise or commotion. As Cheung (26) writes at the end of her introduction to the work of three Asian American women writers, two of whom confront the legacy of incarceration in their postwar written work, "[o]f particular note in [these] works is the inverse relation between spoken and written expression.

Many of their characters . . . distill onto the page what they cannot say out loud. [While many characters] have trouble speaking or *telling* their life stories . . . they all excel on paper: their unspoken emotions break into print."

While this option of "break[ing] into print" whenever one is unable to speak will be discussed in more depth in chapter 4, I call attention to it here to suggest how much we might miss—all those "unspoken emotions" "distill[ed] onto the page"—if we *lost sight* of the visual aspect of attendance.

In addition, by relying solely on the trope of listening, one might "unknowingly erase" its relationship to the tropes of visibility and invisibility expressed in Asian Americanist rhetoric that arose out of the civil rights, liberation, and women's movements that spanned the 1960s to the early 1980s:

Mitsuye Yamada in *This Bridge Called My Back* (Yamada 1983, 40, emphasis added):

> We need to *raise our voices* a little more, even as they say to us "This is so uncharacteristic of you." To finally *recognize our own invisibility* is to finally be on the path toward *visibility*.
>
> people are *still looking right through and around us*, assuming we are simply tagging along. Asian American women still remain in the background and we are *heard but not really listened to*.

Frank Chin, Lawson Fusao Inada, Jeffrey Paul Chan, and Shawn Wong in *Aiiieeeee!*:

> America's dishonesty—its racist white supremacy passed off as love and acceptance—has kept seven generations of Asian-American *voices off the air*, off the streets, and praised us for being Asiatically *no-show*. A lot is lost forever. But from the few decades of writing we have recovered from seven generations, it is clear that we have a lot of elegant, angry, and bitter life *to show*. We know *how to show it*. We are *showing off*. (Chin et al. 1974, xvi)

All aspects of one's intersubjective receptivity are required in order to avoid "looking right through and around" as we learn to *pay attention to*, *be present at*, *take care of*, *apply oneself to*, or, going back to the concept's etymology, *stretch toward*. It is this "stretching toward" that I think both Ratcliffe and Monberg are getting at, stretching toward with mental vigilance, with physical readiness, with intent. Rhetorical attendance.

pay attention, be present, take care, stretch . . .

My own approach began with paying attention to what had already been done in Japanese American studies in both academic and community-based sites of scholarship. This meant combing secondary sources on camp experiences, camp writing, and camp resistance. With over a thousand manuscripts on the subject, I started by focusing solely on "resistance," and as my research evolved, I returned to various sources from other angles to fill in the gaps that I recognized from previous attendances. As Victor Villanueva (2004) writes, "*Memoria* is a friend of ours," and so I came to rely on my friend to tell me *something is missing*, to attend to what was *not* said, to bridge/stretch/direct my energies from my socially shaped but ephemeral intuition toward the concrete material sources that could more easily be shaped into shared knowledge.

Days of Remembrance . . .

Remnants of Portland's J-town . . .

Fifty Years Before, Fifty Years After . . .

Camp Notes, Legends, Syllables . . .

"Gaman, be strong, moto gaman iko, neh . . ."

The Pacific Citizen . . .

Layout tables, the back-lit Tetris-shaped text . . .

Wing Luke. Wooden barracks, enclosed space . . .

The International Examiner . . .

Aiko Herzig-Yoshinaga . . .

Years of Infamy . . .

Uncle Homer, Auntie Chisao, Auntie Peggy . . . a table filled with talk-talk-talk

We are all filled with such attendances, filled with an abundance of epistemological potential. With such fleeting memories, we can learn to "look, listen and look again" and "recognize . . . invisibility" in our research. For me, this translates into a conscious move to claim the memories, my friends—these lifelong attendances of Japanese American writers writing, Asian American performances and texts, Nikkei and pan-Asian American activist rhetorics and material events.

As the daughter of two activists who eventually separated but admirably negotiated split custody *kodomo no tame ni* (for the sake of the child), I was often taken along to meetings, demonstrations, and political and cultural events. My father also took me to his work in the offices of the *Pacific Citizen* and the *International Examiner*, two community vernaculars. As such, my attendances were physical—as in, I was *present at*—but not always fully conscious, as I did homework, listened to music, played on computers, or drew pictures in many of these sites. And yet, like all of us, my cultural/political knowledge was being shaped by the social milieu in which I found myself. Memories were being formed, experiential knowledge was taking root. And this knowledge would be plural, these memories, many; and they would be hard to footnote or cite and yet just as vital as any textual source embedded in what still seems to remain the most legitimate forms of academic inquiry.

Annotated Attendances

Days of Remembrance (1978). Multnomah County Exposition Center. Former assembly center for Portland, Oregon's Nikkei residents during World War II. Portland's first mass public redress event, including former incarceree speakers, music, performances, and paper replicas of incarceree numbered tags pinned to people's clothes. The safety pin pokes my skin, the number flaps in the wind.

Layout tables at the *Pacific Citizen* and *International Examiner*, (1985, 1991). Los Angeles, California, and Seattle, Washington. My father serves as editor, organizing Nikkei and Asian American news. I sit on the floor drawing until he tells me to look at something, shows me how to use algebra to fit columns of Tetris-shaped text in between the square ads. I become used to seeing certain words in print: *camp, commission, 442nd, pilgrimage, hearings, reparations, redress.*

E.O. 9066, Fifty Years Before, Fifty Years After (1992). Wing Luke Asian Museum. Seattle, Washington. My father builds a replica of a barrack as part of the Wing Luke's exhibit on camp. I stop by while he's in progress, touch the tar paper walls, sit on the floorboards, feel the cramped space, imagine the dust storms everyone has talked about. When he is done, some former incarcerees will tell him it's too nice; others will break down in tears.

Family dinner with one of the mothers of redress, Aiko Herzig-Yoshinaga, and her husband, Jack Herzig (1996). Arlington, Virginia. On the East Coast for a family reunion, my father calls Aiko and Jack to have dinner. All fifteen of the Shimabukuros, my father and his siblings and all of us kids, meet the Herzigs for dinner. All I know about Aiko at the time is what my father has told me—that she played a "very important role" in redress, something about finding documents in an archive. As we eat, I am struck by the serious warmth and generous spirit of a Nisei woman I will later learn the government called a "destructive force."

Conversations about the restrictive and expansive meanings of *gaman* with family and friends (1972–2008). Portland, Oregon. Los Angeles, California. Seattle, Washington. I first learned *gaman* as "endure" or "bear with it" or "suck it up." *We will not gaman anymore!* A common rallying cry during the redress movement, as many former incarcerees spoke to the concept as an ideal mode of behavior behind the barbed wire. But lately, rumblings about the term suggest greater complexity with the word implying the cultivation of internal—psychological, spiritual—strength. A good friend recently told me to think of it as "self-dialogue," a way to process the pain internally so as not to impose one's suffering on others around you that suffer as well. That is, to individually gaman is to develop the psychological and spiritual endurance necessary in order to collectively survive any hardship.

The talk-talk-talk of my father and other redress activists at meetings (1979–1984). Portland, Oregon. Flyers, envelopes, stamps, address labels, coffee and soda, bento boxes from Anzen, inarizushi, leftover pickled ginger wrappers, used disposable hashi, half-empty bags of kakimochi, all the makings of a Nikkei meeting. There is much to do, always much to do. But everyone is working, talking, laughing, sometimes saying nothing because nothing needs to be said. I lay under the folding tables, doing my homework, ears open, waiting . . .

But this is not all that there is.

Attendance doesn't stop with these epistemologically rich memories of widely varied and sometimes fleeting moments of intersubjective receptivity. Attendance is vigilant, not passive. One must "apply oneself," must "stretch one's mind," must be "consequent of" what has come before and "follow" with something new.

ATTENDING TO NIKKEI LITERACIES OF SURVIVANCE: WRITING-TO-REDRESS

To attend to the word *redress* in the Japanese American community, I must note its semantic identification with the grassroots reparations movement that began in the 1970s and culminated in the 1988 passage of the Civil Liberties Act. However, Lane Ryo Hirabayashi (1998; see also Nishimoto 1995) has suggested that the collective struggle for redress actually began during the camp period,[9] basing his argument on a historical document that formally articulates demands/requests for compensation. And, as I learned from doing editorial work on the book my father would eventually come to write about the Seattle origins of the redress and reparations movement, the word *redress* means more than compensation for a wrong; broader connotations include the more abstract definitions of "to set right," "to adjust evenly again," or "to remedy or relieve" (Shimabukuro 2001, v). While anyone active in the Nikkei community has long experienced, or at least heard about, the cathartic effects of various stages of the recognized redress movement, as I attend to my memories and to Hirabayashi, as well as to the writing I have both read over the years and more recently recovered in the archives, I would argue that much self- and community-sponsored Nikkei writing from camp suggests a constant use of what I am calling *writing-to-redress*. That is, much writing from camp can be seen as the codification of a desire to set right what is wrong or to relieve one's suffering from the psychological and physical imposition of forced "relocation" and incarceration. In this way, Nikkei writers in camp were engaged in their own version of a "rhetoric of survivance," or the use of language/writing to "survive + resist" (Powell 2002) the conditions of mass incarceration.

As a politically and culturally relevant model of Nikkei literacy, writing-to-redress points to an ongoing literacy practice, what literacy theorists define as a "socially regulated, recurrent, and patterned [set of] things that people do with literacy as well as the cultural significance they ascribe to those doings" (Brandt and Clinton 2002, 342). Taking this kind of practice approach to analyzing literacy requires one to shift their focus away from decontextualized texts to the ways people use writing. As one way of using writing that has developed into a pattern over the past sixty years, writing-to-redress is akin to Jacqueline Jones Royster's Afrafeminist model of "literacy as sociopolitical action," which allows for the understanding that a "consistency of oppressions . . . has been paralleled by a consistency of responses," of which "the use of literacy for social and political change" has been one (Royster 2000, 59). But, as I've argued earlier, in order to see/listen for/become aware of this sociopolitical action in Nikkei community history, we must attend to the historical, material, and cultural particularities impacting the ways incarcerated Nikkei knowingly and unknowingly participated in the socially regulated, recurrent, and patterned activity called writing-to-redress.

Given the particularly complex dynamics of the Nikkei community's postwar "partly real and partly mythical silence" (Chin et al. 1974, viii), realities and myths discussed in the next chapter, attending to the "silent" speech of writing allows us to take heed of and then follow the verbal and rhetorical activity often covered up in the history of our community. We can recover the "quiet" ways people wrote their inner worlds, organized emotion-thought, verbalized dissent, and sharpened awareness of the community's hardship, all in private manners, as guns pointed in at them from the guard towers and barbed wire. We can also recover the "noisy" texts that did "talk back," boldly entering the public sphere, daring to draw the line and say *enough*. And through oral histories and interviews with survivors, we can recover the stories behind these texts, the sheer will and inner strength it took to take both private and public rhetorical action and put it in print. We just need all of our faculties to do so.

The notion is of stretching one's mind toward something

Like historical ethnographers of literacy, I am working across time, not fully able to take part in participant-observation, instead attending to the collective efforts referred to throughout this introduction. What makes rhetorical attendance somewhat different than historical ethnography is the explicit infusion of personal memory and cultural know-how that, together, create a felt sense about the ways we conduct research. In other words, rhetorically attending one's subject requires an explicit awareness and mention that culture and experience inform our decisions about when to ask questions and when to stay silent, about how to contemplate the implications of our work and anticipate the feelings of those with whom we stand. As such, lifelong conversations and eavesdroppings matter as much as feminist rhetorical theory and New Literacy studies. Metaphors embedded in Nikkei poetry, fiction, music, visual art, and cultural practices matter as much as Asian American studies. Across and between not just the disciplines but the moments of our lives, we can learn to look, listen, and look again. This is how we attend to the no-shows, to the what is not said . . .

In order to perform this rhetorical attendance of writing-to-redress, I begin with a close examination of the politics of archival recovery projects for the post–WWII Nikkei community in "ReCollecting Nikkei Dissidence: The Politics of Archival Recovery and Community Self-Knowledge." Contextualizing my choice of archival methods, I explain how Japanese American dissidence during the war has historically been downplayed to the extent that the range of Nikkei resistance to incarceration is still relatively unknown. Historically, this lack of knowledge has been exacerbated by the fact that for several decades after World War II, much of the community still believed the government's rationale of "military necessity" for their imprisonment during the war. It was not until the 1970s and 1980s that the community's collective awareness regarding the government's lie started to shift as part of a larger social movement for redress and reparations. This movement was greatly facilitated by the archival recovery of government documents by two former incarcerees, Michi Weglyn and Aiko Herzig-Yoshinaga, neither of whom were professional scholars but whose scholarship dramatically affected political events. Taking methodological lead, inspiration, and authority from these two mothers of redress, I consider what it means to perform archival recovery work within a community still recovering from history.

Chapter 3, "ReCollected Tapestries: The Circumstances behind Writing-to-Redress," traces some of the social, historical, political, material, and cultural conditions helpful for understanding the activity of writing-to-redress. As noted in the introduction, much of the knowledge shared in this chapter has been exhumed or theorized during and since the redress movement. Detailing prewar community literacy networks, political "blueprints" that laid the groundwork for incarceration, specific material conditions of camp life related to literacy, and cultural "clusters" (Mao 2006) informing writing-to-redress, this chapter is a backdrop for the analyses that follow.

My fourth chapter, "Me Inwardly before I Dared: Attending Silent Literacies of Gaman," points to one form of dissidence recovered in private forms of writing-to-redress. Such self-sponsored writing as diaries, letters to friends, and unpublished poetry was regularly used by incarcerees to gaman, or actively endure by withholding one's emotional reaction to the conditions of mass incarceration. This chapter begins with a discussion of the contested rhetorics of gaman and the ways it has been interpreted and translated as an admonishment to either endure/accept or persevere through oppressive conditions. This discussion of gaman is then developed into a culturally relevant conception of agency and resistance. The theoretical frameworks of King-Kok Cheung, James C. Scott, and Malea Powell all help to illuminate how Writing-to-Gaman served to enable a Nikkei rhetoric of survivance, where incarcerees could both psychologically resist and physically survive by privately articulating their complaints and disillusionment while maintaining both a degree of cultural competence and a veneer of compliance as the US military stood watch.

Chapter 5, "Everyone . . . Put in a Word: The Multisources of Collective Authority behind Public Writing-to-Redress," examines the collective nature of more public forms of writing-to-redress. Theorizing the ways groups of politically marginalized writers come to generate a group-based authority, I draw upon the theoretical frameworks of Abdul R. JanMohamed and David Lloyd's minority discourse, Deborah Brandt's literacy sponsorship, and various scholars' work on authority and petition writing to extend our understanding of the ways public literacy activities are collectively authorized by both friendly and hostile sources as well as those that sponsor literacy from above and amass authority from below. After showing how collective authority gave rise to a number of public writing-to-redress texts and activities, I then apply these concepts through a critical discourse analysis of a text collaboratively written in response to the military draft by the Heart Mountain Fair Play Committee. While the collectivity surrounding the emergence of the literacy activities discussed in this chapter counter a commonly held perception that camp resistance was numerically insignificant, the chapter's analysis also provides a new take on the ways oppressed peoples generate the authority to write back under adverse conditions.

In chapter 6, "Another Earnest Petition: ReWriting Mothers of Minidoka," I build upon chapter 5 by examining the ways collaborative revision serves the process of writing-to-redress. First reviewing the ways women's protest activities have been particularly downplayed in camp history, I then piece together the story of the Mother's Society of Minidoka, an organization made up of predominately Issei (first generation and thus, by law, noncitizen) women who were all mothers of the incarcerated men subjected to the military draft. As some of the first incarcerees to respond in writing to the announcement of the draft, the Mother's Society first enlisted a male Nisei (second generation and citizen) lawyer to serve as a kind of ghostwriter for their letter-petition to the government. However, according to one source, the women found the original version "too weak" and thus decided to rewrite the letter completely. I analyze both drafts in this chapter, focusing on the ways the mothers re/visioned (Young 2004) motherhood and their legal relationship to the United States in the final letter-petition.

In chapter 7, "Relocating Authority: Expanding the Significance of Writing-to-Redress," the focus moves forward in time as I argue that the materiality of writing-to-redress has allowed for its continuance as a rhetorical practice. Drawing on work by activity theorist Yrjö Engeström, literacy theorists Deborah Brandt and Katie Clinton, and multicultural education theorist Tara Yosso (2005), my final chapter highlights the ways the rhetorical force behind writing-to-redress has been re-activated by activist-descendants. After a brief theoretical discussion, I examine three such re-activations that took place across a range of contemporary public forums, including a museum exhibit, community newspapers, a classroom curriculum, and a poetry collection. By calling attention to such rhetorical re-activations, I highlight the potential of literacy to "talk back" to both the authorities of the present and the would-be authorities of the future. Finally, to close, I discuss the ways my own work functions as writing-to-redress, as I position my own critical literacy development in the expanding legacy of Nikkei literacies of survivance.

In this way, over the course of this book, I hope to highlight how writing-to-redress does more than encode or preserve a response. It also serves as a means to expand a rhetorical, and thus, political activity: the collective struggle to relocate authority away from one's oppressors and back into the community itself. This collective struggle, this relocating of authority is an activity in which I see all aspects of this study taking part, including my choice of methodology, rhetorical attendance, and my choice of methods, archival research. While the community-specific politics of my chosen methods are the subject of the next chapter, let me close by performing one more rhetorical attendance: the material sites of my research.

I followed my readings of secondary sources into the always-growing archives. Community archives first, university archives second. Scholars like

Jessica Enoch and Lane Ryo Hirabayashi remind us that attending to materials in an archive means attending to the social position of the archive, an active site of rhetorical remembering and forgetting (Enoch 2008; L. Hirabayashi 1998). I would add that attending to the question of access can also tell us a great deal. Hints can be found in both the discourse and the Discourse[10] of the repository—the naming of its purpose and instructions for its use. Always recognized as a site of official history, the university-based archives I attended required multiple forms, agreements, signatures, "certain restrictions on availability and use," "permissions," "adequate" identification, "prohibitions," lockers, passing through locked doors, pre-paged boxes, notarized photocopies, and inspected laptops. Parking was difficult. Material was recalled from off site. Knowledge protected, sealed off, contained.

In contrast, the community archives that I used relied on a different Discourse. The Hirasaki National Resource Center at the Japanese American National Museum was formed in 1999 "to ensure that the story of Japanese Americans *remains accessible* to everyone" (Japanese American National Museum n.d.). Permissions were required for reproduction but materials were stored on site, and there was no limit to what I could page in a day. By default, the door to the archive room was left open, but I could close it if I liked. Nobody made me open my laptop when I left; nobody had to check my identification. The other archival site I accessed was online. Densho's mission is to "preserve the testimonies of Japanese Americans who were unjustly incarcerated during World War II before their memories are extinguished" (Densho 1997b). But the word *densho* means "to pass on to the next generation" or "leave a legacy," and when one clicks on "About Densho" on the website's homepage, one learns how the mission evolved from simply a desire to "document" these oral histories to that of a desire to "educate, preserve, collaborate and inspire action for equity." Densho uses digital technology to both "preserve *and* make *accessible* primary source materials" and they "*encourage use* of these resources to *expand* awareness of our country's diverse history, to *stimulate* critical thinking, to *develop* ethical decision-making skills, and to help ensure that democratic principles are upheld now and in the future" (Densho 1997a). Access, expand, stimulate, inspire.

This is not a comment about the best way to ensure that sources last. It is a comment about what it means to ensure that knowledge is not kept away from *the people* (this strategic essentialism, another rhetoric of solidarity). It is a comment about the accessibility of knowledge, especially for those whose lives, whose communities, make up the material roots of that knowledge. It is a comment about the importance of attending to a need to not simply *preserve* knowledge but to *use* it, *expand* it, and *pass it on*.

Notes

1. See, for example, work by Keith Osajima (1988), Stacey Lee (1996), David Palumbo-Liu (1999), and Chang and Au (2008).

2. Breaking Silence: An Anthology of Contemporary Asian American Poets (Bruchac 1983); Breaking the Silence: Redress and Japanese American Ethnicity (Takezawa 1995); Shedding Silence: Poetry and Prose (Mirikitani 1987); YELL-Oh Girls! Emerging Voices Explore Culture, Identity, and Growing Up Asian American (Nam 2001); Aiiieeeee! *An Anthology of Asian-American Writers* (Chin et al. 1974); The Big Aiiieeeee! An Anthology of Chinese American and Japanese American Literature (Chan et al. 1991); and Tell This Silence: Asian American Women Writers and the Politics of Speech (Duncan 2004).

3. For discussions of "strategic" uses of essentialism, see Spivak (1987, 205). The notion of "strategic romanticism" comes to me via the work of Jacqueline Jones Royster (2000, 13), who attributes the concept to Amy Shuman and a paper she delivered at the 1997 Colloquium on Women in the History of Rhetoric at Ohio State University. For discussions of "strong objectivity," see Sandra Harding (2004).

4. The Immigration and Nationality Act of 1965 signaled a dramatic change in Asian America, as it "removed 'national origins' as the basis of American immigration legislation" (S. Chan 1991, 145), ending a de facto race-based exclusion policy. While the act resulted in a massive influx of immigrants and refugees from the Asian continent, this group's composite makeup was shaped by the act's new set of immigration preferences, including those given to family members of already permanent residents and citizens; refugees; "professionals, scientists and artists of 'exceptional ability' "; and "workers, skilled and unskilled, in occupations for which labor was in short supply in the U.S." (S. Chan 1991, 146). As such, 1965 marks a dramatic shift in Asian American communities, both in terms of numbers of people and amounts of transnational cultural capital—that is, people of Asian origins were entering the United States with very little cultural capital (in the case of many refugees) and with very much (in the case of professionals and many others of "exceptional ability").

5. Asian American studies scholar Stephen H. Sumida writes that Filipino/as have been in the land now called the United States since the 1760s, when a group of

Pinoy sailors jumped ship in Louisiana while it was under Spanish rule. There they "found refuge in the bayous, where they built homes over the waters like the homes they knew back in their islands" and came to be locally known as the 'Filipino Cajuns.'" The arrival and settling of these "Manilamen" predates the American Revolution, making their descendants even eligible to become Sons and Daughters of the American Revolution (Sumida 1998, 87–88).

6. Hopefully, though, this project can also provide insight to those working on the literacies and rhetorics of those impacted by contemporary hyper-incarceration policies.

7. As Elaine Kim notes, Farewell to Manzanar was published immediately following the civil rights movement, during a period when several Japanese American texts were published and "critical reception was shaped by political concerns at a time when people of color vociferously seeking justice and equality could be shown the example of the non-militant approach of the 'model minority.'" In this context, Kim argues, the book was celebrated for its "'lack of bitterness, self-pity or solemnity' in portraying the wartime incarceration of Japanese Americans" (Kim 1990, 150–51).

8. While I want to be clear that I am primarily reading for a US-based Nikkei practice in intersubjective receptivity, the Japanese origins of which stem from Meiji era codes of behavior and evolved via US-based processes of xenophobia, class struggle, and racial formations, I am taken with the cultural parallels evident in Roichi Okabe's discussion of rhetorical competence in contemporary Japan: "rhetorically sensitive communicators . . . are noted for emphasizing the importance of the role of 'perceiver' more than that of a message sender. They are putting up various antennas, so to speak, to perceive and to accurately tune in to the faintest of signals emitted from their audience even on the nonverbal level . . . The rhetorically competent communicators as sensitive perceivers, therefore, always attempt to adjust, adapt, and accommodate themselves to their audience. In a culture of sasshi or omoiyari (both words meaning 'considerateness'), to communicate competently means for the rhetorically sensitive in Japan means to perceive the inexplicit . . . Sasshi ga ii, or 'being a good mind-reader,' and omoiyari ga ary, or 'being considerate about others' feelings,' are both considered virtues in the Japanese construct of rhetorical sensitivity" (Okabe 2007, 80).

9. While both academic and independent Japanese American redress scholars have noted that individual articulations for monetary redress were made quite early by Joseph Y. Kurihara and Kiyoshi Okamoto, both Nisei men (Maki, Kitano, and Berthold 1999; Hohri 1988), Hirabayashi's discussion is based on Richard Nishimoto's recounting and textual inclusion of a collective document in one of his "autoethnographic" reports as a participant-observer in the Japanese Evacuation

and Resettlement Study spearheaded by Dorothy Swaine Thomas at the University of California, Berkeley. Nishimoto reports that the document was collaboratively written during the All Center Conference in 1945 by both Issei and Nisei men as the WRA prepared to shut the camps down.

10. James Paul Gee (2008, 3) explains that Discourses (as distinct from discourses) "are ways of behaving, interacting, valuing, thinking, believing, speaking, and often reading and writing . . . accepted as instantiations of particular identities." While Discourses "include much more than language" (2), "[l]anguage makes no sense outside of Discourses and the same is true for literacy" (3).

2
RECOLLECTING NIKKEI DISSIDENCE
The Politics of Archival Recovery and Community Self-Knowledge

Any re/collecting of early Asian America . . . must be a revisionist project addressing the conspicuous absence of Asian Americans in "official" histories and correcting stereotypes, myths, and false assumptions.

—*Lee, Lim, and Matsukawa (2002)*

[F]orgetting is not . . . an omission of discourse or of historical writing. Rather . . . forgetting can be seen as a rhetorical act that occurs in the present moment and allows for "the substitution of one memory for another."

—*Enoch (2008)*

Early analysts of camps all wrote from the orthodox point of view and the resource materials assembled as documents, letters, memoirs, and oral history tapes all reflect the biases of the WRA and the JACL . . . Because of that barrier, the revisionists are unable to determine precisely the number of people who actually resisted, the degree of mobilization, the exact role of coercion, and even the forms of nature of resistance.

—*Okihiro (1977b)*

DOI: 10.5876/9781607324010.c002

> [P]reserved writing is itself, in the face of easy losses, a history.
>
> —*Miller (2002)*

> [A]s I opened box after cardboard box and found documents carefully bundled and labeled among my grandfather's papers, I began to feel that he had left them for us—for me—to understand what had happened to him during those war years. This is a story about such bundles, the archival work that brings them back to us, and the process of constructing a community memory.
>
> —*Okawa (2008)*

Nikkei dissidence during the so-called good war has often been portrayed as the sole providence of a few select, almost exclusively male, individuals and/or organizations.[1] Some of these historical representations stem from the period of the redress movement of the 1970s–1980s, as community activists debated what images of the incarceration period they most wished to emphasize during the struggle for reparations from Congress and legal redress in the courts (Murray 2008). But several historians of Japanese America note that internal community struggles over representation long predate the movement for redress, going back even before the incarceration period to early Nikkei struggles amidst both the vast racism they encountered in the United States and the prevailing ideologies set forth by both US and Japanese imperialism (Azuma 2005; Fujitani 2002; Murray 2008; Ichioka 1988; Hansen 2002). Popular, and thus more accessible, accounts of Japanese American history, however, tend to either cover up or downplay the community's long legacy of dissidence.

According to several academic and community-based historians, this cover-up and/or downplay can be traced back to the Japanese American Citizens League (JACL) of the 1940s and 1950s (Murray 2008; Abe 2000; Muller 2001; Lim 1990). An exclusively Nisei organization at the time, the JACL was made up of mostly professional-class Japanese Americans whose prewar legacy emphasized a two-pronged approach of assimilation and patriotism in order to deal with racism (Takahashi 1997, 91; Murray 2008, 105). After Japan bombed Pearl Harbor, and the government arrested and detained without trial all Issei men presumed to be community leaders, the JACL stepped into the shoes left empty by the detained men and claimed to speak for all Japanese Americans, asserting that their membership was almost three times as large as it actually was.[2] As the JACL proceeded to advocate full compliance with every step of the incarceration period, suspicions grew within the community that many JACL members and leaders were government informants, or *inu*.[3] While this suspicion was confirmed years later by government documents recovered by both archival historians and an independent report commissioned by the JACL itself, many mainstream accounts of Japanese American history continue to be shaped by the accommodationist line of the wartime league and its chroniclers.

In such JACL-inspired chronicles, the difficulty and pain of mass incarceration is acknowledged as a great hardship overcome by the community's extreme loyalty, obedience, agreeableness, and quietness. Dissidence of any kind is rhetorically isolated as being caused by only a few troublemakers or disloyals or it is completely ignored. As wartime JACL National Secretary, Mike "Moses" Masaoka retorted to those who would honor Japanese American draft resisters, "Some historians, writing from the *isolation* of their ivory towers, have contended the draft resisters were the real heroes of the Japanese-American story because they had the courage to stand up for a principle. These historians are wrong. The significance is in the *relatively small number* of dissidents" (Masaoka and Hosokawa 1987, 179).

But in her tome of competing "historical memories" of Nikkei incarceration, Alice Yang Murray contends that during the final year of incarceration and the one that followed, the JACL actively promoted tales of wartime heroism performed by Nisei soldiers in order to downplay the significance of any Nikkei resistance that had occurred.[4] As Murray writes,

> At the 1946 National Convention in Denver, JACL . . . members worried . . . that the history of protest within the camps might tarnish the image of military sacrifice the JACL had so carefully burnished. Some felt the league should distance itself publicly from the camp resisters. A few hard-liners even suggested that the JACL go on record as urging the government to deport immediately "those who failed to express loyalty," and require . . . [some of them to] carry special identification cards. The organization ultimately decided that the best approach was to remain silent about the resisters . . . In effect, the JACL hoped to erase the history of internee resistance from public memory by denying its existence. (Murray 2008, 126–28)

However, the wartime JACL and its leaders are certainly not the only participants in this historical downplay. A legacy of US-based racism continues to wreak havoc in the dominant public sphere, as the historical agency of people of color continues to be covered up, distorted, or downplayed in what Nathaniel Huggins (1991) called the "master narrative" of American history. While it is true that more and more people have become suspicious of *any* grand narrative, including that of the "master," these cover-ups, distortions, and downplays still seem to define much of the official curriculums of public schools, including those educating the descendants of former incarcerees and other Asian Americans, impacting how we see ourselves.

While it remains true that official history is, as claimed, written by the winners, recent literacy histories suggest that since the imposition and rise of mass alphabetic literacy across the Americas, the losers have also been writing history in imposed forms, such as standardized English, for as long as they have had the technological access and know-how to do so (Powell 2002; Mignolo 1992; Silva 2004; Cornelius 1991). Whether marginalized peoples have recorded their critical standpoints on history by "bearing witness to negativity," acting as "secretaries" to community struggles (Apple, Au, and Gandin 2009), or "imagining communities" (Anderson 1991), multicultural antiracist histories of literacy suggest that people have "misappropriated" required forms of literacy (Brandt 1998) for as long as literacy has misappropriated them. While these acts of resistant agency are rarely included in official or widely disseminated accounts, the fact that these counter-memories have in fact been written has meant that they can be materially recovered.

This recovery of written text composed as a means to survive + resist oppression takes on particular saliency when key aspects of the truth have been downplayed, distorted, or denied. As Native Hawaiian scholar Noenoe K. Silva writes in her introduction to her book-length study of Hawaiian resistance based on the recovery of nineteenth-century Hawaiian-language public texts,

> Why does it matter [that] this history of resistance is documented and analyzed? . . . We might just as well as ask: How do a people come to know who they are? How do a colonized people recover from the violence done to their past . . . ? Although stories are passed on individually in families, much is lost . . . When the stories told at home do not match up with the texts at school, students are taught to doubt the oral versions. The epistemology of the school system is firmly Western in nature: what is written counts. When the stories can be validated . . . [and] the findings [are made] available to the

community, people begin to recover from the wounds caused by that disjuncture in their consciousness. (Silva 2004, 3)

While recovering texts for Native Hawaiians has helped validate the truth passed down through the mouths of Hawaiian people, for formerly incarcerated Nikkei and their descendants, recovering text has meant recovering truth rarely uttered out loud. As numerous Japanese American studies scholars have noted, very few people openly talked about camp after the war (Nagata 1994; Murray 2008; Ishizuka 2006; Shimabukuro 2001; J. Hirabayashi 1975; Takezawa 1995; Nagata 1993). This silent lack of speech stemmed from a wide variety of reasons, including the pressing pragmatic concerns of rebuilding life interrupted by mass imprisonment (Murray 2008; J. Hirabayashi 1992); the internalized shame and "social amnesia" (Kashima 1980) brought about by the mass trauma; ongoing encounters with racism in the United States; and cultural ideals first inherited from Meiji era ideologies in Japan and subsequently inflected by the experiences of racism before, during, and after World War II. Whatever the reason or combination of reasons, this lack of talk meant very few Sansei (third generation) had a chance "to doubt the oral versions" of what happened to their parents and grandparents, even though many of them have inherited the psychological scars created by the "legacy of injustice" (Nagata 1993).

In a sociocultural and historical context shaped by both multisourced community silence and the symbolic supremacy of writing versus talking, recovering text that offers a glimmer of a more complicated history remains a powerful activity for people whose agency and authority has long been denied. Perhaps because of this complex array of factors operating in the postwar Nikkei community, archival research has played a key role in the movement for redress. But while many progressive male academic historians (few of whom had been in camp themselves) dove into the archives in the 1960s and 1970s to recover a more complex Nikkei history in the face of the monolithic Horatio Alger narrative inspired by the JACL, much of their work was read only by other academics or a few activist students in their fight for ethnic studies programs. That would begin to change when a female former incarceree, a retired Nisei costume designer, recovered some of the same documents and proceeded to redistribute the knowledge they contained back into the community.

"[H]ER OBJECTIVE, GET THE TRUTH OUT": THE MOTHER OF REDRESS AND THE REDISTRIBUTION OF KNOWLEDGE

While even some of the most politically conscious former incarcerees rarely discussed their camp experiences with their children (Takezawa 1995, 154; J. Hirabayashi 1975, Yamada 2001), by the late 1960s and early 1970s, many started to become active in the antiwar and liberation movements of the time (Fujino 2005; Omatsu 1986–1987; Fujita-Rony 2003). During this time, more strident Nisei activists were also taking part in community debates about their representation as the "Quiet Americans" (Hosokawa 1969), organizing camp pilgrimages (Bahr 2007), hosting community slide shows on Nikkei history (Chin 2008), and conducting individual or regionally based small group investigations into the possibilities of redress (Maki, Kitano, and Berthold 1999; Shimabukuro 2001; Hohri 1988). However, even as a collective and public felt sense had started to emerge regarding the injustice of camp, the majority of former incarcerees still retained a sense of collective guilt regarding "the treachery of Pearl Harbor" (Weglyn 1976, 21). Many also still believed the community's mass incarceration was not just the "military necessity" government officials had always declared it to be but that the JACL policy of full compliance was the only option available to prove their loyalty to the US empire, which had never been loyal to them. But in 1976 the community's collective consciousness shifted when one of their own entered the National Archives and took the knowledge she learned to prove that the government had lied.

While academic work written by revisionist historians had already started to appear in academic journals and college bookstores, according to Alice Yang Murray, Michi Weglyn's *Years of Infamy* became the first work on camp to "reach a broad audience of former incarcerees" (Murray 2008, 244). Weglyn herself had been a teenager in camp and went on to not become a professional historian but a costume designer for *The Perry Como Show*. As events such as the "Vietnam War and Watergate scandal opened governmental actions to increasing scrutiny" (Nash 1999, vi), Weglyn found herself wondering about the history of her own imprisonment. As she wrote in the preface to *Years*,

> Curiosity led me into exhuming documents of this extraordinary chapter in our history, which had seen the shattering of so many hearths, lives, careers—of so many hopes and dreams. Among once impounded papers, I came face

> to face with facts, some that left me greatly pained . . . At a time when angry charges were being hurled at heads of state, the gaps of the evacuation era appeared more like chasms. Persuaded that the enormity of a bygone injustice has been only partially perceived, I have taken upon myself the task of piecing together what might be "forgotten"—or ignored—parts of the tapestry of those years. (Weglyn 1976, 21–22)

According to historiographer Murray, "Weglyn spent seven years conducting research at the National Archives, the Library of Congress, and the Pentagon," while her husband, "a Jew who avoided the Nazi death camps by hiding in eleven different places when he was twelve years old," became chief sponsor of her efforts to "document the suffering of internees" (Murray 2008, 245). And document she did. Over her time in the archives, Weglyn collected a vast array of government documents that proved their own public rhetoric regarding "military necessity" to be a lie and recounted some of the harshest abuses that incarcerees like herself had endured during camp years. With Weglyn's incorporation of such textual markers of authority as extensive block quotations, reproductions of full documents, and endless footnotes and references, *Years of Infamy* gained "immediate credibility" (Nash 1999, vii).

But even as the trade book received positive reviews from a number of sources, one Asian American studies historian heavily critiqued the book as "nothing more than old wine in a new bottle," arguing that the "falsity of the government's claim" had already been exposed before by academics (Okihiro 1977a, 168, 168–69). The government's lie was not the "untold story" Weglyn claimed it to be. Despite what story had already been distributed among the halls of academia, Okihiro must have been disconnected from what story, or knowledge, had been redistributed among the Nikkei community at large. In *Historical Memories of the Japanese American Internment and the Struggle for Redress* (2008), Murray refers to several vernacular responses to Weglyn's text:

> "I don't think anyone who lived through the 'camp experience,' reviewer Mary Karasawa declared, 'will be able to finish reading this book without experiencing every range of human emotion—much of which has been lying dormant for the past 30 years . . . You will swear, you will cry, you will feel bitter, but you will surely begin to see the pieces of the puzzle come together." *Years of Infamy* enabled Karasawa "to develop further insight into racism" and "the politics and rationale of expediency in some national decision making" . . . Ruby

> Yoshino Schaar, stalwart of the JACL, expected to dislike the book because she had heard that it criticized the league's wartime leaders. But two days after receiving it, she called Weglyn to tell her that she "couldn't put it down." She then sent numerous letters to JACL chapters, media representatives, and friends promoting the book. (quoted in Murray 2008, 245–46)

> Edison Uno declared the book a "must for every library in the land and must reading for every American . . . No other book contributes so many new facts: the shameful conspiracies, the official deceptions and cover-up." Uno thought the book was "a masterful contribution to the rewriting of that part of our history too long distorted and misrepresented." Nisei Paul Tsuneishi thanked the publisher for providing what "most of us within the Japanese American community are finding to be the most meaningful book of the evacuation and internment experience." (quoted in Murray 2008, 247)

> Activist Kiku Hori Funabiki praised the book for boldly revealing "events which were not widely known to the community." (quoted in Murray 2008, 248)

Murray (2008, 244) contends that many formerly incarcerated Nikkei were particularly drawn to the fact that the book had been "written by a former internee with no formal training in historical research," despite Okihiro's claims that the book put "to rest the myth that what is needed in the literature of the camps is more works by authors of Japanese descent" (Okihiro 1977a, 167). Female former incarcerees seemed particularly taken with the book, as "[p]eople couldn't believe 'that any Nisei, let alone a Nisei woman, could write with such passion and conviction.'" As Joy Yamauchi, editor of the *Tozai Times*, explained to Murray, "People were amazed that Weglyn, who was not a historian, could write a simple truth in a way that touched all who read it. In essence, Weglyn forced people to re-examine all of camp history. Her painstaking careful research uncovered government duplicity and propaganda . . . It kicked off discussions and debates, opened up the community and more than a few wounds. It began the healing process for all those touched by the evacuation process" (quoted in Murray 2008, 247).

While I would not personally read *Years of Infamy* for another fifteen years, after I graduated from high school, Weglyn touched my own life after the book was recommended to my father at his first redress meeting. That afternoon, he asked the Nisei sitting next to him, Homer Yasui, if he knew of anything he could read to "find out more about this stuff." Homer handed him a long list of books, the first of which of which was Weglyn's. As my father recounted in his own book's preface,

> I took it home and thumbed through it. The first photo: two children who looked like my cousins, accompanying an elderly woman, perhaps a grandmother, all with what looked like baggage-claim tags attached to their clothing. The caption read, "Most of the 110,000 persons removed for reasons of 'national security' were school-age children, infants and young adults not yet of voting age."
>
> Estelle Ishigo's drawing of toilets and showers followed, as did newspaper clippings about "riots" in the camps. Next came 300-plus pages of text and documents describing the events leading up to and resulting from Executive Order 9066, its legislative corollary Public Law 503, and all the proclamations that "justified" corralling and incarcerating more than 120,000 persons of Japanese ancestry "on a record which wouldn't support a conviction for stealing a dog."
>
> I read Weglyn's book in one long sitting, taking time to eat, maybe to nap a bit. It was an intensely emotional weekend. I was angry, bewildered, anguished, sad. And the two kids wearing the baggage-claim tags haunted me . . . (Shimabukuro 2001, xiv)

At some point in the long sitting, my father would have read Colonel Bendetsen saying that "if they have drop of Japanese blood in them, they must go to camp" (Weglyn 1976, 77), extending his initial felt identification with "two children who looked like [his] cousins" to children like his own "mixed-race" daughter. Soon after that, he and I would sit on the cracked linoleum floor of our living room and look at photographs edited by Maisie and Richard Conrat in *Executive Order 9066* (Conrat, Conrat, and Lange 1972). It is in this moment that he tells me what happened, why all of these people—even the kids—have paper tags hanging from their jackets, why folks are getting on the trains with covered windows. And then he says we would have both had to go. I am silent.

But this is not the experience I wish to redress here. Who cares what happened to a seven-year old hapa girl whose blood relatives weren't even in camp? Re-focus. Attend to the matter at hand . . .

Rhetorical attendance is not about individual lives but a complex interacting array of knowledge still being collected, still being shared, still being redistributed back to the people whose material lives served as the source of that knowledge. And this is what was so powerful about Weglyn's work. Her book reached the people whose lives had been directly impacted by the material conditions that shaped that covered-up knowledge. She redistributed the wealth of knowledge stolen from people's lives. As another former incarceree and long-time dissident Nikkei reCollector, Aiko Herzig-Yoshinaga recalled that when *Years of Infamy* was first published, she heard Weglyn speak not at an academic conference of historians, but in Herzig-Yoshinaga's church. It was there that she "could tell . . . her objective, get the truth out" (Herzig-Yoshinaga 1997, s4). Collecting texts with the rhetorical intent of redistributing knowledge, Michi Weglyn was perhaps our first reCollecting Nikkei dissident after the war, dissidently reCollecting and redistributing documents in such a way that she would come to be known by most Nikkei activists themselves as the "mother of redress" (Murray 2008, 247).

"[S]EEING MORE THAN WHAT WAS WRITTEN": AIKO HERZIG-YOSHINAGA ATTENDS (TO) THE NATIONAL ARCHIVES

After Herzig-Yoshinaga heard Weglyn speak, she approached the community scholar and the two quickly developed a friendship that would prove vital to the redress movement, now beginning to gain steam. Like many formerly incarcerated women struggling to rebuild their lives and raise their families in the postwar years, Herzig-Yoshinaga did not often "engage in the discussions of history" (Murray 2008, 330), recounting in several interviews how "apolitical" she was until she became involved with the New York–based Asian Americans for Action (AAA) during the late 1960s. According to Thomas Fujita-Rony, this group, started in 1969 by two Nisei "activist women, Shizuko 'Minn' Matsuda and Kazu Iijima," was "the first of its kind on the East Coast." While not exclusively a women's or Nikkei organization, the membership of AAA was made up of a majority of formerly incarcerated Nisei women. It was this organization that Herzig-Yoshinaga asserts " 'turned [her] around' and got her thinking more actively about 'minorities, about equality, about ethnic relations' " (Fujita-Rony 2003, 41). By the time Weglyn came to Herzig-

Yoshinaga's church in 1976 to talk about *Years of Infamy*, she knew how important the work would be. As Herzig-Yoshinaga explained in a 1997 Densho interview, Weglyn's "work was just so meticulous, and she was not about to put anything in that book that she couldn't say, 'I got this information from the government.' No one could refute it" (Herzig-Yoshinaga 1997).

A few years after Weglyn's talk, Herzig-Yoshinaga remarried and moved to Washington, DC, to join her new husband. It was there that she found herself faced with a new privilege of not having to work for a living, so she decided to take the time to look into the National Archives to see what it had on her family (Fujita-Rony 2003, 44). At first, she was amazed at what the government had collected, but then she realized that, while in camp, everyone was always "fill[ing] out forms"; "So why shouldn't they have this . . . they kept everybody's papers: school records, dental records, medical records, letters that went in and out of camp. They kept everything . . . putting them in individual folders for each person. If you were a child, your papers may have ended up in your mother or father's folder. But . . . sometimes there were individual folders . . . for children, too. I remember seeing some drawings, report cards, things like that" (Herzig-Yoshinaga 1997).

As Herzig-Yoshinaga worked her way through her own family's papers, the archivists told her that there was an abundance of materials on the camps that very few people were actually requesting and offered to help her look at any of it. Given the growing movement for redress, her newfound time, and her admiration of Weglyn's "meticulous" research, Herzig-Yoshinaga decided she too would "exhume documents" to see if she might learn more about the history of incarceration (Herzig-Yoshinaga 1997).

Herzig-Yoshinaga's story and status as a Nisei female re-collector of Nikkei history has already been persuasively narrated and analyzed by camp studies scholar Thomas Fujita-Rony, who argues that Herzig-Yoshinaga's extensive postwar clerical training and work during her "apolitical" years enabled her to finesse the skills she would use to become the researcher she did. While Fujita-Rony focuses not on literacy per se and instead on Herzig-Yoshinaga's "gendered labor," his study also serves as a perfect illustration of what Deborah Brandt has referred to as women's "appropriation" of literacy sponsorship, where "deeply sanctioned" forms of women's literacy, like clerical work, can "become grounds for covert, innovative appropriation" (Brandt 1998, 182). As such, I will refer extensively to Fujita-Rony's article but will read it through the twin lenses of cultural rhetorics and literacy theory.

Many historical scholars had combed the archives prior to Herzig-Yoshinaga, including Weglyn, but no one had ever found any redress-related evidence that could be used in court. Herzig-Yoshinaga knew this when she started but proceeded nonetheless, drawing upon the literacy skills she had developed as a clerical worker since the war, as she developed detailed records of each and every incarceration-related file and an elaborate cross-referencing system that sometimes included up to ten separate index cards per document (Fujita-Rony 2003; Herzig-Yoshinaga 2008).

As Fujita-Rony (2003, 44) notes, such a "painstaking process is extraordinarily time-consuming . . . and demands strict attention to detail at all times." Given the "strict attention" such a time-consuming process entails, I would argue that Herzig-Yoshinaga *rhetorically attended* the National Archives, first becoming *present at*, then *taking charge of*, and then *applying herself to* the archives as she *stretched her mind toward* what was not readily obvious, all with the intent of helping facilitate social change. Herzig-Yoshinaga's rhetorical attendance meant contending with the files of several government agencies, including the Justice Department and the War Relocation Authority. But the WRA records by themselves consisted of "several million pages of documents" that lacked a complete index. Thus, Herzig-Yoshinaga's attendance became "roughly equivalent to indexing all the information in a library, working from a card catalog that only gave a subject description by shelf without individual book titles or authors" or even direct access to the stacks (Fujita-Rony 2003, 45).

In order to find that "single needle in a field full of haystacks," Herzig-Yoshinaga rhetorically applied herself to the archives. There she drew upon "[h]er years of clerical work and her previous political activism," where she developed "a sensitivity to implicit meanings, or as she put it, 'seeing more than what was written on the paper.'" In addition, though, Herzig-Yoshinaga also "took the unusual extra step of noting when documents she looked at mentioned other documents" (Fujita-Rony 2003, 45) and created not just a re-collection, but a massive intertextual web of information.

Such rhetorical attendance would eventually allow Herzig-Yoshinaga to identify documentary evidence that the government not only knowingly engaged in unconstitutional reasoning to justify the mass incarceration but that it had also explicitly attempted to cover up that reasoning by destroying early drafts and rewriting reports (Fujita-Rony 2003, 49). Herzig-Yoshinaga had found several memos between various officials regarding an original draft of what would eventually become the government's final report on the mass incarceration, including both detailed editorial requirements that included "what page, what sentence, what word should be changed" (quoted in Fujita-Rony 2003, 49) and instructions to destroy all of the ten original copies. But other documents suggested that only nine had been recovered and destroyed. It was not until a few years into her research that she would happen upon a copy of the report, with a different binding than the final version, just sitting on the archivist's desk. Never one to ask, Herzig-Yoshinaga instead rhetorically attended to the redress movement (and the Nikkei community at large) by attending to this spontaneous moment in the archives and opened up the text, where she "noticed all these notes written on the margins" (quoted in Fujita-Rony 2003, 50). It was the missing tenth copy. According to Fujita-Rony, this original version of the report illustrated the "racist basis" and "utterly unconstitutional rationale" of senior government officials regarding the plausibility of "determining the loyalty of Japanese Americans." Assistant Secretary of War John McCloy fully recognized that the original version would expose the illegality of the government's wartime policy, which is why he had demanded revisions in memos, hoping to cover up the fact that government agencies knew they were engaging in unconstitutional behavior (Fujita-Rony 2003, 49). While Michi Weglyn had proved the government's rationale to be a lie, Herzig-Yoshinaga had just found proof that the government had actively sought to cover-up the fact they knew it was a lie. This proof would be instrumental in more than one redress case that would soon be reargued in front of the US Supreme Court. But no one would have known the significance of the marked-up copy of the final report sitting on the archivist's table without the elaborate web of documents Herzig-Yoshinaga had not only reCollected, but had organized, and cross-referenced, rhetorically attending the National Archives to help set right what she could now prove the government knew was wrong.

RECOLLECTING AFTER THE MOVEMENT: ATTENDING MYSELF ATTENDING COMMUNITY

> What I do in terms of Asian American history goes beyond the processes of gathering/assembling/accumulating information for study . . . Since we

> operate in terms of a world that is framed by conscious and unconscious assumptions and constructions, we must actively and reflexively struggle to achieve a modicum of clarity. We must reread, rethink, reconceptualize, and reconstruct in order to be able to recover our pasts, if only because dominant society hegemony is such a powerful influence. Its premises and biases shape the very intellectual environment through which we view and interpret data, as much as it shapes the form and content of "the data" themselves.
>
> —*Hirabayashi*

In the same review where Gary Okihiro critiqued Michi Weglyn's work for being "nothing new," he claimed what remained "untold" was not the story of government abuse and lies, but "the history of the Japanese internees themselves, their innermost aspirations and fears, and their daily struggle for survival." As Okihiro continued, "I find no comfort in [the] portrayal of Japanese as passive, faceless beings manipulated by white administrators and historically worthy of mention only because their history fits the needs of the wider society" (Okihiro 1977a, 169). Later, he accused Weglyn of hypocritically "castigating white racists for stereotyping Japanese," only to follow in their footsteps by "adopt[ing] their terminology . . . describ[ing] the Japanese in such terms as 'orderly Japanese fashion,' 'a people to whom indolence was foreign,' 'self-effacing,' and 'cultural imperative unquestioning obedience'" (171).

While Weglyn herself was quite critical of the JACL and its wartime leaders, who advocated compliance at every stage of the incarceration period (as seems fairly clear when one reads her book), Okihiro's critique nonetheless explicitly aligned *Years of Infamy* with the "liberal-JACL" tradition of Japanese American history (Okihiro 1977a, 168). Such accounts of Nikkei history, perhaps most clearly embodied by Bill Hosokawa's *Nisei: The Quiet Americans*, typically downplay incarceree agency and resistance and/or turn the history of camps into one more obstacle to be overcome by playing the rules and waiting out the incarceration period.

Given the enormous impact Weglyn's book had on the community and the movement for redress—an impact, Murray writes, that Okihiro (1977a, 247) later acknowledged—the overall tone of Okihiro's critique may have been misplaced at the time. However, his argument about incarceree stereotypes and agency is important—and something that lingers even today, twenty years after the passage of the Civil Liberties Act, even among progressives interested in social justice. For example, in 2008 the progressive education magazine *Rethinking Schools* published an article by Sansei writer Carol Tateishi, "Taking a Chance with Words: Why are the Asian-American Kids Silent in Class?" (Tateishi 2007–2008). In her introduction, Tateishi notes that while she spent most of her 1950s social life among Japanese Americans, because she "attended predominately white schools," her father raised her and her siblings "to make [their] way in the dominant culture." A conscious decision on her father's part in the shadow of mass incarceration, learning to "make one's way" included "hav[ing] the words and the confidence to speak up and use language like full-blooded Americans," in contrast to the "proper Japanese" who were raised "not to speak," resulting in the community's "lack" of "leaders who could make [their] case and resist government forces" during the 1940s (Tateishi 2007–2008, 20). While this narrative is merely constructed as an introductory kickoff into a much needed discussion about Asian American students' lack of participatory talk in classes that require class participation, the stereotype of the quiet Japanese Other lingers in Tateishi's construction of the Nikkei community, where presumably no dissidence ever reared a public head. Against this constructed backdrop, readers are implicitly encouraged to see "full-blooded American" moves, like the talk-filled, child-rearing choices of Tateishi's father, as individually heroic acts in the face of Japanese silence and insecurity.

Along with the interdisciplinary gaps outlined in the last chapter, it is these seemingly progressive myths of Nikkei oppression and Nikkei (lack of) resistance that led to this project. Even with my lifelong attendance, I was raised amidst these progressive-at-the-time myths that while Nikkei who "talked back" or complained (or retained any bitterness at all) were individually heroic, they were still numerically few. Japanese people didn't talk back; hell, they barely even talked! You never heard them on TV, never heard them in a movie. I could barely hear my own father when he spoke, even though my stepmother always said that in his mind, he was yelling. And as much as I remember each and every intimate moment that I spent with my Nikkei grandmother—the feel of her hands, the smell of her clothes and hair, the shape of her smile—not only did I never hear her complain about *anything*, I'm not sure I ever heard her at all. To this day, I can't remember the *sound of her voice*, and as a poet obsessed with sensory memory, I remember sound.

Meanwhile, as my father's activism heated up, books poured into our home: *Shedding Silence*, *Breaking Silence*, even *The Quiet Americans*, all without any conversations about differences or nuances in meaning. And in the roughly 50/50 White/Black post-busing public schools that I attended in Portland, Oregon, many of which had started to attend to heroic accounts of African American struggle, Japanese Americans were barely known. Mass incarceration, if taught at all, was something *I* brought into classrooms or mentioned to my teachers. And since my schools seemed so race-conscious, I often presumed the myths that seemed progressive at the time must be true: that while camp was clearly *bad*, very few incarcerees engaged in conscious struggle; that those who did were "numerically insignificant"; that Nikkei incarcerees were generally quiet or even silent; that this silence meant that they were passive; and that, really, it took the Sansei to "make some noise" and spur the old folks to redress all they had endured.

Of course, there is no reason to share any of this unless (in an obligatory I-was-blind-but-now-I-see rhetorical move) I now know *these myths were wrong*.

RECOLLECTING AFTER THE MOVEMENT: ATTENDING MYSELF ATTENDING WRITING-TO-REDRESS

> And so I started to examine those records, and they grabbed me, absolutely grabbed me.
>
> —*Herzig-Yoshinaga*

As eager as I was to enter and access the archives at the Japanese American National Museum (JANM) and Densho, I couldn't have been prepared to find what I did, especially at the JANM: diaries in both Japanese and English, multiple drafts of petitions, quick-sketched poetry, neatly labeled letters, chaotic files of news clippings and notations, mimeographed handbills and flyers, handwritten script, fading paper, crossed-out text, illegible notes . . . the more I found, the more I could barely remember to breathe. The feelings alternated between utter excitement and utter embarrassment. Sometimes I felt my face burn, ashamed I did not know. Each piece of paper, a slap in the face: *How could you think we wouldn't write? How could you think we would just sit there in camp? How could you think we wouldn't try to make and remake our lives?* There in the archives, I had to face myself facing the vast display of written activity spread across the table; I both had and had not believed the lies. Like so many other progressives before me, I had, at various points in my life, maintained the myth of the passive American so I could individually proclaim *that's not me*.

And yet, there it was. Nikkei dissidence. The quiet and loud complaints, angst, swearings, bitterness, protests, and resistance I had hoped for but was not sure that I would find. In JANM, I could touch the paper, touch the words, touch the penciled script or mimeographed ink. I could see the quick-drafted poems on pages of preprinted diaries, uneven dashes typed in the dates, spiral-bound paper handwritten and wide-ruled, tiny drawings filling in space between all the text. On some documents, crossed-out text and handwritten notes projected images in my mind of real hands writing, committed to making the words perform the writer's intent. And in Densho, in a newer form of literacy, digital access allowed me to attend video testimonies far from the physical location of the agents who voiced their memories in public. Memories of women and men pilfering time for poems written in camp hospitals, rewriting questions on the infamous "loyalty" forms, hand cutting stencils of flyers for mimeographs, or hiding illegal agendas and handwritten notes inside a basket of freshly ironed clothes.

In other words, amidst the drafts and diaries and descriptions and details, my own archival re-collecting became not a close reading of texts but a close reading of activities, a reading of practice, of literacy-in-action. While individual examples of both polished and draft forms of found writing were fascinating in themselves, the more I attended these reCollections of writing, the more compelled I grew by the sheer amount of it all—the patterns of social activity, the multiplicity of involvement. While my research is far from quantitative, it became harder and harder to believe that writing-to-redress could be "numerically insignificant." The written responses I found to the announcement of military conscription alone numbers fifteen completely different collectively authored or signed documents originating in eight out of the ten WRA camps. And by attending to the drafts and accounts of these literacies-in-action, I was able to see how the process of such public writing-to-redress was always the source of much conscious, collective, and active struggle. The material and ideological sponsors, the multiple authors, the shared distribution of material, the intellectual and emotional labor—all of it enabling public performances of dissidence, all of it enabling writing-to-redress to enter the public sphere.

As I started to conceive of this type of public writing-to-redress, I came to see it as a form of literacy-in-action meant to interrupt the status quo of the processes involved with incarceration. In other words, these collectively authored and authorized texts were meant to make a public commotion or, in the discourse of Hip Hop, make some noise. These were the literacy activities performed out in the open, collaboratively composed or agreed to in public spaces, or whose text was intended for wide distribution in camp or beyond the barbed wire fence to government officials. In other words, this writing-to-redress was meant to be seen, meant to be read. Even if the immediate and named audience were other incarcerees, participants in this activity knew and perhaps intended that government officials and agents would see it. For this reason, participants in this activity would have wanted us to "hear" it and receive it; and the only reason we have not is because it has been silenced by what Jessica Enoch calls "rhetorical forgetting."[5] As writing that took place in public, this writing-to-redress, these texts and accounts, are ones we should have been long able to attend.

Not so with the other forms I was finding. There, amidst all the texts and accounts of public literacies-in-action, were also private forms of writing—letters, diaries, notebooks, handwritten poems and drafts. I found most of these at JANM, some were found in other digital archives I eventually stumbled upon, much of it written in English.[6] Unlike the participants of public writing-to-redress, authors of these "hidden literacies" (Finders 1997) did not intend their activities and texts to enter the wider public sphere, did not intend their writing to be circulated in camp or beyond the barbed wire. These writers were more likely to presume that government officials and agents would not see their texts.[7] Private but present, quiet but active, these sites of literate activity allowed incarcerees a space to engage in private protest, struggle for psychological strength, and bear witness to specific incidents of injustice. As such, this writing became another form of literacy-in-action—a rhetorical way to do something with writing but without making noise or a public commotion, as incarcerees made use of a tool that could both "speak" and remain quiet at the exact same time, all in order to survive and resist the psychological effects wrought by their imprisonment.

Over the course of my research, these roughed-out types of writing-to-redress, private / silent / quiet and public / noisy / loud, slowly became my two broad subcategories of choice. While maintaining this distinction runs the risk of reifying problematic dichotomies (especially public/private), for the sake of this study I believe in the efficacy of "discourses of measurement" (Cintron 1997, 210). As literacy and rhetoric ethnographer Ralph Cintron once explained, even though such imposed "creations of order" can contain/limit our thoughts about the world, they can also, simultaneously, allow for "deeper and deeper levels of reflection" (229–31). In other words, "discourses of measurement" can allow for a much-needed rhetorical attendance of what has been previously downplayed and/or covered up. In my own case, separating writing-to-redress into categories relative to the intended private or public circulation of texts allows me to attend to the difference between literacies-in-action whose silence has been *chosen* and literacies-in-action whose silence has been *imposed*. By examining private writing-to-redress together, I can attend to patterns across texts and activities whose silence was chosen by their authors. Choosing to come to voice without making a sound, these writers codified complaints, bore witness to negativity, and held arguments with the self. In contrast, by examining public forms of writing-to-redress, I can attend to the patterns of texts and/or activities whose participants intended to make a public commotion: male and female participation, wide use of public space, collaborative authorship, struggles over wording, multi-draft texts. These are the literacies-in-action we should have known about but generally do not, as they are the texts and activities of public commotion and dissidence, subsequently downplayed, rhetorically forgotten, and/or archived away from mainstream accounts of history. In others words, the writing-to-redress whose silence was imposed by authorities in the government, JACL leadership, and/or "official knowledge" (Apple 2000) of the past.

Which is all to say that thinking in terms of public/noisy/loud and private/silent/quiet writing-to-redress allows me to attend not simply to History but to the ways history has both been *hidden* and/or selectively *used* against Japanese and other Asian Americans. If public writing-to-redress allows for a redressing of the myth that few incarcerated Nikkei ever "wrote back," private writing-to-redress allows for a redressing of the myth that silent means passive and/or acquiescent. Archival recovery retains an ability to reveal such silent and silenced activity, downplayed or covered up even in a community's own collective memory. As such, it remains a vital political project for those of us who too often believe the lies they/we tell about ourselves. While literacy and composition studies taught me to see writing as a practice, and ethnic and feminist rhetorics taught me how to understand that practice, Nisei women activists are the ones who showed me a method: archival recovery as a means to bring truth to power, as a means to hear what's been denied. Attending to my mentors across all my lifeworlds, I began to stretch my mind across the archives and attend the activities they offered.

Notes

1. Joseph Kurihara, Harry Ueno, and Kiyoshi Okamoto or singularly unique organizations like the Heart Mountain Fair Play Committee, or ideological fanatics aligning themselves with Japanese imperialism.

2. According to Alice Yang Murray, right before "evacuation," JACL leader Mike Masaoka testified before the Tolan Committee that the JACL was 20,000 members strong with sixty-two chapters in 300 communities across the United States. But during the war, Togo Tanaka, another JACL leader, "admitted that the organization 'exaggerated' its membership to 'impress the government.'" The actual membership was closer to 7,500 (Murray 2008, 120–21).

3. Literally, "dog" in Japanese.

4. All the while eliding the fact that the JACL-designed plan of recruiting Nisei volunteers out of the camp had fundamentally failed—3,000 had been hoped for while only 1,200 volunteered and only 805 were actually accepted. It was not until the draft was re-implemented that incarcerated Japanese American men entered the military in the "numerically significant" numbers typically implied (A. Herzig-Yoshinaga, pers. comm.).

5. Citing the work of Barbara Zelizer, Enoch (2008, 2) writes that "forgetting can be seen as a rhetorical act . . . [when it] . . . allows for 'the substitution of one memory for another.'"

6. I found even more private writing in Japanese, writing I could not read—a fact I attribute not only to the legacy of language loss in the Nikkei community after World War II but also to an even longer legacy of Eurocentric language-learning options in US public schools. I can only hope that future biliterate scholars will attend to these Japanese-language "hidden" literacies and either translate or offer up their analyses.

7. Due to the working definitions I have outlined above, I do not look at letters to and from the Department of Justice (DOJ) camps, where many Issei men were imprisoned as "enemy aliens" separate from their families. There, the stated policy

was that mail to and from these camps would be heavily restricted and censored. For an overall discussion of mail to and from the DOJ camps see Fiset (2001). For personal accounts of these letters, see Kanemoto (2003), Ichikawa (1999), Akashi (2004), Akutsu (1997), and Groves (1998). For discussions of the legacy of DOJ literacies in general, see Okawa (2003, 2008).

3
RECOLLECTED TAPESTRIES
The Circumstances behind Writing-to-Redress

> Persuaded that the enormity of a bygone injustice has been only partially perceived, I have taken upon myself the task of piecing together what might be called the "forgotten"—or ignored—parts of the tapestry of those years.
>
> —*Weglyn (1976)*

Four years after Michi Weglyn, the "mother of redress," published *Years of Infamy*, growing grassroots agitation for redress finally forced the US government into forming the Commission on Wartime Relocation and Internment of Civilians (CWRIC), complete with (now paid) research associate Aiko Herzig-Yoshinaga, and opening public hearings on the experiences of former incarcerees. The commission was controversial among activists since many thought the process stalled an active movement that had started to gain momentum and potentially prevented redress for Issei former incarcerees, many of whom were dying (Hohri 1988; Shimabukuro 2001). But in retrospect, even some of the CWRIC's more vocal dissidents acknowledge the

DOI: 10.5876/9781607324010.c003

cathartic role that the hearings played for the community. Over 750 former incarcerees, their descendants and supporters, and a few apologists testified for twenty days across ten cities, with many airing their bitterness and dissidence for the first time in public (Kashima 1997, xvii). Beyond the emotional catharsis for its participants, though, the public hearings also played a significant role in shifting the government's official position on the mass incarceration in the public sphere. Prior to the publication of *Personal Justice Denied*, the CWRIC's report based on the hearings, the US government had either completely evaded the episode in mainstream public accounts of the history, like sanctioned public school textbooks, or they had steadfastly maintained the apologetic myth of "military necessity" (Kashima 1997, xix). But as Tetsuden Kashima (1997) notes, after the hearings, the CWRIC's subsequent report, and the passage of the 1988 Civil Liberties Act, the US government formally admitted they had been wrong as they issued the commission's recommended apology along with token reparations for all living former incarcerees. Unclaimed allocated money was turned over to the Civil Liberties Public Education Fund, out of which many community historians, including my father, would eventually be granted funding to help raise awareness about Nikkei struggles during and after the incarceration period. Between the testimonies recorded, the report published, and the fund created, the community's dissidence continued to enable re-collection of Nikkei life, as subsequent studies, community projects, artwork, and film often referred back to, or received funding from, one of these government sponsors of collective memory.

Through such studies, projects, artwork, and film, the majority of which came into being after the Civil Liberties Act was passed, we have been able to re-collect quite a lot of history that had previously been downplayed or covered up. For my purposes, these rhetorical re-collections have provided helpful context to the literacy activities of both private and public writing-to-redress. As such, in this chapter, before I turn to the writing I found, let me attend to some of the broader historical, political, material, and cultural circumstances in order to expand the "limits of the local" (Brandt and Clinton 2002) and better understand this recurrent practice of Nikkei literacy.

TIGHT CONFIGURATIONS: NIKKEI LITERACY NETWORKS BEFORE THE WAR

Although poor
I will never give up my subscription
To the Hokubei Jiji
I look forward to the news from my poet friends.

—Sue Yoneyama
Hokubei Jiji, March 16, 1934
(translated by Sachiko Honda)

By several accounts, the Issei were a particularly literate immigrant group (Ichioka 1988; James 1987; Tamura 1994). While definitions and measures of Japanese literacy have varied (Rubinger 2007), prior to their arrival in the United States, Issei men had typically attended school in Japan for somewhere between five and seven years, while women had attended for three to six (Tamura 1994, 252n47). This amount of schooling should have been enough to read with some facility and even write simple things in *kana*, the syllabic forms of Japanese script.[1] Thomas James (1987, 11) claims that this relatively high degree of immigrant literacy (90 percent of all Issei over age ten could read by 1910), allowed for the rise of a "tight configuration of community institutions" that included Buddhist, Christian, and other kinship or ethnic organizations; economic cooperative arrangements; and a vibrant Japanese-language press.

The origins of this press can be traced back to 1888, when a group of exiled student laborers started a transnational weekly to critique Meiji government reforms.[2] According to Eileen Tamura (1994, 71), by 1920 periodicals serving the Issei on the "mainland" would amount to roughly fifteen. According to Kazuo Ito, Seattle alone saw the rise of five different daily vernaculars serving Nikkei in Washington, Montana, Utah, and Idaho. In addition, Ito notes that over thirty-five different Japanese-language weekly papers and monthly magazines were also published and circulated in the Seattle area, although some only lasted three or four issues (Ito 1973, 729). The community vernaculars seemed to reach many Nikkei households, as circulation numbers cited range from 4,000 to 25,000 during a period when the Issei population in the western states ranged from 50,000 to 65,000.[3]

As vibrant counterpublics in their own right, these vernaculars served as rhetorical sites for the community's creative expression of emotion as well as their ideological battles. While several vernaculars published traditional forms of poetry, many editorials, articles, and letters to the editor debated how Nikkei residents should most appropriately affiliate with an increasingly imperialist Japan or how they could best respond to the increasing amount and degree of racist exclusion acts and laws in the United States. In addition, within the papers' pages, Issei community members debated various aspects of the community's "second generation problem" as they weighed the linguistic, cultural, and political ramifications of being both neglected by and caught "between empires" (Azuma 2005).

In addition to the newspapers, prewar Japanese-language and literacy networks included a vast number of tanka, haiku, and senryu clubs that arose up and down the West Coast, where both men and women regularly gathered to write, read, and critique each others' work (De Cristoforo 1997a; Nomura 2001; Honda 1989; Yamada, Yasutake, and Yasutake 2002; Sumida 1988). In addition, Junko Kobayashi (2005, 23–24) has pointed to a multistate Japanese-language literary association that emerged in the 1930s called Bungei Renmei, where writers collectively sponsored their own magazine, *Shukaku*, which served both as a creative forum and a mode of communication between writers as they published poems, short stories, essays, critiques of previously published work, reports on local literary events, and letters to the editor.

While these US-based Nikkei clubs and associations have been noted in Asian American poetry anthologies, oral histories, and literary scholarship, they must be understood transnationally. Audrey Kobayashi, for example, suggests that Issei poetry clubs in Canada descend from nineteenth-century literacy practices in Japan, where, by the end of the century, poetry had become a highly popular pastime, such that "no village was without at least one poetry circle" and most children (including future Issei) had become "well-versed in the classic forms of poetic expression" (A. Kobayashi 1995, 217). In addition, Junko Kobayashi asserts that *Shukaku* was simply a US-based *dojin zasshi*, a type of literary journal sponsored by members of the publication's parent association. Popular in Japan during the 1920s, dojin zasshis derived their name from martial arts *dojos* (studios/practice places), as the journals were seen as types of studios-in-print where writers could "collectively polish and improve" their writing via published discussions or letters on previously published work (J. Kobayashi 2005, 24–25). As such, many Issei and Kibei (those born in the United States but educated in Japan) who took part in such literary clubs, associations, and magazines, were drawing on preexisting literacy practices, transnational "funds of knowledge" (Moll and González 1994), to negotiate life and meaning in their new home.

But for US-educated Nisei, full access to such networks of Japanese-language literacy was limited. Somewhere between 30 percent and 70 percent of Nisei living on the West Coast attended Japanese-language schools before the war,[4] but by several accounts, the schools were more successful at introducing the moral codes of Meiji era Japan and strengthening other forms of ethnic identity than they were at fostering reading or writing in Japanese. As such, while most Nisei could speak and understand some Japanese, few were literate enough to read and write in their heritage language. As far as literacy was concerned, most Nisei were English-dominant.

Fully aware of this reality, Issei community leaders moved to develop English-language forums for the subsequent generation. According to David Yoo, some language schools regularly sponsored English-language essay contests "with the bridge of understanding as the theme—so much so that it seemed that the contests were held for the purpose of promoting the idea" (Yoo 2000, 31). Meanwhile, during the mid-1920s, Nikkei vernaculars began to include English-language sections, as different publishers and editors rhetorically positioned their papers as either representative of or mentor to the Nisei. For example, when the LA-based *Rafu Shimpo* started their English-language section, the space was explicitly advertised as "for the Nisei by the Nisei." Others followed, like the *Shin Sekai* in 1929, the "Daily Friend, Counseler [*sic*] and Servant" of the Nisei (Yoo 2000, 70–71). According to Yoo, the English-language sections in most of the Issei-run papers "promoted an ideology of racial responsibility that encouraged Nisei to respond to racism by embracing life in America as loyal, hardworking citizens who would 'prove' their worth" (74).

But Los Angeles was also home to *Doho*, a leftist-oriented paper started in 1938 whose English section, titled "Socialist leaning," accused other papers of not representing ordinary Nikkei concerns. *Doho*'s columnists, like John Kitahara, would regularly challenge the community's own class structure by pointing out that when other papers advocated for "the protection of Japanese industry," they really meant "only the protection of the interests of the Japanese owners and very little protection for the workers," insinuating that this approach was all "a clever scheme to dupe the [Nisei] workers" (Kitahara quoted in Yoo 2000, 75).

In addition to these Issei-sponsored, ideologically heterogeneous forums, a few Nisei-run, English-only publications emerged before the war. For example, in 1928 the Seattle-based *Japanese American Courier* became the first English-only Nikkei paper when it was started by Nisei publisher and editor, James Sakamoto. One of the JACL's "founding fathers" (Ichioka 2006, 97), Sakamoto is perhaps best known for espousing the idea that the Nisei should, in his words, "'lower the anchor' into American life" (quoted in Ichioka 2006, 95) and serve as "a bridge of understanding between Japan and the United States" (quoted in Ichioka 2006, 92–93). In addition to the *Courier*, another important prewar Nisei-run English-language publication was *Current Life* magazine, published and edited monthly by James Omura in San Francisco. Touted as the "Magazine for the American Born Japanese," *Current Life* dealt with Nisei arts and politics and either featured or highlighted the work of Nisei journalists who edited and wrote the English sections of Nikkei vernaculars and emerging Nisei literary figures like Toyo Suyemoto, Toshio Mori, and Hisaye Yamamoto.

What is difficult to discern, however, is the degree of Nisei consumption of all the community-based English-language writing discussed above. While Yoo (2000, 72) speculates that Nisei youth read the English sections of whatever papers their parents subscribed to, Yuji Ichioka points out that during the 1920s and 1930s, the majority of Nisei were children and teenagers and may have only been marginally interested in content beyond sports or community affairs. In Seattle, specifically, most adult Nisei at the time were either "working-class people with little interest or time to devote to international or national affairs" during the Great Depression or they had progressive politics at odds with Sakamoto's anti-labor bias (Ichioka 2006, 117). As such, Ichioka claims that the *Courier*, for example, appealed to only a "small group of college-bound and college educated Niseis" (118).

Regardless of how many Nisei, or even Issei, were taking part in these pre-WWII Japanese- and/or English-language literacy networks within the community, these "tight configurations" helped create and foster a transnational but US-based community orientation toward the use of writing to navigate one's social, political, and cultural circumstances, including those that transpired both before and after the bombing of Pearl Harbor.

"BLUEPRINTS": DRAFTING THE POLITICAL CONDITIONS OF MASS INCARCERATION

According to many histories of Nikkei life in the United States in scholarly, narrative, and oral forms, mass incarceration came not as a complete aberration but as part of a history of anti-Japanese racism, both legal and "everyday" forms. Whether Nikkei residents were racially conscious or not, legalized racism affected everyone—from the laws preventing the Issei from becoming US citizens or owning any property, including all the previously barren land Nikkei families cultivated into rich farmlands up and down the West Coast, to restrictive housing covenants in cities like Seattle and Los Angeles that prevented Japanese Americans and other people of color from buying homes in certain neighborhoods (Yoo 2000, 51; Shimabukuro 2001, xvi). In contrast, everyday experiences of racism ranged in both quality and quantity for members of the Nikkei community, as different patterns of experiences depended on urban versus rural realities, gender roles and expectations, social class position and cultural capital accrued in both Japan and the United States, citizenship status, dominant language forms, and various regional idiosyncrasies. Some Nikkei residents, for example, regularly experienced name-calling on the street or in school, discrimination in hiring practices, or racialized harassment and/or violence in both the mainstream and the community press. Others remember more benevolence and friendship in their multiethnic, multiracial communities and/or schools prior to Japan's bombing of Pearl Harbor.

For most formerly incarcerated Nikkei, however, December 7, 1941 is indeed a day that lives "in infamy." Oral histories, memoirs, testimonies, and diaries all attest to the fact that Nikkei residents collectively experienced an increase in anti-Japanese hatred that day. My choice of a phenomenological clustered verb—*collectively experienced*—is purposeful here. As Tetsuden Kashima has recently argued, it is perhaps more accurate to think of anti-Japanese racism as a "backdrop" to the events that transpired post-12/7. In his *Judgment without Trial*, Kashima amply demonstrates that the US government and its agencies had secretly been creating a working "blueprint" for the mass incarceration since 1931, after Japan invaded and occupied Manchuria and US agencies began to actively surveil and compile data on Issei residents, including extensive details on their daily activities and associations (Kashima 2003,

16). By 1940 this blueprint took on an institutionalized form when Congress passed the Alien Registration Act (Smith Act). According to Kashima,

> Under [these laws], all foreign nationals were to be fingerprinted, registered, and prevented from possessing "firearms, explosives, or radio transmitting apparatus." It also became illegal . . . to be a member of an organization promoting the destruction of the US government. The government developed a questionnaire for aliens that requested information on citizenship status, occupation, residence, biographical data, and organizational memberships. When the registration process ended, the United States had rosters and life histories for 4,921,452 foreign nationals. This list constituted a significant data source from which the government could create sublists of particular groups and individuals and their locations. (23)

Amidst all the covert and overt profiling of Japanese nationals (who were banned from becoming US citizens), however, government officials often blurred the distinction between foreign- and US-born Nikkei residents in their public and interoffice rhetoric (Kashima 2003, 16). This prewar blurring served to racialize away the legal distinction between citizens and noncitizens, thus preparing the ideological groundwork necessary for the mass incarceration of "all persons of Japanese ancestry" along the West Coast.

While the Issei, of course, knew they were being asked for extensive personal information along with being required to be fingerprinted and registered as "foreign nationals," the degree to which most Nikkei residents knew of this larger ideological blueprint seems to have been limited. Instead, within most personal and historical accounts, Pearl Harbor marks the beginning of mass imprisonment. In the months that followed, most Nikkei living along the West Coast would destroy, give away, or sell at absurdly low prices most of their property and belongings after being informed they would be allowed to take only what they could carry. By spring, over 110,000 residents, two-thirds of them legal citizens, would be forcibly removed from their homes, placed behind barbed wire, and surrounded by uniformed men with guns.

BAD ENOUGH: THE MATERIAL LIFE BEHIND WRITING-TO-REDRESS

> [A]t the time of the newscast she could only ask the more immediate questions, such as "What was it like?" and "Did you have enough to eat?" How

could she know that they were the wrong questions? The only possible response was, "Really, it wasn't that bad."

—*Yamada*

Memories of the material experience of mass incarceration have been difficult for many former incarcerees to articulate out loud; this was especially true before the mass hearings. Today, though, numerous personal, sociological, and historical accounts exist that chronicle the ways camp conditions were simultaneously *bad* and—in contrast to the *other* camps of World War II—*"not bad enough"* (Omori 1999). While many of these bad and not-bad-enough conditions will be threaded throughout the book, let me offer a brief overview here of some general conditions that impacted the activity of writing-to-redress.

Communal Living/Lack of Privacy

After the US government forcibly removed Nikkei residents from their homes, it first "relocated" them to assembly centers constructed on racetracks, fairgrounds, and livestock pavilions located on the outskirts of major West Coast cities. There, the majority of incarcerees were forced to live in horse stalls and stadiums in makeshift "family apartments" divided by thin half-wall partitions. As Michi Weglyn (1976, 80) so bluntly put it, there, in places that had such ridiculous euphemisms as "Camp Harmony," inmates "ate communally, showered communally, defecated communally."

The lack of privacy followed people throughout the whole incarceration period, even though it was not as severe at the more permanent WRA camps. By a few accounts, it did limit how much people would write. Because the walls were thin, typing could not be done at night, especially if the content needed to be kept a secret. And those who had access to typewriters were sometimes presumed to be spies. At times, people would stop writing or reading because the light was bothering other people or the noise of others was too distracting.

These reactions were understandable given the cramped, flimsily constructed quarters. In most cases, families of five to eight members were assigned bare rooms, without inside walls or ceilings, measuring twenty by twenty-four feet, while smaller families shared rooms of sixteen by twenty

FIGURE 3.1. Two children walking among barracks at Minidoka, Idaho. (Photographer unknown, 1940s, Wing Luke Asian Museum Collection, Densho.)

feet. However, in 1983 the government's own Commission on Wartime Relocation and Internment of Civilians reported that two families had doubly occupied over 900 rooms (US Commission on Wartime Relocation and Internment of Civilians 1997, 158). Each barrack held four to six families, while twelve to fourteen barracks composed a block of 250 to 300 incarcerees; one block shared a mess hall, laundry room, latrine, and recreation hall (Weglyn 1976, 84). For the writing-to-redress involved in collective action, these common areas became crucial locations of writing-to-redresss, as mess halls often became the places where resolutions, demands, and manifestos were read, debated, and passed, and the walls to latrines or mess halls often served as bulletin boards for dissident flyers. Forced into semi-communal living, incarcerees took advantage of what they had to organize as they needed.

Other Subpar Living Conditions

In more than one contemporary account of camp, historians and/or former incarcerees recount the completely inadequate living conditions the community had to endure (Mackey 2002; Harth 2001; Chin 2002; Uchida 1982;

FIGURE 3.2. Incarcerees lining up at a mess hall in Manzanar, California. (Photograph by Ansel Adams, 1943, Ansel Adams Collection, Densho.)

US Commission on Wartime Relocation and Internment of Civilians 1997; Yamada 1976; Omori 1999; Nishimoto 1995; Weglyn 1976; Hayashi 2004; Inada 2000). In fact, aside from the 1943 loyalty questionnaire and the 1944 reinstatement of the draft (both of which will be discussed in chapter 4), subpar living conditions served as the most common instigator of writing-to-redress. From the sack mattresses incarcerees had to fill with straw to the tar paper walls and roofs that barely withstood the harsh summer or winter weather of the desert camps, to the inconsistent availability of running, hot water, to the lack of promised winter clothing, to the shortage in adequate medical facilities or practitioners, to the absence of culturally relevant or even nutrient-filled food, subpar living conditions continuously sparked writing-to-redress, as incarcerees frequently wrote up individual and collective complaints in order to set right what was wrong and relieve the immediate suffering of their community.

Occasionally these conditions even called forth more organized, public protest. In June 1942, for example, the lack of decent food tipped off a strike in the largest assembly center, Santa Anita, as 800 Nisei who had, in a show of patriotism, volunteered to help make camouflage nets, sat down on the job complaining of hunger (Weglyn 1976, 81–82). For some, like twenty-something Nisei Mary Nakahara, early collective actions such as these would spark an intense, inner debate worked through in private writing over the value of Nikkei protest against racist discrimination (Nakahara 1942a, June 16). And yet, despite how people may have felt about public protest, access to substantial and nutritious food remained an issue throughout the camp years, serving as a tipping point in some places—like Manzanar—for individual actions followed by collective revolt (Ueno et al. 1986).

Collective strikes, protests, petitions, and written complaints regarding living conditions would also continue throughout the camp years. While most of the collectively organized and public writing-to-redress emerged in reaction to the registration and the draft, some of these literacies of public intervention seem as though they were built upon the collective authority generated through the redressing of day-to-day conditions. For example, within Chica Sugino's papers on the draft at the Japanese American National Museum, both handwritten and typed notes contained what appeared to be possible phrasing the Poston Nisei might use for their collective response. Phrasing referencing their status as "wards of the government" with "shoddy outworn or outgrown apparel" and plain-worded admonishments such as "fix things so we shall have a little more to be fighting for" both suggest that daily conditions were still on the community's mind as rationales for their written dissidence-in-progress. As such, in many ways we might understand earlier pragmatic forms of writing-to-redress not simply as reformist literate activity but as rhetorical training grounds for subsequent, broader-visioned writing-to-redress that challenged the entire logic of mass incarceration. That is, as incarcerees wrote to redress all the bad but not-bad-enough living conditions they encountered each and every day, they were collecting and codifying their knowledge, feelings, and arguments in order to set right what was wrong and relieve suffering, both in the immediate now and in the distant later.

Access to the Tools of Writing

From the very beginning, government officials had planned to run the incarceration camps like small colonial townships. As such, there would be somewhat elaborate bureaucracies to manage, both inside and outside the barbed wire. And as with all mid-twentieth-century bureaucracies in the United States, an elaborate use of literacy was required in order to make the camps run. A survivable running of the camps, though, was made possible only through the hard work, determination, and underpaid labor of incarcerees,[5] whose commitment to community was exploited by government agencies. Even so, camp workplaces such as WRA schools, camp newspapers, community councils, post offices, libraries, hospitals, and mess halls, required people to fill out forms, organize data, write reports, record inventories, plan menus, take minutes, announce policies, translate rules, draft agendas, transcribe interviews, type letters, maintain files, and dissuade dissent. As such, many incarcerees had, at their jobs, regular access to tools such as typewriters, mimeograph machines, stencils, notebook paper, and pens.[6]

Outside of work, incarcerees had some writing tools, but, according to one former incarceree, mass amounts were not necessarily easy to acquire (Emi 2008). Some materials were certainly brought along in original collections of what could be carried, but other materials that were not borrowed or pilfered from work sites had to be bought at camp stores, via mail order catalogs, or in town by incarcerees who received temporary privileges to leave camp, using camp wages or savings from home (Emi 2008).[7] For those attempting to organize using reproduced copies of flyers or manifestos, access to typewriters and mimeograph machines, along with all necessary ribbons and stencils, was critical; in some cases, siblings and other supporters facilitated this access to resources, widening the sphere of collectivity surrounding the writing. In any case, no matter how resources or access to resources were acquired, people knew they could not expect endless amounts, so in any given act of writing-to-redress, incarcerees tended to use their resources wisely.

Degrees of "Freedom in Confinement"[8]

Whether incarcerees were complaining about a lack of hot water or demanding the unconditional release of men from the stockade or drafting speeches that denounced WRA policy and its community-based spies, much writing-to-redress, ironically, seems to be predicated on the degree of "freedom" incarcerees had while imprisoned. This was particularly true for the women involved in this literacy activity.

More than one historian of Nikkei women's experience has pointed to the pattern that Weglyn poetically noted when she wrote, "Mothers and grandmothers inured to dawn-to-dusk drudgery were all of a sudden ladies of leisure, no longer confronted by the day-to-day struggle for survival" (Weglyn 1976, 82; see also Nakano 1990; Matsumoto 1984). While it is important not to romanticize any aspect of camp, the communal organization of life under mass incarceration did release many women from several of their gender-assigned chores, allowing for a greater amount of time to "choose" among work and leisure activities. Many Nisei women, for example, suddenly found themselves able to be paid for work for which they had been trained, such as typing or other forms of clerical work, but for which they had been unable to find jobs before the war because of racist hiring practices. Others gained work experience they never would have had access to in their beyond-the-barbed-wire sphere. Cherry Kinoshita, for example, a budding young Nisei writer, applied and was hired for a job on the *Minidoka Irrigator*, the WRA-sponsored camp newspaper, where she wrote a weekly column for women, Feminidoka, on how to attend to beauty and fashion amidst harsh camp conditions (Kinoshita 1997, S1). Issei women also worked, tending to gravitate toward mess halls or camp hospitals, places where they could draw upon their extensive knowledge managing the previously private, domestic sphere (Nakano 1990, 63). And all working Nikkei women also experienced a higher degree of pay equity in camp since there, low wages were in fact "equal pay for equal work."

As the days of mass incarceration stretched into weeks into months into years, incarcerees who, for physical, political/ideological, or even classist reasons, did not work for the WRA needed to find ways to fill the time forced upon/allowed by the government agency. For some, writing filled this void, as haiku and senryu clubs that continued in camp from prewar communities became WRA-sanctioned but relatively ignored spaces to maintain, craft, and even publish Japanese expression (De Cristoforo 1997a; J. Kobayashi 2005).[9] Most children and teenagers eventually attended WRA schools, where the mostly white teachers and their Nisei assistants struggled to promote an "ideology and curriculum" (Apple 2004) based on Americanized notions of democracy to the citizen youth who had been imprisoned without trial (James 1987). Adult education courses were also eventually instituted, and many Issei took advantage of the English courses actively promoted by the WRA.

FIGURE 3.3. High school history and English class in Tule Lake, California. (Photographer unknown, 1943, National Archives and Records Administration, Densho.)

Ironically, these freedom-in-confinement locations of literate activity—camp jobs, Japanese poetry clubs, camp schools, and adult English classes—all played, directly and indirectly, intentional and unintentional roles in sponsoring much writing-to-redress. For this book, I have limited my focus to self- and community-sponsored acts of writing-to-redress in order to highlight the ways incarcerees actively composed/drafted their knowledge, feelings, and arguments away from WRA eyes and without permission. In effect, this means not attending to the vast amounts of prose composed by camp newspaper staff or students in school. While I do not doubt that writers in these rhetorical locations also maintained a degree of freedom in confinement, previous scholarship and former incarceree recollections suggest that all newspapers were subject to WRA censorship (though the degree to which it was instituted remains under debate) (Hosokawa 1998; Kessler 1988; Mizuno 2001, 2003), and students were often discouraged from making full-throated critiques in school assignments.[10] However, these points are not to say that these WRA-sanctioned locations of writing did not help facilitate self- and community-sponsored writing-to-redress, as will be made clear in some of the accounts and texts referred to in subsequent chapters. Having access to typewriters and mimeograph machines or more complex English-language literacy, or linguistically "private" spheres of Japanese expression, or even *time* to compose and draft, were vital to the ways in which people wrote to set right what was wrong about and relieve suffering caused by mass incarceration.

INVENTED CLUSTERS: FIXING CULTURE ACROSS TRANSNATIONAL NIKKEI HISTORY

Within camp and redress studies, seemingly passive cultural concepts such as *shikataganai* (it cannot be helped) and gaman (endure; persevere) are continuously offered as reasons why more incarcerees either did not protest or rebel against the entire project of incarceration or did not talk about the experience afterwards (Muller 2001; Takezawa 1995; Nagata 1993; Ina 1998; J. Hirabayashi 1975; Kikumura and Tanaka 1981; Nakano 1990; Ishizuka 2006; Matsumoto 1984; Nagata 1994). While gaman's contested rhetorics (including its passive and active connotations) will be discussed in depth in chapter 4, it is important to note that these two terms are, within camp studies, often discussed together. As such, within the collective discourse that constitutes camp studies, these terms have evolved into what cross-cultural rhetorician LuMing Mao might consider a conceptual "cluster," such that the interpretation of any one word has become intricately laced with the other (Mao 2006, 31).

This conceptual cluster of shikataganai-gaman can be seen in a number of texts. Take the work of legal scholar Eric L. Muller, whose critically acclaimed chronicle of Japanese American draft resistance employs the two terms in order to construct a contrasting backdrop of Nikkei compliance during the incarceration years: "There was little talk among the Nikkei about refusing to comply with the removal program. Most understood that they were up against the power of the federal government during wartime and that resistance would be pointless. Moreover, every Nisei had grown up hearing his Issei parents recite the phrases *shikata ganai* and *gaman suru*—'it can't be helped' and 'just endure it.' It was thus a virtue, or at least a feature, of Japanese culture to accept what could not be changed" (Muller 2001, 26). Or Gil Asakawa, in his historical and cultural "JA sourcebook" on *Being Japanese American*:

> The main values that have held Japanese American communities in check (and in the process made them practically invisible to the American mainstream) can be encapsulated with two phrases: *gaman* and *shikataganai*. Both helped people of Japanese descent through the injustice of the forced evacuation and internment during World War II. And both still have a powerful hold over many of us.
>
> *Gaman*[,] or endure, is invoked when you are required to bite the bullet and quietly accept hardship, such as the forced evacuation and internment, with very few (if any) protests. *Shikataganai*, which means "it can't be helped," was used to keep the anger, especially of the younger JAs, in check during the internment years. It helped prevent mass community upheaval against what was clearly an injustice. (Asakawa 2004, 42)

While containing some elements of truth, such culturalist explanations have unfortunately tended to fix and objectify Japanese essence, such that the presumed lack of protest is attributed to something quintessentially (and almost biologically) Japanese. As Takashi Fujitani notes, in many such accounts, Japanese culture has become reified as "a culture of resignation that encourages subservience or compliance to authority," despite the fact that many Nikkei in both Japan and the United States have, throughout history, regularly "chose to shape their own futures," assuming an ethos of *ganbaru* (persevere in struggle) just as often as any of the presumed passive concepts noted above (Fujitani 2002, 23–24). Fujitani argues that such impressions of Japanese culture are not only reified by orientalist perspectives within the United States but also stem from "invented traditions" set forth during Japan's Meiji era, a time of both concerted nation-building and ravenous imperial projects. Like all budding empires, including that of the United States, Japan was in great need of a loyal and obedient body of national subjects, and the ideologies of their national ethics curriculum reflect this need (Horio 1988; Hoffman 1999; Shibata 2004; Lanham 1979). The majority of the Issei in the United States would have been educated during this era in Japan; as such, many of their notions of ideal behavior and "common sense" that they would have passed on as culturally distinct (and perhaps, somewhat fixed) would have been formed under the era's "ideology and curriculum"

(Apple 2004). However, as any teacher knows, just because a particular set of behavior and ethics are prescribed "from above" (especially in school) does not ensure that they will be embodied "from below." It is simply racist to presume that some groups of people are *by nature* more inclined to internalize the rules of what they are told to do.

But I would also follow Fujitani by arguing that cultural traditions are still under invention, still being formed, still being impacted by both the material experiences people encounter in the present and the ones they carry from the past. As such, the meanings of such concepts and clusters as shikataganai and gaman are not done being made.[11] For now, though, it should suffice to say that regardless of whether people did or did not accept and/or comply with mass incarceration, there is nothing essentially Japanese about the acceptance of or compliance with oppression. Fujitani and others continue to remind us that transnational Nikkei history is filled with rebels and rebellions—male and female dissidents who dared, both individually and together, to stand up or sit down and say no. And whether we get to know about them or not does not change the fact that they did.

Nonetheless, regardless of Fujitani's persuasive arguments and historically grounded cultural analysis, it is important to note that the conceptual cluster of shikataganai-gaman continues to inform the recollections of many former incarcerees. As such, it would seem that they, directly or indirectly, impacted how literacy, including writing-to-redress, was used by incarcerees. As formerly incarcerated writer Hisaye Yamamoto told King-Kok Cheung about the "whole etiquette structure" of gaman, since she was "brought up like most Nisei . . . [she] imagine[s] [her] writing has been influenced by such behavior patterns—it would be strange if it wasn't" (quoted in Cheung 1993, 31). It is for this reason that I will attend both the rhetorics and the literacies of gaman in chapter 4. For now, it is just important to remember that cultural concepts have material histories; that they are formed and re-formed in dynamic interaction with evolving material conditions; that they can, like any and all signifiers, "slip" in various directions and become occupied by different ideologies; and that they may, at any time, be actively rejected or reused resistantly by those subjected to its sedimented meanings.

The wide range of literacy networks, political blueprints, material conditions, and cultural clusters described above all serve as large parts of the broader rhetorical contexts for writing-to-redress. With these contexts in mind, I turn to more detailed discussions of the ways incarcerated Nikkei used writing, in both private and public manners, to set right what was wrong and relieve community suffering during the experience of mass incarceration.

Notes

1. According to Richard Rubinger, Kikuchi Dairoku, Japan's minister of education from 1901 to 1903, asserted that four years of an average Japanese education enabled a child to read and also write in kana. Dairoku further noted, though, that was not completely sufficient, "as almost everything is written with admixture of Chinese ideographs, and as children learn only 500 of them, they cannot read most ordinary points" (quoted in Rubinger 2007, 141). Dairoku's concern reflects the great debates taking place in Japan around the turn of the century over the state of mass literacy; intellectuals, writers, and government officials debated the amount of kanji, or Chinese ideographs, one needed to know in addition to kana in order to function as an effective subject of the Meiji empire. According to several sources, this period brought about a mass reduction in the amount of kanji used in Japanese textbooks and newspapers. More recently, Laura Miller referred to an unnamed scholar who suggests that today, knowledge of 500 kanji plus kana is sufficient to understand 75 percent of all Japanese media (Miller 2004, 360).

2. These student laborers were political exiles from Japan's People's Rights Movement, which regularly challenged the Meiji government's domestic policies via demonstrations, publications, and armed uprisings (Ichioka 1988, 16, 19)

3. In 1920 the total Nikkei population on the West Coast numbered 104,282; in 1930, 131,669; and in 1940, 120,927 (Niiya and JANM 2001, xvii). However, according to Ron Takaki, by 1930 roughly half of the community was Nisei (Takaki 1998, 181).

4. Noriko Asato (2006, 109) writes that 42 percent of all California Nisei attended, whereas only 30 percent of all Washington Nisei went. David Yoo (2000, 28) writes that 69 percent attended, though this figure may include Hawai'i, where attendance was much higher.

5. The wages for incarcerees in the camps amounted to "$12 a month for unskilled labor, $16 a month for skilled labor, and $19 for professional employees" (US Commission on Wartime Relocation and Internment of Civilians 1997, 166). In the assembly centers, the wages for the same categories of labor were even less: $8, $12, and $16 a month, respectively (Herzig-Yoshinaga 2009).

6. This was less true in the Department of Justice (DOJ) camps, where many Issei men were held apart from their families and where, according to Gail Nomura, a lack of access to writing materials meant the traditional poetic forms of tanka,

haiku, and senryu, all of which were quite short, became "ideal forms" for the pent-up emotions of the internees. For example, Nomura (2001, 302) notes, one DOJ poet "scribbled a hundred poems on the only two sheets of paper" he was able to carry with him between detention centers.

7. According to the CWRIC, the WRA wage "system caused severe financial hardship. Evacuees could not afford to meet even their minimal needs inside the centers. Sometimes the barest essentials in the Sears catalogue, such as shoes for the children, were out of reach . . . [Plus,] it was insulting. A WRA librarian received $167 a month, while her evacuee staff received $16 a month." As the government's own report prepared by the CWRIC noted, "Perhaps the best that can be said of the mean system is that no one starved" (US Commission on Wartime Relocation and Internment of Civilians 1997, 167).

8. Nakano (1990, 62).

9. Junko Kobayashi (2005, 76) notes that Japanese-language literary publications in camp followed the same sponsorship pattern as before the war, publishing poems with the funds generated from membership dues and sales of the magazines.

10. This is not to say this was always true for students, as Hui Wu (2007) argues. But Kats Kunitsugu and Henry Miyatake, former incarcerees held at two different camps, related stories available in the Densho archives of teachers either rewriting harsh critiques they had drafted (Kunitsugu 1995) or expelling them from school for critiques they had composed (Miyatake 1998).

11. The ongoing reinvention of cultural concepts can be seen in a poem recently written by Mari Oye, the granddaughter of former incarcerees and a 2007 presidential scholar who first made news by confronting President George Bush with a letter signed by forty-nine other presidential scholars calling on him to reject torture and to treat all suspects in the "war on terror" humanely. Oye's poem "Redress" was subsequently published in the 2008 holiday issue of the Pacific Citizen; it closed with two lines about her grandfather: "he taught me to say shikataganai / before he died, but not to mean it" (Oye 2008). With these closing words, Oye lovingly embraces the common refrain of the incarcerated generation even as she simultaneously suggests that the full meaning of the term's invocation has always been more complicated than it seems.

4
ME INWARDLY BEFORE I DARED

Attending Silent Literacies of Gaman

Beyond the visible forms of resistance, between the occasional petition, strike or riot, is the true nature of Japanese resistance to white control.

—*Okihiro (1973)*

Gaman shite	Endure!
gaman shite iru	We are enduring
hifu no iro	by the color of our skin

—*Sanada Kikyo (Hayashi and Yamanaka 1976)*

I sought to seed the barren earth
And make wild beauty take
Firm root, but how could I have known
The waiting long would shake
Me inwardly, before I dared
Not say what would be gain
From such untimely planting or
What flower worth the pain?

—*Suyemoto (1942)*

DOI: 10.5876/9781607324010.c004

ATTENDING GAMAN: TRACING A NIKKEI RHETORICS OF SURVIVANCE

The word *gaman* first entered my vocabulary via Nobuko Miyamoto, long-time singer, dancer, and actor, well-known among the first generation of pan–Asian American activists for the politically inspired, race-conscious, and consciousness-raising music she wrote and performed with Chris Iijima and Charlie Chin on the first "Asian American" album, *A Grain of Sand* (1973). I met Nobuko in 1985 when I was thirteen. I had traveled to Los Angeles to spend the summer with my father, who had recently left Portland to become the assistant editor at the *Pacific Citizen*, which featured weekly stories on issues pertinent to the Japanese American community, including the then-current social movement for redress and reparations. That summer I palled around with Nobuko's son, Kamau, who, even more than myself, had been raised amidst a massive transcontinental community of activists. Always involved in some show or another, Nobuko recruited both Kamau and myself for one of her performances with the East West Players that summer, showcasing the music of her new album, *Best of Both Worlds* (Miyamoto 1983). A budding performer at the time, I eagerly agreed.

While the fine details of the full show blur into my memory, I can still hear the melody of Nobuko's verses today:

Walking to mess hall
I hold Obachan's hand
Passing rows of barracks
We fight the wind and sand.
Why do they hate us so
Will we be here all our lives?

Waves of dust-colored fabric snap behind and in front of myself and others. We move slowly across the stage, stretching our arms around our heads as if we are walking headfirst into an unbearable wind. Over the same music, Nobuko's voice offers a shield, as she chants a strong, melodic, back-of-the-throat whisper of a chorus into the wind that surrounds us:

GAMAN . . . be strong
Motto gaman shite iko, neh[1]

While I don't know the literal meaning of each and every word at the time, I do know what they mean altogether. They are the first conceptual "cluster" (Mao 2006, 31) I personally associate with gaman: a race-conscious and consciousness-raising voice encouraging me to *keep going* and *be strong*.

Nobuko's song is only one of many English-dominant Nikkei performances of gaman. This cultural ethos has been noted again and again by Nisei former incarcerees as being one model of ideal behavior put forth by either their Issei parents or their teachers in Japanese school. Today within US-based communities, gaman is most often translated as either "endure" and/or "persevere," but it has also been defined by Japanese Americans in a number of ways including "stick things out at all costs" (Kikumura and Tanaka 1981), "bear up" (O'Brien and Fugita 1991), develop "self-discipline" (Murase quoted in Northwest Nikkei 1996) and "control over [one's] emotions" (B. H. Suzuki quoted in Adler 1998).

Amidst and across these definitions, though, gaman has often been interpreted by both Nikkei and non-Nikkei alike as a call to quietly accept oppression, especially in relation to camp. And this interpretation is not without warrant. As early as 1942, incarcerees were publicly writing about the term as one that circled around them. In "Concentration Camp: U.S. Style," an article published in *The New Republic*, Nisei Ted Nakashima wrote from the Puyallup Assembly Center, euphemistically called "Camp Harmony," reported such a strikingly candid description of conditions that the magazine had to print an editorial at the US Army's insistence rebutting Nakashima's description some six months later (Editors 1943). Nakashima spends most of his text rhetorically comparing life in camp, where "[m]ealtime queues extend for blocks" and they are surrounded by "wet mud that stinks when it dries" with life back in his "fine American home," replete with "highballs" and an abundance of "American friends" (Nakashima 1942, 822). And then, drawing a distinction between himself and others who might be uttering words of advice all around him, Nakashima proclaims toward the end of his description that he doesn't "have enough of that Japanese heritage '*ga-man*'—a code of silent suffering and ability to stand pain" (823).

Twenty-seven years later, sociologist Harry H. L. Kitano would encode his translation of the term during a year of popular uprising around the world. First published in 1969, the same year as Bill Hosokawa's *Nisei: The Quiet Americans*, Kitano's text, *Japanese Americans: The Evolution of a Subculture* would become, for many years, one of the most cited works on the Japanese American experience. In the midst of a chapter prescriptively labeled "The Culture," Kitano defines gaman as one "value" among others that "explain[s]" why the "Japanese" have a "low degree of acting out, overt rebellion, and independence," translating the term as the "internalization . . . and suppression of anger and emotion." Further describing/delimiting the function of this cultural ethos, Kitano offers a family anecdote: "The author's father often tells of early episodes of discrimination and mistreatment to which he was subjected. A simple walk down the street, in 1919 in San Francisco, often resulted in being shoved into the gutter and called a 'damn Jap.' But father would *ga-man*, that is, take no retaliatory action, and the incidents never escalated into serious conflict" (Kitano 1976, 136).

Given discussions like these, it is no wonder that gaman has been interpreted as a call to internalize or accept oppression without complaint. Especially given the historical sources of this ethos as an "invented tradition" during the Meiji era in Japan. As Takashi Fujitani argues, values like gaman were promoted because they were seen as "the most conducive to development as a nation and control over people." Fujitani follows his assertion with an illustration of a historical figure, Ninomiya Sontoku, a peasant sage of Japan who "encouraged common people to work hard and practice frugality." While Sontoku lived during the Tokugawa years, right before the Meiji era, it was the Meiji government who turned him into a "national icon" by "erecting statues of him carrying a load of firewood on his back."[2] Fujitani's point then becomes clear: so-called Japanese cultural values are far from authentic in an ahistorical sense. Rather, such values are ones "that existed among some people and in some places in Japan prior to the Meiji era, that were taken up and fostered by the Meiji government . . . because they . . . appeared congenial to . . . creating a modern and powerful nation" (Fujitani 2002, 32).

Given Meiji era nation-building, consolidation, and imperial ventures, one can certainly see how gaman as "silent suffering" or the "internalization . . . and suppression of anger" might serve any oppressive body governing Nikkei bodies. However, just as Fujitani argued that most cultural traditions were invented for particular purposes, so are they still being invented, still being formed, still being shaped by the contemporary rhetorics of transnational Nikkei communities.

Take, for instance, the Japanese American National Museum's recent *Encyclopedia of Japanese American History* (Niiya and JANM 2001). Under the entry "gaman," the encyclopedia begins with the usual definitions of "endure, persist, persevere" but then immediately follows with "or to do one's best in times of frustration and adversity." This one-line summary is followed by a short paragraph first citing, then complicating, Kitano's definition:

> According to UCLA sociologist Harry H. L. Kitano, *gaman* is a concept that refers to "internalization of, and suppression of, anger and emotion." Thus, Kitano maintains that "to gaman" is to take no aggressive retaliatory action against one's misfortunes. Betty S. Furuta asserts that the employment of gaman by, for example, the Issei during World War II in order to endure the humiliation and hardships of incarceration, is mistaken by many non-Japanese to indicate a lack of assertiveness or initiative rather than strength in the face of difficulty and suffering. (Niiya and JANM 2001, 170)

Here, the authors carefully attend gaman both by waiting upon its "classic" definition by a noted sociologist and by following with something new: a revision of gaman's connotation from passivity to strength.

This shift in connotation is one many Japanese American psychologists specializing in the legacy of incarceration would embrace. As Donna Nagata notes, an ethos of gaman appears to have been quite influential in the resilience of at least some incarcerees after incarceration. As "Sachi," the subject of one of Nagata's case studies, explained, "*Gaman* means to endure adversity . . . My father used to say in response to the slightest pain, 'You have to endure.' I'm quite sure it helped me cope. It wasn't a conscious thing and it's only in retrospect that I've come to realize that I learned to *gaman* in camp." While Nagata is careful to point out that gaman "did not resolve the feelings of stigma or vulnerability" brought about by mass incarceration, it did, she suggests, provide Sachi a framework for "managing her emotions." As such, Sachi believed that gaman, in Nagata's words, "increased her sense of resiliency." As Sachi explained, "I'm a survivor. I learned to cope and just as I learned that there was life after internment, I know there was life after the death of my child, after divorce, or any kind of loss. It helped me in my coping with adversity . . . I remember each time thinking, 'This too will pass' because I had gotten through the internment experience and I never fell apart. I remained strong for the rest of my family and I think this was because I learned to gaman" (quoted in Nagata 1994, 123–4).

While Sachi's use of gaman as a self-rhetoric cannot be said to be shared by all incarcerated Nikkei, there does seem to be ample evidence from psychological studies that the concept was employed by a number of people to cope with and push through the psychological havoc that mass incarceration wreaked on their inner selves (Nagata 1994; Kinoshita 2001; Ina 1998; Nagata 2000). For this reason, gaman could also be seen as Nikkei kin to what Malea Powell calls American Indian "rhetorics of survivance," or the use of language/writing to "survive + resist" oppression (Powell 2002). While the historical circumstances for Powell's rhetorics of survivance (policies of mass genocide) greatly differ from that of Japanese American incarceration (policies of mass imprisonment), her analysis helps us see more broadly how writing to *resist* cannot be seen as fully separate from writing to *survive*. After all, we must first survive if we are ever going to end oppression, and, I would add, we must not only do so physically. Just as critical to oppression's demise is the survival of what we might consider our inner world/s. That is, the vitality of social and political movements against oppression depends a great deal upon the psychological and cultural health of the people who form them. For people like Sachi, then, gaman, as a guiding principle of ideal behavior, was employed to survive + resist the rampant racism, enforced curfews, military orders, forced "relocation," barbed wire fences, watchtowers, and military guards with guns that marked the incarceration period. More than simply that Japanese code of silent suffering, gaman, for some incarcerees, became a Nikkei ethos of survivance.

It is important to understand however, that while gaman is often discussed in terms of individual survivance, it has, at its base, an ethical commitment to a collective good. For example, my longtime friend Ken Matsudaira, a bilingual Sansei whose parents were both incarcerated during the war, recently told me that he always thought of gaman as a call for "self-dialogue," especially in the midst of others experiencing a similar hardship (Matsudaira, personal communication, 2008). That is, people should gaman in order to avoid inflicting additional psychological or emotional strain on others by endlessly (and thus, selfishly) complaining about something *everyone* is experiencing. Indeed, Mei Nakano seems to agree, as she claims that the ethos of gaman is intricately tied to the belief that one should develop an "acute consciousness" of oneself as a social being, as someone whose actions affect other people, in that it often "require[s] superseding one's private needs for the good of the larger group" (Nakano 1990, 106). In this way, I have come to see gaman as an ethos implicitly concerned with collectivity, or the well-being of others as interdependently related to the self.

The idea that the well-being of others is interwoven with the activity of the self recalls LuMing Mao's discussion of *shu*, or a notion of the self that can, perhaps, more accurately be glossed as "reciprocity." According to Mao (2006, 87), the "discourse of [*shu*]," which can be translated as either "reciprocity" or "putting oneself in the others' place," stands in somewhat of a contrast to the discourse of individualism as it has arisen in Europe and the United States (though Mao would caution us against exoticizing the conceptual difference). In Mao's words, the Chinese concept of *shu* "constructs self as irreducibly social, . . . forever intertwined with other selves and with an ever-expanding circle of relations" (91), and, in doing so, "encodes and celebrates a network of interdependence and interrelatedness" (93). Reading Mao's discussion, I was taken with what I started to think of as a point of conceptual kinship between shu and gaman: the attention to those beyond oneself.[3] While part of me hesitates to include this point in my discussion of gaman for fear that it simply reifies any number of subservient stereotypes about people of Asian ancestry, especially women, it is also important to note that for some Nikkei, attention to others is a key component of gaman.

However, in full rhetorical attendance of gaman, I must cautiously avoid any assertion that the somewhat celebratory connotation of attending to others is shared by all. Indeed, for many incarcerees and their descendants, the ethos of gaman merely exacerbated subservient behavior along with any and all forms of internalized shame and anger over camp. It is for this reason that you could hear the call during the redress movement of the 1970s and 1980s "We will not gaman any longer!," meaning, essentially, we will not silently endure what camp did to us anymore. It is only recently, in the so-called post-redress era, that any revisitation of the rhetorics behind gaman can be performed without seeming to condone those who would urge people *not* to publicly redress the period of mass incarceration.

Which is why, in my attempts to attend to this ethos and all its competing definitions and implicit rhetorics, I have tried to stretch my mind toward a common denominator across all meanings. Given the strength, silence, internalization, forbearance, self-discipline, suppression, and emotional control, it seems that, no matter whether one is simply accepting of or persevering through adversity, in order to gaman one must strive to focus inwardly while maintaining an outward silence, all to endure hardship so as not to inflict further emotional strain on others. That is, to gaman one must simultaneously develop an interpersonal awareness of self and cultivate the self-discipline necessary to exert control over one's emotion-thoughts, all in order to attend to the larger community's well-being.

BREAKING INTO PRINT: THE ACTIVE LITERACIES OF GAMAN

> Mother and Father quietly reading, Kay asleep, the mending on my lap, my mind protested: How long are we to be here in this forsaken place? What will I tell my son when he grows up? I could not openly speak of the pain I felt or ask the questions that assailed me, and poetry was my outlet:
>
> Time threads the needle.
> I sew blindly, because tears
> Obscure my slow hands.
> Grief chokes in my throat.
> I cannot speak
>
> —*Suyemoto (1942)*

> [W]riting does not occur suddenly against a background of pure speech.
>
> —*Collins and Blot (2003)*

Moving toward this more complicated understanding of the rhetorics of gaman, I began to see the similarities between this community ethos and the non-individualist possibilities of personal or private writing.[4] Just as gaman relies on an active and dynamic conception of an inner self that is capable of developing self-control or order, proponents of self-writing imagine the activity of composing as a process that retains the potential for helping one "bring order and composure to our inner selves" (Dixon 1975, 13). Particularly true in contexts of imprisonment, Lynn Bloom notes that such periods of "[e]nforced leisure" sometimes provides "unusual time for reflection" such that personal writing can become "a means of gaining perspective on [a] cramped existence, [and] of coping . . . perhaps through verbal escape" (Bloom 1976, 796–97). Because writing can, as Ralph Cintron (1997, 231) put it, "interrupt or shape an amorphousness that might otherwise melt us into everything else," it can offer us an "illusion of control" through an "opportunity of reducing language and experience to something manageable" (229). In this way, several comp/rhet scholars have noted the ways that self-writing can serve as a powerful "act of survival," as it can help collect or "recuperate" a self or social identity that processes of oppression have fractured, alienated, or denied (Herrington and Curtis 2000, 135).

While gaman shares with personal writing this kind of opportunity to compose oneself, gaman also relies on a socially conscious use of inward focus and outward silence, or lack of public utterance. In this way, the contested rhetorics of gaman allude to recent work on the rhetorics of silence, especially work that calls attention to power differences. Calling upon the relationship between silent meditation and private forms of literacy, Pat Belanoff (2001, 403) argues for the rhetorical efficacy of "attending inward," pointing to how, historically, those who have been "robbed of the right to speak" have found silent reflection/meditation to be an empowering "doorway out of the constraints set up against their voices" (406). In addition, both Anne Ruggles Gere and Cheryl Glenn have noted how some public silences are inherently ethical or political, in that a refusal to disclose the details of hardship may simply be a refusal to participate in the pain or exploitation of others (Gere 2001, 213–14) or a way to take social "responsibility all the while refusing to be compliant" (C. Glenn 2004, 155). That is, for Gere and Glenn, one can embody an ethical commitment via a combination of outward public silence and inward dissident emotion-thought.

However, while the rhetorics of silence help complicate meaning/s behind such outward public silence, such discussions can also easily conflate two modes of verbalization: speech and writing. For many folks in comp/rhet, silence serves as the converse of speech, suggesting that silence is without words or verbal activity. For example, even as Cheryl Glenn (2004) attempts to rescue the rhetorical possibilities of silence in *Unspoken*, she generally sticks to discussions of the semantic range of nonverbal communication. But ten years before Glenn published her study, Asian American studies scholar King-Kok Cheung discussed the ways Asian American writers both exploit and comment on silence's "articulate" possibilities. Within her discussion,

Cheung notes that the character for "silence" in Chinese and Japanese is not so much the opposite of "speech" than it is the opposite of " 'noise,' 'motion' and 'commotion' " (Cheung 1993, 8n11). We are reminded, via Cheung, that silence is not simply the absence of *verbal action* but the absence of *noise* or *outward commotion*. This distinction is important as we consider not just the ethos of gaman but how that ethos might be served by *writing*, a means of expression and communication that is different from, but not opposite to, speech. As noted earlier, Cheung points to this difference at the end of her introduction to the work of three Asian American women writers, two of whom confront the legacy of incarceration in their postwar written work,

> Of particular note in [these] works is the inverse relation between spoken and written expression. Many of their characters . . . distill onto the page what they cannot say out loud. [While many characters] have trouble speaking or *telling* their life stories . . . they all excel on paper: their unspoken emotions break into print. (Cheung 1993, 26, emphasis in original)

It is this "break[ing] into print" whenever one is unable to speak that allows one to remain quiet and be active at the exact same time, allowing writers to both verbalize feeling and thought, all the while never making a sound. As a longtime proponent of personal writing, Peter Elbow reminds us, private writing remains an "ideal medium for exploring our thoughts or feelings" in ways that "*no one else will hear them*" (Elbow 2000, 40). In other words, the silent speech of private writing allows for both an active exploration of emotion-thoughts and provides a safe passage or a "hush harbor" (Nunley 2004) for this inward activity to take place amidst one's ethical (cultural, political, social) commitments to remain outwardly silent in public. In this way, private writing provides a technology for gaman to be put into rhetorical action.

Hints of how writing provides for gaman can be found in a few trace discussions of Nikkei writing. In her preface to an anthology of translated haiku from the incarceration camps, Mayumi Nakatsuka writes that " much of the haiku expresses the *Gaman* of the detainees" noting that "their poetry must have been an irreplaceable comfort in such a difficult period . . . [and] must have provided them intellectual and spiritual sustenance (quoted in De Cristoforo 1997a, 12). Similarly, in her preface to her collection of translated haiku written while she was incarcerated at Tule Lake, Violet Matsuda de Cristoforo explains her reliance on gaman as an ethos of survivance and her turn to writing amidst the "harsh conditions of camp life": "[S]tripped of dignity, self-respect and purpose, and with no access to radios or outside newspapers, rumor was rife and our lives were subject to uncertainty and doubt . . . It was only 'Gaman'—our ability to endure hardship and humiliation without complaint—that enabled us to survive. But, under those oppressive conditions, I became more and more introspective and found solace in my Haiku" (De Cristoforo 1987, E ix).

For all of these reasons, I have come to see gaman as one of the ethoi guiding private Nikkei literacies-in-action under mass incarceration. Far from being a traditional Japanese genre of rhetoric, Writing-to-Gaman, as I have come to call the activities and texts of this private form of writing-to-redress, speaks to the use of this quiet technology to privately organize one's emotion-thoughts and/or verbalize dissent while sharpening an awareness of oneself as connected to others enduring hardship. In other words, I offer up Writing-to-Gaman as a culturally relevant lens with which to view the conscious and unconscious use of a community ethos to both individually write and collectively survive + resist. In doing so, I am attempting to complicate a discourse of cultural deficiency that has already surrounded gaman in previous years by striving for an additional discourse—one of cultural *efficacy*—that assumes the rhetorics of gaman served the community well. This is not to deny that gaman continues to retain the potential to stifle verbal activity, as can be seen across the term's history. But this ethos of presumed passivity also has the potential to *cultivate* such activity, as we will soon see below. It is only through this kind of revised cultural lens that we can even begin to "critically imagine" (Royster 2000, 83; Kirsch and Royster 2010) the meaning of incarcerees breaking into print, or their active participation in a literacy practice that enabled them to collectively survive + resist the hardships and humiliations induced by their own government.

Examples of this soundless verbal activity are available in memoirs, oral histories, and the primary texts themselves, including English-language diaries, private letters, and unpublished poems donated by the authors or an author's family to the public archives of the Japanese American National Museum, the online Densho archive, and miscellaneous university-sponsored archives in California, both physical and virtual. In other words, while this writing was at one time written and kept among the private papers of the incarceree writers, it has since been made public by the writer or her/his descendants.

This is an important distinction because much writing by incarcerees was collected both openly and surreptitiously by the US government (alluded to by Herzig-Yoshinaga in chapter 2) or by anthropologists working for the University of California, Berkeley–based Japanese American Evacuation and Resettlement Study (JERS), the US government's Bureau of Sociological Research, or the War Relocation Authority's Community Analysis Section. As such, the authors of such collected writing, which is not included in my analysis, were either unaware that their writing was being "published" for government eyes, or they already felt comfortable enough to have their personal writing exist as part of a public record.[5]

Which is all to say there are, of course, limitations to my sample, and thus, my discussion. Aside from my reliance on work discussed in or donated to the archives noted above, the writings discussed here were all composed in English. For a fuller perspective on what Writing-to-Gaman might have looked like, Japanese-language diaries, letters, and unpublished poetry would have to be included. As scholars like Brian Hayashi (2004) and Junko Kobayashi (2005) have argued, Japanese-language texts remain underused in camp studies, a fact related to the legacy of camp and its Americanization emphasis playing out across generations, such that even if some descendants of incarcerees have successfully struggled to reclaim their heritage language, most remain illiterate in Japanese. Given my own lack of Japanese-language literacy, I do not make arguments regarding texts and activities beyond those I studied; but based upon my personal and lifelong familiarity with various rhetorical sites of Japanese America, I would speculate that Writing-to-Gaman could serve as a rich analytical framework for private genres of Nikkei writing, no matter what language dominates the text.

In order to choose my data, I asked JANM archivists to pull whatever English-language diaries, personal papers, and personal letters they had in their stacks. With Densho, I conducted online word searches relevant to private writing, survival, resistance, protest, and values associated with gaman. During this same time, I also learned of the Online Archive of California (OAC), which digitally links university and museum archives across the state, and I decided to search for private writing through their online search options. While OAC led me to volumes of Japanese-language sources held in the Japanese American Research Project at the University of California, Los Angeles, it also unearthed a few additional English-language diaries, one of which I knew had been published in book form and another that was now digitally available through another California-based digital collection, the Japanese American Relocation Digital Archive (JARDA).

After gathering a range of materials and an increasing amount of sources awaiting further exploration through these in-person and online searches, I decided to further limit what I would include for my study. First, I set aside all letters written between family members in the WRA camps and the Issei fathers held in the Department of Justice camps, where an official (and thus well-known) censorship policy was in effect and so directly impacted what was written.[6] Second, I decided to set aside the diaries of Nikkei researchers who were incarcerees themselves and who also took part in the JERS study, such as Charles Kikuchi, Richard Nishimoto, and Tamie Tsuchiyama, as these writings were not truly private in that they were submitted publicly as part of their fieldwork notes (see Nishimoto 1995; Hirabayashi 1999; Kikuchi and Modell 1973). In the end, I limited my analysis to the texts of and/or references to private writing written by eighteen Nikkei incarcerees[7] whose collected private writing ranged from a single poem inscribed in a scrapbook to discussions of writing at work in a camp hospital, to digitized diaries, to boxes and boxes of personal papers.[8]

Once I had narrowed the writing I would examine, I studied what I had for prominent patterns. I began by looking for ways that the private writing seemed to redress any facet of incarceration. Within that sample, four themes emerged that seemed to umbrella the private redressing taking place: witnessing, complaining, internal struggling, and rehearsing/verbal preparation. Using these themes, I coded what I had; but despite their prominence in the data I had gathered, I still wasn't happy with my choices. As I sorted text and slices of transcripts into my working charts, I grew increasingly aware that my "discourses of measurement" were not allowing for the "deeper and deeper levels of reflection" that Cintron suggested good writing/analysis can do (Cintron 1997, 229–31). Instead, my choices stuck to the surface.

At the same time I was busy flattening a literacy activity I so earnestly wanted to define, I sorted through my research of gaman, trying to organize the ideas that make up the first part of this chapter. Working through the term's social dimensions—the ways gaman implicitly asks us to attend to others—the problem with my codes suddenly hit me: they had not emerged from an "indigenous" understanding of gaman. While "witnessing," "complaining," "internal struggling," and "rehearsing" were indeed rhetorical modes of political expression, I had not let the patterns arise from gaman's own internal logic. I had not fully allowed for gaman to operate as a rhetorical lens. Once again, I needed to engage in a fuller attendance—"look, listen and look again"—and stretch my mind not only toward my data but my own stated, culturally relevant lens. Of course, in doing so there is a risk that I will overstate or exoticize rhetorical difference, especially considering most of the incarceree writers under discussion here were born, raised, and schooled within the United States. However, as Nisei writer Hisaye Yamamoto told King-Kok Cheung, "most Nisei" were "brought up . . . with Japanese ideas like *gaman* . . . and that whole etiquette structure." As such, it would seem that even for the Nisei educated in the United States, we might, as Yamamoto further stated about her own writing, "imagine" that Nisei writing was "influenced by such behavior patterns. It would be strange if it wasn't" (quoted in Cheung 1993, 31). Even as I do not deny the presence of my first choices of political themes more familiar to most US-based readers, my intention here is to point to another way to view the political in private writing, another way to view "survivance," another way to attend Writing-to-Gaman, by relying on gaman's own logic built on its own ethical assumptions. By doing so, I was able to develop a more culturally relevant set of themes and see how this activity of private writing allowed incarcerees to (1) organize emotion-thought, (2) verbalize dissent, and (3) sharpen an awareness of others enduring hardship.

With my new themes, I more confidently saw the efficacy of Writing-to-Gaman. However, it is important to note that Writing-to-Gaman as a concept does not exhaust the range of what it meant to write in private under mass incarceration, nor does it exhaust the range of what I examined for this study—after all, much of the text I looked at did not suggest the use of Writing-to-Gaman.[9] But much of the writing I looked at did. Writing-to-Gaman merely provides a culturally relevant heuristic with which we might better understand a literacy practice that grows out of a specific historical moment and, as I will argue in my conclusion, retained the potential to foster additional redress activities. In the immediate discussion that follows, however, my focus remains with the actual literacy activities and texts of Writing-to-Gaman, as Nikkei incarcerees used writing to cultivate both a stronger interpersonal awareness of themselves and the psychological discipline necessary to control public displays of emotion, all in the interest of collective survivance.

WRITING-TO-GAMAN: A LITERATE ACTIVITY OF NIKKEI SURVIVANCE

In March 1942, a few weeks before her forced evacuation, an anonymous Nisei writer wrote in her diary of her conflicted feelings about the needed "sacrifice" all "evacuees" were making and followed with a discussion of her and other "Nisei mothers'" concerns, already noting the government's seeming lack of attention:

> Dealing with the ~~problems~~ social problems created and growing more intense among our (Japanese) community now . . . Treasury Dept to date make no definite provisions for storage of our goods. Hampering efforts of evacuation. Wish something could be done! Something must be done! Something's gone wrong with the effort of the JACL and United Federation. People are lost in thoughts because have lost faith in what they are so hard endeavoring to do to lessen confusion! ~~Army calls for evacuation 16 hrs notice.~~ We Nisei mother a few of us privately, decide to get together and attempt to help at this time of confusion. (Anonymous 1942, notations in original)

The handwriting of this entry seems fast, the script is relatively tight, the letters close together, the pages full on both sides. The underlined words are done so two or three times, with the words crossed out in such a way that they can still be read. I was taken with the pace when I first read it in JANM, taken with its placement in a small, 7-inch by 10-inch three-ring binder that contains only a few loose-leaf diary entries; a handwritten draft of one letter to "Mr. Lindley" on the "hot water (etc) situation" dated October 27, 1942; and several pages of handmade typed charts that read, "As of today," "When occupied," "Laundry-Hot, Cold, None," "Showers-Hot, Cold, None," "Toilets, Yes, No," "Water, Hot, Cold, None," with four rows of handwritten answers in the corresponding columns, each of them with same answers: "cold, closed, yes, cold."

I can only assume the writer subsequently followed her own urgings that appear in her March entry: "Something must be done!" Here, in what appeared to be a private notebook, she organized her observations of camp conditions in an impressively systematic fashion, out of which she appears to have at least prepared a letter to some administrator named Mr. Lindley. But the writer also seems as though she may have Written-to-Gaman in order to develop the self-discipline she would need to help "lessen confusion" and attend to the needs of her community. Closing her March entry, the writer articulates an anxious desire to ease people's lives all the while legitimizing the community's gaman-like ideals: "I feel so much I want to contribute—my mind runs around at a crazy speed—can hardly control it—I wish I could be more calm—I must cultivate it—I must—otherwise people will not respect me because I am such a rattle brain . . . I know it and yet—I must endeavor to correct it !!!!!!!) (Me—no good) But then I feel the fight in me" (Anonymous 1942, notations in original). This writer's struggle to "cultivate" her mind is striking, in both the immediate context of an entry noting the ways other people are "lost in thoughts" and the broader context of a notebook that suggests that her cultivation did in fact take place, that the writer did in fact "contribute" by attending to the lack of hot water in camp, a condition affecting a large number of people.

Encompassing all aspects of Writing-to-Gaman, the entry articulates the need to cultivate one's inner world in order to more properly attend to others. But it also seems to have provided a safe rhetorical space to critique the government that is "[h]ampering efforts" and, to a lesser degree, the JACL, with which "something" has apparently "gone wrong." Indeed, several texts I attended over the course of my research seemed to perform one or more of these activities that make up this Nikkei literacy practice of survivance. But in my continued hopes of allowing for Cintron's "deeper and deeper forms of reflection," I will separate these activities into their own discourses of measurement in order to better attend the practice of Writing-to-Gaman.

CULTIVATING A "RATTLE BRAIN": ORGANIZING/DISCIPLINING EMOTION-THOUGHTS

This use of writing to privately cultivate and/or organize one's emotion-thoughts was evident in several diaries I attended. Heart Mountain teenager Stanley Hayami's (1942–1943), for example, includes both statements of intent that he will write "tomorrow" "about what [he] think[s] about post War planning" after a disheartening argument with one of his friends (January 10, 1943) and a fully capitalized, multipage essay-statement regarding his "VIEWS OF THE EVACUATION." Written a couple of months before Hayami joined the military and subsequently died overseas, this diary entry is framed by topic sentence-like questions that explore different aspects of the mass incarceration:

> FIRST OF ALL, DO I THINK THAT IT WAS CONSTITUTIONAL? NO I DO NOT. . .
>
> DO I THINK RACIAL ~~PQEDD~~ PREJUDICE WAS INVOLVED? YES I DO. . .
>
> DO I THINK THAT IT WAS WORTHWHILE FROM THE STANDPOINT OF THE GOV'T. THIS IS A VERY TOUGH QUESTION AS I DON'T ~~THINl~~ KNOW ALL THE FACTS . . .
>
> DO I THINK THE EVACUATION DID OR WILL DO SOME GOOD? YES . . . (Hayami 1942–1943, June 6, 1943, notations in original)

By the end of Hayami's (1942–1943) essay-entry, he seems to have come to some conclusions based on his reasoning through the various questions he has laid out for himself.

> WELL NOW THAT I HAVE GONE OVER THE WHOLE GODDAM SITUATION WHAT DO I THINK IN THE FINAL ANALYSIS.
>
> I THINK THAT THE WHOLE MESS WAS UNNECESSARY AND A LOT OF TROUBLE COULD HAVE BEEN AVOIDED. HOWEVER IT DID SOME GOOD—THAT OF BREAKING UP THE CLIQUES. I PERSONALLY WILL PROCEED TO FORGET THE WHOLE MESS, WILL TRY TO BECOME A GREATER MAN FROM HAVING GONE THRU SUCH EXPERIENCES, KEEP MY FAITH IN AMERICA, AND LOOK FORWARD TO RELOCATION AND THE FUTURE. (June 6, 1943)

But Hayami was not the only young man to lean on formal written qualities to help him organize his thoughts in private. James Yamasaki, who was held in Colorado at the Gila River Relocation camp, explored the pros and cons of the military's 1943 proposal that there should be an all-Nisei unit in the army made up of Nisei volunteers from camp:

> Problem: All Nisei division in army.
>
> Favorable: If Nisei were placed in the same division, there would be no discrimination as to advancement in rank. There would be no antagonistic interaction within the group. They would be able to show their ability as a group and bring honorable distinction in themselves thru courageous combat. If they, as a group, are placed on duty as cleaners or some dirty job, then they may protest as a group; whereas, if they separated into different divisions, then they may have to take orderly jobs and no one know too much about what kind of work they are doing.
>
> Unfavorable: After the war the Nisei would not have made Caucasian friends and assimilation would be very hard. There would always be in the minds of the Nisei the thought of discrimination and segregation. As a group they may be placed in certain unit as cleaners, ditch diggers, etc. There would always be objections to government plans because the Nisei would consider the worst of the plans concerning them, thus causing disunity and disloyalty. There would no complaints if Nisei were separated from each other. The Japanesy element will be involved, and Japan is our enemy.
>
> Conclusion: I am in favor of an all Nisei division.
>
> Propaganda is truth, half-truth and lies spread to gain faith and support on a certain issue. (Yamasaki 2003, 85, February 5, 1943)

Perhaps the most striking use of a journal to think through or organize one's emotion-thoughts can be seen in a notebook kept by Mary Nakahara. Titling her journal "The Bordered World," Nakahara wrote frequently during her time in California's Santa Anita Assembly Center, where she and her family were held from April to November 1942 before being assigned to a WRA-camp in Jerome, Arkansas. Within the pages of the notebook, Nakahara continually responds to events and conversations around her. Sometimes her response takes a defensive tone, as she privately argues with the opinions of other incarcerees: "This is my country . . . and it'll always be my country, no matter what happens in the future. Most likely I'll be hated by the Japanese for thinking the way I do, and prejudiced and looked down upon by the Americans because of my race. But so what? As long as I can refrain from ever hating anyone else, then, the fight for my way of life was worth it" (Nakahara 1942b, July 20). Other times, Nakahara bravely reexamines her own beliefs: "It's strange. I never felt like this before. In fact, I never gave much thought to the Japanese people. I never thought of myself—as being a part of a nation, so prejudiced I never gave much thought to that word, 'nationality' or thought of people according to their race,—but just—that they were individuals" (Nakahara 1942a, May 13).

Often, though, Nakahara's twists and turns can be seen in the same entry, as she thinks through her own perspective after talking directly to other people about their lives:

> Yesterday I wrote we should feel grateful to the government—and I certainly hope I always shall, but after some of the incidence I heard today by different hospital workers, I wonder about some things myself.
>
> So many of them got such raw deals and tough breaks just through prejudice and discrimination. It doesn't seem fair.
>
> But then again, everyone's life regardless of what nationality he is has sorrows scattered throughout a period of time. And one seldom knows who has gone through the most. Usually those who seem the happiest, and complain the least have tasted the most of life's bitterness . . .
>
> Within camp are the great number who have taken the "easiest way out" by blaming someone else;—by blaming the government, the people, or some incidence. Perhaps it might ease ones mind, but usually it's only temporary, because the only ease would be the consolations from sympathizers. When those "seemingly" kind words die down, and such a person can't "take" the bad breaks, then the same procedure would begin—For what? For more consolation. Complaints, word of sympathy, ease of mind, for short while and back again to complaints.
>
> Perhaps I'm looking at such situations a little too coldly,—but sorrows, after all, are a part of life, and I feel we should "take" it. Yet again, sympathies are comforting and helpful as long as it doesn't bring about self-pity. (Nakahara 1942b, July 7)

Nakahara's ending note here recalls the ethos of gaman—what is the point of "blaming someone else"? It does not bring about change, only an endless cycle of "complaints, word[s] of sympathy, ease of mind . . . and back again to complaints," especially since "sorrows . . . are a part of life" that people "should 'take.'" And yet Nakahara is clearly concerned about the "raw deals and tough breaks" experienced by the people she meets, and so we see her using writing to struggle through contradictory feelings, trying to organize them in such a way that helps her make sense of the world.

EXPLODING AT THE MOON: VERBALIZING DISSENT IN PRIVATE

While Hayami, Yamasaki, and Nakahara seem to have struggled with a range of contradictory feelings and thoughts brought forth by mass incarceration, private writing by others suggests less conflicted feelings—camp was simply bad. But given the isolated desert or swampland locations, the surrounding barbed wire fence, the soaring MP towers, and the army guards with guns, verbalizing dissent in public, for many incarcerees, did not seem politically prudent. In the face of such potential public danger, the private literacy spheres of unpublished poetry, diaries, and personal letters seems to have offered several hush harbors for incarcerees to talk back by breaking into print.

Writing in the no-man's-land of the Colorado River Relocation Center/ Poston, Chica Sugino privately articulated her dissent in a number of genres. In an unpublished poem found loose among her papers at the JANM, Sugino describes the stark atmosphere of "this earthly hell," where "tar/ papered barracks, row on row," "stretch" across a "barbed desert" and "new power drunk" MPs "had glared with gun" against a child's kitten, which apparently was forbidden in camp. Too much for Sugino, she "explodes at the moon," only to "rush inside" to "pray" that she can do her "share to end this . . . cursed the war" (Sugino n.d.).

Sugino also verbalized dissent in private letters to sympathetic friends beyond the barbed wire, especially those whose friendship she said she found "pacifying" to the "surging and writhing" "indignations" in her "raw subconscious," though she seemed to struggle with her feelings about "the things . . . now being perpetuated" (Sugino 1943b). As she bluntly articulated in a typed letter to Mabelle Shelp,

> Everything is pretty unsettled here now . . . I try not to think; I try to go from one day to the next in a dead beat of work and study and try to live impersonally. To think is to boil or be thoroughly beaten neither of which is good for any body's equilibrium. Perhaps that is why I shy away from writing letters these days. It takes me back to associations, human associations. We live as caged animals and we try to live the resigned animal life. Well I'm het up so I'll close. We usually keep our feelings locked up. (Sugino 1943c)

Here, in the midst of her verbalized dissent signified by such word choices and phrasing as "dead beat," "boil," "live impersonally" and "as caged animals," Sugino points to both the pain and the possibility of writing to others under mass incarceration: the capacity to help one remember one's humanity in the midst of inhumanity by decidedly *not* keeping one's "feelings locked up."

Sugino was not alone in using private letters as a means to unlock one's feelings. Stanford professor Yamato Ichihashi (quoted in Chang 1997, 108) regularly wrote to his friends Payton and Jessie Treat, complaining about his living conditions: "we are fast being converted into veritable Okies." About the War Relocation Authority he wrote, "Criticisms relative [to] any matter are not tolerated by the management" (111). Meanwhile, in his private journal, Ichihashi railed against the "hideous sleeping place" provided by the WRA, which consisted of "two dangerous wooden cots" and bags that needed to be packed "with straw for mattresses" (103). And as early as June 1942, Ichihashi was willing to call the WRA's management of camp, as he saw it, an "autocracy enforced by a veritable Gestapo" (124).

While Yoshiko Uchida might not have gone as far as Ichihashi, she did seem to use writing to release her own indignations, even though years later, in her memoir of incarceration, she would attribute her "survival" of the camps to the fact that her parents "taught her to endure" as they did, with "dignity, stoic composure, disciplined patience, and an amazing resiliency of spirit" (Uchida 1982, 148). Uchida paired the gaman-like qualities of outward dignity, composure, patience, and resiliency with inwardly written diary entries, where she employs repeated textual strategies to verbalize her dissent. On January 16, 1943, for example, Uchida writes that she just heard that "Calif. is going to demand that citizenship rights of J's be revoked." "How disgusting!" she writes next, adding that the state is also considering excluding Japanese from California completely, demanding their repatriation to Japan. "If that doesn't sound un-democratic, I don't know what does!!—To h—with Warren!," she swears (but rhetorically bleeps what we can only assume is "hell") at California Attorney General Earl Warren (Uchida 1943, January 16, notation in original). Two weeks later, Uchida declares that the proposed draft of already-incarcerated Nisei men makes her "SICK!" capitalizing each letter, ending with an exclamation point, and underlining the word twice for additional emphasis (January 31, notation in original). And in February, she rhetorically sticks out her tongue at the announcement of the Nisei's segregation in the army, punctuating "fooie!!!" with three exclamation points (February 9).

Uchida's most dramatic "explosion" comes in response to the murder of "a 63 yr old bachelor," James Wakasa. An Issei resident of Uchida's camp, Wakasa was "shot + instantly killed" by a guard in April 1943, and Uchida uses her now common textual strategies to scream about the injustice through her journal entry. According to her entry, the guard "claim[ed] [Wakasa] was trying to crawl through the fence . . . [and] wouldn't stop after 4 warning shots," an assertion she quickly dismisses: "The body was found 40" inside the fence—that's the inexcusable part. Ye Gads—how could the man hear—if some one yelled from a guard tower about 200 feet away . . . a warning shot should always be fired over-head first! . . . it's . . . so inexcusable! Hope the d—fool who shot him is jailed for life!" (Uchida 1943, April 12, notations in original).

Dissent, however, was not always expressed against the United States or its agents; at times, private writing was used to complain about community actions, as incarcerees tried to make sense of what was taking place. Nakahara, for example, used her diary to complain about the Santa Anita sit-down strike, a "rather shameful thing," which took place among 800 incarcerees who had volunteered to make camouflage nets for the military. According to Nakahara, the strike involved workers who claimed that "they were not receiving enough food, that their pay was too small, that this work was injurious to health, and that they were drafted to this project." Consistent in her use of her diary to sort through her thoughts, Nakahara writes through some counterarguments even as she questions her full understanding of the situation. But in the end, she clearly disapproves of what, from other accounts, seems to have been a well-supported strike (see Weglyn 1976, 81), which she attributes to being merely an issue of "personal rights":

> Japanese have always been so showy when professing Americanism. In the papers they have time and time again printed dynamic articles on such topics as "Nisei Americans," "Nisei Loyalty to Stars and Stripes," and "Americans All," and yet soon as situations became tough going, they have to pity themselves and say "they are martyrs, people without a country"; "getting raw deals."
>
> It is true that there have been prejudices shown, but much of what has taken place (such as evacuation) was for national security, which comes before personal rights. (Nakahara 1942b, June 16)

Nakahara's professed concern for "national security" (or the public rationale for "evacuation") was not uncommon among many Nisei who fervently believed in the benevolence of the United States in contrast to the evil Axis of Germany, Italy, and Japan. But in the moment of a strike, this would have been an unpopular point of view, and Nakahara would have known as much, making the refuge of her diary an important outlet for her dissenting thoughts.

And Nakahara was not the only one who used writing to privately complain about public forms of collective protest. In his diary, Stanley Hayami (1942–1943) complained about the "Manzanar riot" in December 1942, which, by mid-month, he had heard about in Heart Mountain. While Hayami disassociates himself from the "Japanese" and blames the "Kibeis and isseis" for the state violence that ensued, he seems to find the private space of his diary the perfect arena for his free-flowing anger that is, if not misplaced, understandable:

> Now the politicians and such are starting all over again in trying to take Jap Americans citizenship away and make things more strict in camp. Heck those guys should remember that over half are loyal Americans and the rest are Kibeis and isseis. I don't see why us innocent and good guys half to pay for stuff the Japanese do. Things like what Happened at Manzanar make all of us look like bad sabateurs when just a minority are the ones causing trouble. Darn it anyhow us loyal Jap Americans have no chance. When we're outside people look at us suspiciously and think we're spies. Now that we're in camp the Japs look at us and say we're bad cause we still love America. And now that people outside want to take our citizenship away from us as if we're the bad ones, when its really the Kibeis and isseis. If they take our citizenship away from us we'll be people without a country! Cause, gee whiz! Who in the hell wants a Japanese citizenship. I wouldn't go there for nothing! (Hayami 1942, December 14)

As a Nisei teenager whose camp diary also suggests an ongoing concern with doing well in school and a stated lack of bitterness toward the government over his forced relocation, Hayami would not have been likely to support the Manzanar rebellion/riot, especially since he would have most likely only heard about it via mainstream US newspapers or those sponsored by the WRA. But his complaints here that "what Happened at Manzanar make all of us look like bad sabateurs" and "loyal Jap Americans have no chance" were, at the time, still examples of dissident rhetoric. That is, his writing expressed disagreement with such prevailing racist rhetoric as General John DeWitt's famous words, "A Jap's a Jap" (quoted in Niiya and JANM 2001, 66) or the pre-incarceration editorializing printed in Hayami's hometown paper, the *Los Angeles Times*: "A viper is nonetheless a viper wherever the egg is hatched . . . So, a Japanese American born of Japanese parents, nurtured upon Japanese traditions, living in a transplanted Japanese atmosphere and thoroughly inoculated with Japanese . . . ideals, notwithstanding his normal brand of accidental citizenship almost inevitably and with the rarest exceptions grows up to be Japanese, and not an American" (59).

Given the nature of such public rhetoric, Hayami's written disgust, or even his stated resistance to potential policy—"I wouldn't go there for nothing!"—serves as a sharp example of a young man Writing-to-Gaman, who, like all the others, wrote to survive + resist the broader circumstances of mass incarceration by verbalizing dissent on a quiet but word-filled page.

"NOT JUST MY OWN": SHARPENING ONE'S AWARENESS OF OTHERS ENDURING HARDSHIP

Even as Hayami's and Nakahara's individual dissent counters what seems to have been a larger collective sentiment, it is important to note that in both entries quoted, the writers state a concern that the strikers/protesters are not thinking about people beyond themselves. For Hayami, the "Kibeis and isseis" involved in the "riot" "make all of us look . . . bad" and could potentially cause "us loyal Jap Americans" to have "our citizenship" taken away. For Nakahara, "national security" has to come before "personal rights." While both sets of rhetoric send chills down my spine as I write in the post-9/11 era of the Patriot Act, racial profiling, and the harassment and arrests of Muslim and seemingly Muslim human beings, I am nonetheless taken with a presence within these words of another aspect of Writing-to-Gaman: sharpening one's awareness of others enduring hardship.

For Nakahara, this "sharpening" began weeks before her anti-strike entry. Her journal begins with an explicit but broad desire to avoid writing anything that would, in her words, "hurt, humiliate, look down, blame or show dislike for any person, nation, race, religion, or station in life," as she wrote on the cover of her journal. But in camp, the first time Nakahara lives solely among other Nikkei, she begins to learn endless, specific stories of anti-Japanese discrimination from older coworkers. A month after her arrival at Santa Anita, Nakahara reflected a "conversation of opinions" (Nakahara 1942a, May 12) between Nikkei doctors and nurses at the camp hospital where she worked as an assistant. Calling their comments "undoubtedly" representative of "the majority of the people" in camp, Nakahara writes that she is

> slowly coming to understand the problems of the Japanese people; problems I never gave much thought to . . . [t]he evacuation, in itself . . . and all the problems and conflicts that go with it. The positions, many were resigned to give up; the paycheck that is no longer theirs; the property and homes that to be sold at such disadvantageous costs; the unfair dealings by those who were prejudiced; the plans and hopes that are now shattered; the loss of faith in other people; the darkness of the future to look forward to; the broken homes that were accounted for; in that the equality with other people, that seems meaningless, and the freedom that is now limited. (Nakahara 1942a, May 12)

The next day, she learns of the incarceree pay scale, including the "worse than disgusting" salary for the hospital's Nikkei staff. "As for myself," she writes, expressing more concern for others than herself, "monetary pay is of little interest, <u>BUT</u> to think that these doctors and regular nurses, who give all of their time and effort to their work, [will] only . . . receive $16.00 a month" (Nakahara 1942a, May 13, notation in original).

As Nakahara continued to learn more about the range and depth of hardship that the Nikkei community faced, she reminded herself that even if their experiences contradicted her own "high principals [*sic*]," she should never "forget . . . co-workers and friends," proclaiming her hope that she wouldn't "forget to see things through other people's eyes, not just my own." (Nakahara 1942b, July 29).

And she never seemed to, at least in her diary. The most remarkable example of Nakahara's "not forgetting" came when she learned about a prospective nursing student, a young Nikkei woman she never met, from one of her coworkers. In an entry dated September 9, Nakahara writes that she is "recouping 14 letters received by a ~~Japanese~~ Nisei girl who wished to go into nurse training . . . from the hospitals she wrote to, asking for admittance." After stating bluntly that "not one would accept her," Nakahara struggles with her own reaction:

> Could hardly believe that public sentiment could be so strong against the Japanese-[Americans] ~~of American birth and rearing.~~ But not until I myself actually come up against prejudice and discrimination, will I really understand the problems of the Nisei. When that time comes, I hope I can take it without blaming anyone else,—or whining . . . and hope I can still cling to the ideals I once set before me . . . and deep within, still feel that I'm an American.
>
> I'm grateful to —— for letting me recopy these letters (Nakahara 1942b, September 9, notation in original)

Nakahara follows these thoughts with ten handwritten pages of what appears to be texts and excerpts of the fourteen letters denying the young woman's admittance, all of which cite race as a factor but employ passive-like discourse to attribute the real reasons to prejudices of the town, the patients, and/or other nursing students. As a young female hospital worker herself, Nakahara seems to identify with the young woman, as she writes after the last of letters, "I wonder how I would have felt if I were the one to have received 14 such letters" (Nakahara 1942b, September 9). But she also seems to simultaneously see the adverse experience as beyond herself: "not until I myself actually come up against prejudice." As a whole, this remarkable entry, which is the longest in the journal, suggests a need to witness hardship, even if only for oneself—perhaps convincing the self that one is living among others who are truly being impacted by negative forces.

This heightened awareness of others beyond the self is also evident in Sugino's unpublished poems, several of which call upon other incarcerees to persevere through camp. Even though Sugino never uses the word *gaman* in her English-language poems, the feeling is evident in such stanzas as this one found handwritten into her day planner/diary for 1942: "Oh our comrades weaken not / That justice nor liberty are withheld / Men before us of this native land / Were imprisoned upon these fordless tracts / By men who spoke of lofty thoughts." (Sugino 1942, September 20). This slice of Sugino's private writing encourages incarcerees to not only persevere ("weaken not"), but to do so because others ("Men before us of this native land") have also been forced to endure hardship ("imprisoned upon these fordless tracts"). And yet, Sugino could just as well be writing to her Self, reminding her to think of herself as being among (historical) others. Poems are, after all, thought by many poets to be arguments we have with ourselves, and this poem ends on a sad note of "Love and faith and hope to bear / Vanish in the blazing sun," suggesting that the hardship of camp, and thus the argument that one must gaman, is ongoing.

In addition, while this poem (which may or may not have been made public later) was found written in Sugino's private day planner/diary, preprinted for 1942, poems dated later found loose among Sugino's papers suggest an ongoing struggle for collective perseverance. In "EVACUEE, MY EVACUEE," for example, found typed on a loose index card, Sugino admonishes other incarcerees not to "cower in the dust" and to instead "[r]emember Sakura no hana[10]/ its splendid essence so sublime" (Sugino 1943a).

Regardless of whether Sugino meant "comrades" or "EVACUEE[s]" to include herself or not, either way, the ethos of gaman as both perseverance + awareness of others enduring hardship remains a strong theme in Sugino's poems. For Sugino, the sharpened sense of others also seems evident in her praise of collective action, which she, unlike Hayami and Nakahara, seemed to believe served the community well. "Inspired by [the] unity of demonstration" displayed at Colorado River/Poston in November 1942, Sugino wrote "Rebirth" into her day planner/diary:

I saw the spirit of my people ebb last December;
I saw my people mauled this way and that like a thing accursed
Watch adazed their children shorn of every right,
And their lifelong savings melt into the night.
Resigned to fate meekly bowing without one remonstrance
Suddenly came to life and startle:
Enough's enough. It's gone far enough!"

I saw my people as dead since the war
Come to life today to say:
"Before God, we've still got some human rights!
'Tis better to die fighting than die like this
Caged beasts, meekly cowed by men
Who flaunt democracy but deign to give an ounce
Axis-ly interning innocent men
Who before God love American as much as they."

Kneel ye before thine own judgement throne
Who is to say American is thine or mine?

Has not each toiled to make this land divine?
God grant to each thy love to share. (Sugino 1942, November 18)

For Yoshiko Uchida, her awareness of herself among others seemed to grow sharpest during the "registration" period in early 1943, when the US government, at the urging of the JACL, "announced the formation of a special all-Nisei . . . combat unit" to be made up of young Japanese American men who had, for the past year, been ineligible for the draft (Niiya and JANM 2001, 260). This announcement led the military to recruit incarcerated Nisei men of draft age, but not before requiring them to complete what came to be known as the "loyalty questionnaire," which presumably tested incarceree loyalty to the US government by asking them, among other things, if they would "swear unqualified allegiance to the United States . . . and forswear any form of allegiance to the Japanese Emperor" (261). This questionnaire was soon extended to the entire camp population as a way to sort the "loyal" incarcerees from the "disloyal" incarcerees and subsequently caused great distress within the already distressed community, as it forced the Issei into a position where they would either be labeled "disloyal" or they would become people without a country (since they were ineligible for citizenship). For the Nisei, the question was insultingly racist—as US citizens, there was no inherent reason they would have allegiance to the Japanese emperor in the first place.

For Uchida, as for several others, this painful period brought forth much writing-to-redress, both in public and private forms. Taking note of her father and other Isseis' active attempts to redress registration with the outside "neutral" party of the Spanish consulate, Uchida complained, "at least the Issei can register their gripes—but we Nisei—have no country to gripe to—since our very own country puts us behind barbed wire. What a sorry state we're in!!!—" (Uchida 1943, January 19). But a couple of weeks later, Uchida writes about a "Citizens Mass mtg" she attends about the proposed "Nisei Combat Unit." In an entry dated February 4, 1943, Uchida responds to the "tragic" policy: "It seems so tragic—it is so tragic, so unjust to put the Nisei on such a spot—Saying now is their chance to show their loyalty + yet trying to put them in a 'yellow' unit—for cannon fodder most likely. If they don't volunteer I suppose we'll all be called disloyal. Yes, such a mess— + such an awful predicament. I couldn't sleep for a long time when I tho't of this whole tragically confused world." While the policy asking Nisei men to volunteer for the army while their families stay incarcerated does not impact Uchida directly, she is clearly concerned for "them," knowing that "their" actions could affect all of them—"we'll all be called disloyal." But unlike Hayami, who blames other incarcerees for the community's collective hardship, Uchida sympathizes with those who have been "put . . . on such a spot," acknowledging the hardship of being forced into a position that could result poorly no matter which choice—"cannon fodder" or "disloyal"—is made (February 4, notations in original).

Hayami, however, did not simply write to privately accuse other incarcerees for not thinking of people beyond themselves; he also wrote to remind *himself* to think of others. Often writing about his struggles for privacy in camp to study, write, and even think, Hayami also struggled with himself to remember to be considerate of those around him. For example, Hayami (1942–1943, January 10) wrote about a disagreement he had with one of his friends over what would be the best plans for after camp. Clearly heating up as he wrote, he finished relaying the dialogue and then exclaimed, "Hell! I've got a lot more to write but everyone else is sleeping already so I'd better turn the light off so they can sleep better." Eight days later, he complained, "Doggone it! Our room is so noisy that I can't study" but immediately tempered his complaint, reminding himself of other people: "Oh well, I should crab, everyone is entitled to his part in this house. I'm not the only one living in it. Anyhow I'll have to devise a means so I can concentrate better" (January 18).

Late in Nakahara's diary, though, we can see a culmination of this attention to others, the effects of a sharpened awareness of what it means to be connected to other people enduring hardship. Several months after Nakahara first arrived in Santa Anita, she finds herself needing to "write of the many things . . . racing through [her] mind." By this entry, coincidentally dated September 11, Nakahara seems reconciled to the idea that any "statements" made by a "good three-fourths of the people" in camp do not (as we might presume she previously thought) stem "from bitterness, but from summarizing actuality." Rhetorically moving to summary herself, Nakahara writes,

> Yes, it's true that the Japanese people from the time they came here have had raw deals, one after the other. And it's true that they've tried to fight for equality in chances for good positions but lost out because of racial prejudice Yet, the isseis saw to it that their children would be educated. Sacrifice meant nothing to them . . . and thus thru the span of twenty and thirty years, the majority of Niseis have received more than just high school education.

> They've made good grades in school. Their standards have been high . . . yet what happened when they got into the outside world? Racial prejudice and discrimination told them that the school-world and the work world were two different "hemispheres;" that what Caucasian teachers tried to instill in every student was only meant for the Caucasians; that the black and orientals would be looked down upon; that obstacles would be many.
>
> And how natural then, that bitterness seeped into the hearts of the great percentage of Niseis long before the war broke out.
>
> Yet just as M— said, the Niseis' love and loyalty, inspite of what their parents and themselves have gone through, rests in the heart of America. Deep within, below bitterness and hurt—lies hope and faith in the American that is theirs.
>
> As I listened to her—I'm sure something gripped me—and touched me in such a way—that I feel I want to fight, shoulder to shoulder with every Nisei, for the right to the same opportunities as the Caucasian.
>
> I can't do much—but I can do the little things in own capacity—to help and build what has been torn from them.
>
> Even if it's just writing letters, I'll write then—as I've never written before. (Nakahara 1942b, September 11)

While Nakahara followed through on her pledge to do "little things in [her] own capacity" by later mounting a strident letter writing campaign to Nisei soldiers who had either volunteered or been drafted out of camp (Fujino 2005, 43–46), it is in this entry that we can see the culmination of Nakahara's process tracing her commitment to sort through her ideas in private all the while attending to others by increasing her awareness of the difficulties they face. And like Hayami, Uchida, Ichihashi, Sugino, and the anonymous Nisei mother, Nakahara broke into print, actively engaging in a culturally relevant literacy practice in order to survive + resist mass incarceration.

LITERACIES OF GAMAN AS HIDDEN TRANSCRIPTS

> This camp is quiet and peaceful because the residents here have no guts and they are willing to put up with the WRA no matter how it treats them without complaints . . . [I]f there are those who are capable of thinking, they remain completely in hiding.
>
> —*Ichihashi*

While Writing-to-Gaman may have done little immediate rhetorical work to set right what was wrong about mass incarceration, this literacy activity enabled incarcerees to organize and verbalize unspoken emotion-thoughts all the while strengthening their awareness of themselves as human beings living among others enduring hardship. For those Japanese Americans who believed that their lives would be better off if they could just persevere through the duration of camp, the activity of breaking into print helped these incarcerated Quiet Americans both physically survive and psychologically resist mass incarceration. And thirty years later, this survivance would enable many to participate in the redress movement of the 1970s, a hard-fought public commotion filled with survivors making noise.

In this way, I have come to think of Writing-to-Gaman as one part of writing-to-redress. Calling upon the double-meaning of *to* as a signifier of "in order to" and of "toward," over the course of attendance, I have come to view this private activity not only as one performed *in order to* redress the circumstances of mass incarceration, but also as one that enabled the community as a whole to move *toward* a collective redress movement, a movement made possible, in part, by the community's explicit values of perseverance, strength, and attention to oneself among others.

In this sense, Writing-to-Gaman shares much in common with James C. Scott's (1990) "hidden transcripts." Describing these "arts of resistances," as the "whole range of practices" (14) that occur "'offstage,' beyond direct observation by powerholders" (4), Scott explains that hidden transcripts are made up "of what cannot be spoken in the face of power" (xii). While Scott's metaphor encompasses more than literal (written) "transcripts," the activities and texts of Writing-to-Gaman fit Scott's description of those "practices" that signify resistance to "ideological insubordination" (xiii). But Writing-to-Gaman also fits with Scott's notion in another manner. In his second-to-last chapter, Scott writes for some length about whether or not the practices of hidden transcripts function as what are commonly thought of as social "safety-valves" (185). In this interpretation, hidden practices of ideological resistance become merely practices of release, rhetorical moments where the oppressed can "let off steam" such that they become "[a]t best . . . of little or no consequence [and] at worst . . . an evasion" of the real inequities in power (184). However, Scott argues that such practices do not supplant "actual resistance" but instead just as often function to "sustain" it. "*It would be more accurate,*" Scott emphatically asserts, "*to think of the hidden transcript as a condition of practical resistance rather than a substitute for it*" (Scott 1990, 191, emphasis in original).

Following Scott, then, we might think of Writing-to-Gaman as both a private writing activity performed in order to redress one's adverse circumstances and as a private writing activity used to *(pre)-condition* oneself among others for subsequent public acts, whether performed via the activities of writing or otherwise. In this way, Writing-to-Gaman becomes akin to what Kimberly Harrison (2003, 244) calls "rhetorical rehearsals," where "personal rhetorical negotiations . . . result in [a] public presentation of the self." As Harrison makes clear, private writing can serve as a clandestine activity of ideological *preparation* and practical *training* necessary for public acts. Where Writing-to-Gaman differs, though, is that the activity rests on a preexisting ethos that sees the individual as interdependently connected to other people who are also undergoing "personal rhetorical negotiations" of their own. One may be *individually* Writing-to-Gaman but only because she/he lives among a *collective* group of people who are all enduring hardship together. In addition, I would argue that Writing-to-Gaman does not simply hold the potential to "result in [a] public presentation of the self," but instead holds the potential to result in a public presentation of the collective hardship. Writing-to-Gaman should be seen not as a *soloist's* rehearsal but as an act of individual preconditioning for an *ensemble* performance. In this case, individually writing *toward* collective movement.

Which is why separating the private activities of Writing-to-Gaman from the public acts can be misleading. After all, I would argue that several writer incarcerees who engaged in this private literacy activity ended up writing *toward* collective movements to redress, or "set right what was wrong" and "relieve suffering." Former writer incarceree Mitsuye Yamada has spoken of the ways her poems, silently tucked away in a shoebox after being written during her night job at the camp clinic were, in her words, "coaxed" "out of the mothballs" by the editors at Kitchen Table Press into the public form of a book published in the mid-1970s.[11] For Mary Nakahara, the private use of her journal to organize her emotion-thoughts not only allowed for the development of an early commitment to social justice, it also served as a political training ground for the work she would come to be known for after she married, claimed her Japanese name, and became the organizer

Yuri Kochiyama, whom many activists across the United States have come to know as the "heartbeat" of many public struggles for justice (Fujino 2005) and who actively called upon "We Japanese in America" to "speak up now" during the redress movement (Kochiyama 1981). Toyo Suyemoto, who wrote that poetry was her "only outlet" when she could "not speak," has since been hailed as the Nikkei "poet-laureate," as she continued to author both private and public poems throughout the camp years, publishing in both camp newspapers and in the *Yale Review* while she was still incarcerated (Schweik 1989; Streamas 2005). And who can say how Yoshiko Uchida's silent swearings in her diary enabled her to distill her writing into award-winning prose for children and young adults, including the first children's book I read with Asian American characters (Uchida 1976). Meanwhile, Chica Sugino never restricted her camp explosions at the moon to the private realms of personal writing, authoring protest letters, reports, and articles intended for public consumption beyond the barbed wire.

While I'm not in a position to argue that these incarceree writers consciously wrote toward a collective movement as they wrote to gaman, I can point to one more theme implicit in the rhetorics of gaman—that of waiting for a different future. This theme can be noted in several locations, as Mei Nakano (1990, 29) wrote, "Indeed a mood of 'no matter what' underscored the immigrants' outlook. They would gaman (*be patient*, persevere), no matter what, to survive." Similarly, my friend Ken Matsudaira added to his description of self-dialogue that the closest analogy he could make was "this too will pass." And psychologist Donna Nagata noted that gaman was one value that helped Nikkei families rebuild after incarceration since it "led many Nisei to avoid dwelling on the past" (Nagata 1993, 101).

Whether or not one thinks this attitude of patiently looking to the future in the midst of oppression is politically wise or psychologically healthy, it is certainly another sign that gaman was not an ethos of passivity but, instead, one of conscious activity. As my father commented to me after reading a draft of this chapter, he always thought of gaman as akin to the concept of "struggle" as used by his activist friends in African American communities. Citing Frederick Douglas's famous mantra, "If there is no struggle, there is no progress," he further explained that "obviously, struggle is a positive, active concept. You can struggle in silence, but it is still an act" (Shimabukuro 2008). Which brings us to the great lesson of Writing-to-Gaman. Despite what Ichihashi insinuated in the opening epigraph of this section, "remaining in hiding" is not the same thing as being "passive beyond imagination" (Chang 1997, 305). Nor is the internalization of emotion-thought in the midst of others enduring hardship. Despite all the history of oppression that has accompanied its ascendance as a distinctly Nikkei concept, gaman is so much more than a passive "code of silent suffering." It is strength, endurance, self-discipline, an awareness of others, and the ability to keep the future in sight. For many incarcerated Japanese Americans, gaman became a rhetoric of survivance. And in breaking out across a word-filled page, several found ways to practice this code of behavior by writing—outwardly unspoken, inwardly expressed, preconditioning themselves for public acts to come.

Notes

1. "Let's try to endure / hold out a little longer, okay?" I am grateful to Meiko Shimura, lecturer in the Japanese Language program at California State University, Fullerton for this translation.

2. Dedicated to "Issei pioneers," there is also a Sontoku statue in Little Tokyo, Los Angeles (Several 1997).

3. An argument could probably also be made for a historical relationship between the two concepts, as gaman was one of many "codes" put forth during the curriculum of *shushin*, the Meiji era moral education required of all schoolchildren (including those that would become the Issei). According to comparative education scholar Michiya Shimbori, the word shushin "is Confucian, literally meaning 'cultivating oneself.' In the Analects we find a phrase: shushin, chikoku, heitenka ('man should first cultivate himself, then govern his country, then bring peace in the world'). The time sequence of these three processes is teleological; that is, man should cultivate himself in order to govern his country, which in turn strives for peace. It can be translated also in the casual sense: 'man cannot govern his country if he has not cultivated himself and he cannot bring world peace if he cannot rule his nation.' The objective of self-cultivation is the well-being of society" (Shimbori 1960, 98n4).

Shushin, as a discipline, was also in place in some US-based Japanese schools attended by the Nisei (Tamura 1994, 154, 155), though because these schools were often sites of ideological struggles within Nikkei communities, it is difficult to say to what extent it was part of their curriculum (Asato 2006; Nakano 1990, 56; Azuma 2005; Ichioka 1988).

4. It is, of course, equally important to remember that there was a vibrant and public print culture within the prewar Nikkei community. See chapter 2.

5. See, for example, writing by Joseph Kurihara, one of the more notorious public dissidents during mass incarceration, some of which can be found at the JANM. Also, National Archives research by Rita Takahashi Cates indicates that the government's Office of Censorship kept a file of examples of "Political, Evacuee bitterness," which was made up of intercepted letters from the WRA camps, even though a censorship policy was only officially in play for the Department of Justice camps, where noncitizen Issei men were held during the first year or so of camp (Takahashi Cates 1980, 96n4). While not the focus of this study, the examples Takahashi Cates cites suggest that these files in the National Archives would constitute compelling data for further study.

6. See work by Louis Fiset (1997, 2001) on such letters. Also, Gail Okawa's (2008) recent research examines the literacy practices of Issei men in these camps.

7. I also refrained from examining the writing of Estelle Ishigo, one of the Euro-American women that "voluntarily" accompanied her Nisei husband to camp.

8. I examined a number of writings from various sources. From the JANM collection: camp diaries by James Yamasaki, Mary Nakahara, Stanley Hayami, and an anonymous "Nisei mother"; the personal papers of Chica Sugino (including her day planner, loose poems, and mimeographed copies of personal letters); and a poem written by Min Yasui sent to and inscribed into the scrapbook of his father, Masuo Yasui. From Densho: video histories and interviews of Mitsuye Yamada, Roger Shimomura (2003), and the Nakano family (Yaeko, Hiroshi, Kenishi, and Stanley); the family letters of Joe Nagano; and an unnamed diary from the Ikeda collection. From the Online Archive of California's link to the Japanese American Relocation Digital Archives: the diary of Yoshiko Uchida. From subsequently published texts: a diary and letters written by Yamato Ichihashi (Chang 1997) and a memoir, including previously unpublished poems, by Toyo Suyemoto (2007).

9. This is especially true for the private writing I looked at that was written by men, suggesting that a gender and literacy analysis would be in order for future projects.

10. Cherry blossoms.

11. Yamada's writing-to-redress will be discussed in more depth in chapter 7.

5
"EVERYONE . . . PUT IN A WORD"
The Multisources of Collective Authority behind Public Writing-to-Redress

> But resistance requires authority, and the source of that authority in Bakhtin's universe comes from what he calls "internally persuasive discourse" . . . Internally persuasive discourse is the constellation of voices we appropriate . . . These voices speak through us, and allow us to "be" who we need to be in a given circumstance.
>
> —*Mortensen and Kirsch (1993)*

Like most Japanese Americans that grew up during and around the redress movement, I came to know of individual resisters like Min Yasui, Gordon Hirabayashi, and Fred Korematsu as a child.[1] And later, during the 1990s "post-redress" era, I would learn of James Omura and his famous words to the Tolan Committee, asking the US government point-blank if the "Gestapo had come to America." Given this background knowledge of individual and heroic resisters, I believed, at times, the JACL chroniclers in their assertions that camp resistance had been numerically insignificant (Masaoka and Hosokawa 1987, 179). And so I began my research with the suspicion that

DOI: 10.5876/9781607324010.c005

I would find most writing-to-redress to be of a private nature, that, generally speaking, I would find accounts and examples of Writing-to-Gaman.

To my surprise, the majority of what I found and learned about seemed much more public—that is, intended for public circulation. For example, in a 1986 issue of *Amerasia Journal*, Kazu "Always A Rebel" Iijima shared memories of her life before, during, and after camp.[2] Iijima tells Glenn Omatsu that even before everyone had been rounded up, she and the rest of the all-Nisei Oakland Young Democratic Club wrote a statement in spring 1942 condemning the "evacuation" order as an act "of fascism in a war for democracy." She never forgot the literacy event, that moment an act of reading or writing took place, Iijima says, "because we were angry. We were a small group—only a dozen of us—but everyone wanted to put in a word. So it was formulated by the group" (Omatsu 1986–1987, 93).

Like so many other public acts of writing-to-redress, the Young Democratic Club's statement was ignored, even after the group sent it to several newspapers (Omatsu 1986–1987, 93). But regardless of whether the statement was published, the story of its event is a powerful testament to the ways groups of Nikkeis used writing to talk back and did so in a unified, collective voice in order to be heard in public. It was learning of writings like this—letters to editors and government authorities, petitions and manifestos—that have helped me understand the lie of "numerical insignificance"—that, in fact, many incarcerees wrote to interrupt the policies of camp, to change some procedural aspect of incarceration or make day-to-day life more bearable.

But what I have also found is that such public literacy acts often grew out of a group-based authority, similar to the one hinted at by Iijima. Unlike the writers who privately "broke into print" and individually Wrote-to-Gaman, these writers publicly "made some noise" and Wrote-to-Redress collectively, as a group. To do so, however, these incarcerees needed to develop a collective felt sense of their right to talk back. Such collective authority, as I have come to think of it, seemed to begin in response to the shared experience of forced "relocation" and incarceration and subsequently developed strength via a multitude of material and ideological sources. In addition, I believe that the collective authority behind public writing-to-redress gained further strength from the synergy of incarceree struggle itself—that is, incarcerees also generated authority from the collective energy amassed during organizing. Examining the activities and texts of collectively authorized, public writing-to-redress, this chapter focuses on the literal and metaphorical ways multiple interests and ideologies, parties and people "put in a word," as incarcerees formulated a way to write back to incarceration and did so as a group.

ATTENDING PUBLIC WRITING-TO-REDRESS

Unlike the exact document composed by the Young Democratic Club, much public writing-to-redress remains in the collected memories of former incarcerees, collected reports of camp anthropologists, and collections of papers held in university and community archives. In order to find these accounts and texts of writing first intended for public circulation, I rhetorically attended the sites of Japanese American historiography, stretching my mind toward my sources, their citations, my chosen archives, my memory, and my political/rhetorical commitments.

First, I revisited the primarily social science work of camp resistance scholars like Gary Okihiro (1973, 1997b, 1984, 2001), Arthur Hansen (2002; Hansen and Hacker 1974), Lane Ryo Hirabayashi (1998; see also Nishimoto 1995), Michi Weglyn (1976), Eric Muller (2001), Susan McKay (2001), Lon Kurashige (2001), and Frank Chin (Chin 2002). I reread these accounts and analyses of resistance, noting places where self- or community-sponsored writing seemed to be employed as part of the protest or resistance or response. From there, I followed up on several citations of writing-to-redress that seemed particularly noteworthy, tracking down less known sources: secondary, like Rita Takahashi Cates's dissertation (Takahashi Cates 1980), and primary, like exact texts collected by camp anthropologists whose records are held in places like the University of California, Berkeley's Bancroft Library.

In addition to this spiraling attendance, I also attended the hard copy archives of the Japanese American National Museum and the online archives of the Densho: The Japanese American Legacy Project. At the JANM, I first asked for English-language materials that had been written during camp that were not sanctioned by the WRA and which publicly sought to change some aspect of incarceration. In addition to sending me a list of materials the archivist thought would fit my needs, she thought I might be interested in a collection of papers that had recently been donated but not yet cataloged in full detail: the collection of Chica Sugino, a former incarceree who had been held in Poston and worked, for a time, as a research assistant for the Community Analysis Bureau, one of the government-sponsored agencies conducting social science research in the camp.

In terms of Densho, my rhetorical attendance began with my choice to include this online archive of video histories. I have known of Densho since it began, as my stepmother, Alice Ito, was one of the first employees of the project, conducting many of the interviews available in the database. At family dinners or other gatherings, I listened as Alice talked of her work, the patience it required, and the stories people were willing to tell on tape. I knew Densho was accumulating memory to pass on, to make use of, and to enable others to know a community as well as a community to know itself. I also knew that the video histories were painstakingly transcribed, coded, and cataloged before being made available to the public. As such, I knew I could search hundreds of video histories that had been collected ethically and in the community's interest. Using various versions of the words *writing*, *protest*, *petition*, *censorship*, and *resistance*, I searched the database of histories, attending the memories of others as they recalled individual and collective acts where writing may have helped them redress incarceration.

THE SIGNIFICANCE OF COLLECTIVE AUTHORITY IN PUBLIC WRITING-TO-REDRESS

As I first combed the secondary works and then attended the archives of the JANM and Densho, I soon learned that writing-to-redress had, throughout the incarceration period, continued to take public form. Gone were the images of passive Nikkei masses I had always been told about. Instead, digital and hard copy files soon filled both my computer and hardwood desktops, all with eclectic titles that labeled icons and manila folders filled with images, texts, and transcriptions: "Minidoka Boilerman Strike 1943," "Voice of the Nisei," "GILA," "Writing No-No." Some of it referenced public writing-to-redress individually performed, like essays submitted to *Reader's Digest* or the *Saturday Evening Post* that were never published[3] or accounts of people rewriting the loyalty questionnaire refusing to answer in the ways the WRA had instructed.[4] But much of the writing-to-redress I learned about or read seemed to draw authority from a collective body of Nikkei incarcerees who either debated wording, signed their names, or contributed their labor to the given literacy event. That is, much of the work enabling the public writing-to-redress I was finding seemed inherently collective.[5]

By *collective* I mean something different than the given understanding in composition and rhetoric that writing is inherently social. All writing is, of course, enabled by social processes, ranging from community ethoi and cultural clusters (Royster 2000; Mao 2006), discursive heritages and affiliations (Lu 2004; Smitherman 1977; Canagarajah 1999); sociopolitical circumstances and exigencies (Duffy 2004; Young 2004), audiences imagined and invoked (Ede and Lunsford 1984), and access to the material resources and know-hows of literacy (Brandt 2001; Duffy 2007; Cornelius 1991).

And yet, even as we know that writing is social—that it is, in many ways, a collective process—at times it is still difficult to see how writing under adverse conditions comes to be taken up *in a collective manner* by those who might otherwise choose to be publicly silent. Many community portraits composed in comp/rhet are amalgamations of individuals writing in a single geographical or racial/ethnic/cultural community. For example, comp/rhet ethnographers such as Ellen Cushman and Ralph Cintron paint powerful portraits of individuals in working-class communities of color taking up "the struggle and the tools" (Cushman 1998) in order to "*create respect under conditions of little or no respect*" (Cintron 1997, x, emphasis in original). Jacqueline Jones Royster draws upon the mixed methods of historical ethnography, "critical imagination," and Afrafeminist methodology to analyze how individual elite African American women writers "construct a sense of an empowered self amid disempowering forces and use the energy generated by this process to act" (Royster 2000, 70). In addition, John Duffy analyzes the rhetorical uses of literacy by individual Hmong immigrants as they talk back through their "letters to the Fair City" (Duffy 2004).

These studies greatly help us see how communities of writers have taken up the struggle and the tools to create respect where there is little or none offered from the powers that be, as does work in Asian American rhetorics over the past twenty years. Scholars such as Terese Guinsatao Monberg, Haivan Hoang, and LuMing Mao have examined the meaning of rhetorical performances (including, but not limited to, acts of literacy) by different groups of Asian Americans in response to historical and contemporary wrongs (Monberg 2002; Hoang 2004, 2015; Mao 2006). In addition, and most related to my work, Gail Okawa has examined individual and collective petitions to the government written by Issei men held at the internment camps reserved for targeted male Issei leaders in the prewar Nikkei community (Okawa 2011).[6]

Through such studies we are given a sense of how individual writers lay claim to rhetorical agency when / as their community's own authority is denied and the kinds of discourses or performances employed by groups asserting their agency in the face of a collective wrong. Collectively, their scholarship suggests that the authority one draws upon to Write-to-Redress does not always stem from an obvious, single source.[7] Instead, we come to see the ways writers struggle with the conditions of their lives and "use the energy generated by this process to act" and *write* with conviction, dignity, and pride.

Following these scholars, then, we can more deeply understand how such a struggle manifests out of the conditions of life—in this particular case, mass incarceration—such that a group-based authority can be generated to collectively and publicly Write-to-Redress. For my own work, that meant looking at the ways writing-to-redress was sanctioned, or authorized, not only by the writers themselves but also by the larger camp community and the broader social conditions of the exact moment in history. This collective sanctioning, or authorization, seems to have been key to much collective incarceree authority that brought forth public writing-to-redress and yet seems to have developed out of several competing processes working to enable or suppress these public literacies. As Deborah Brandt and Katie Clinton (2002, 350–51) remind us, "literate practices can be shaped out of the struggle of competing interests and agents . . . [and] multiple interests can be satisfied during a single performance of reading or writing . . . 'Agency' does not have to be sacrificed through such an analysis, only recognized as multisourced."

If we understand that rhetorical agency is multisourced—that it stems from a "struggle of competing interests and agents"—then we must understand what those interests and agents are. We must understand that vastly different processes, ideologies, institutions, and individuals combine to enable a rhetorical performance of literacy and that processes, ideologies, institutions, and individuals do not always have our best interest at heart. In other words, for any given rhetorical moment, we navigate between and across concrete and abstract processes that have bumped up against our lives—some of which, intentionally or unintentionally, encourage us to rhetorically act and others that, intentionally or unintentionally, discourage us.

Amidst these competing tensions, we may or may not take to writing or we may take to writing in some moments and not others. And sometimes the struggle between these contradictory processes can provide the energy to act. For a great amount of the public Writing-to-Redress I looked at, such struggles seemed to give incarcerees a kind of permission, or authorization, to rhetorically make use of literacy to respond to incarceration.

But that struggle, and thus, that authorization, emerged from competing interests. It was multisourced. Born out of the oppressive reality of mass incarceration, it drew upon material and ideological resources available from both friendly and hostile sponsors and gained strength as a collected synergy developed among incarcerees who organized against their conditions. What follows are detailed discussions and examples of each of these types of sources. The chapter closes with an analysis of multisourced authority in one specific act of collective Writing-to-Redress, that of the Heart Mountain Fair Play Committee's manifesto against the draft.

THE MULTISOURCES OF COLLECTIVE AUTHORITY: DAMAGE, SPONSORSHIP, AND AMASSING

Out of Damage Inflicted: Damage as an Authorizing Force

> At rhetorical borderlands, we border residents are deeply situated and our rhetorical practices are intensely social. We therefore face enormous constraints, for example, on what we say, on what relations we enter into, and on what subject positions we occupy. In turn, such constraints exert structural effects on how we form our knowledge and beliefs, on how we establish our social relationships, and on how we cultivate our social identities . . . However, Fairclough reminds us constraints are enabling, too. That is to say, socially situated participants are "only through being so constrained that they are made able to act as social agents" . . . and in fact being constrained, for Fairclough[,] is "a precondition for being enabled" (Mao 2006, 30).

To understand the emergence of the collective authority behind writing-to-redress, we must first consider the role that the constraints of oppression plays in both authoring and authorizing oppressed groups of people to use writing to come to public voice. As Abdul R. JanMohamed and David Lloyd assert, given the "historically sustained negation of minority voices"—which I would argue is a sustained act of rhetorical not-listening—"minority discourse is, in the first instance, the product of damage." Such damage, JanMohamed and Lloyd go on to explain, is "more or less systematically inflicted . . . by the dominant culture. The destruction involved is manifold, bearing down on variant modes of social formation, dismantling previously functional economic systems, and deracinating whole populations at best or decimating them at worst" (JanMohamed and Lloyd 1990, 4). It is in this context that the discourse of minorities, written or otherwise, is formed and expressed, articulating the pain, anger, frustration, and/or rage that boil up in oneself as part of a collective community facing that "damage."[8] In this way, the experience of large-scale oppression can grant an oppressed group of people the right to come to public voice and do so in a collective manner. Or as JanMohamed and Lloyd put it, "Out of the damage inflicted on minority cultures . . . emerges the possibility of a collective subjectivity formed in practice rather than contemplation" (9). This collective identity emerges, they further explain, because "minority individuals are always treated and forced to experience themselves generically"; but while they may be "[c]oerced into a negative, generic subject-position, the oppressed individual responds by transforming that position into a positive, collective one" (10).

And such transformation from negative-generic to positive-collective is partially enabled by the technology of literacy. While not about damage, collective authority, or literacy per se, the work of rhetoric historian Susan Zaeske on nineteenth-century antislavery petition campaigns by white middle-class women says much about the ways people excluded from the dominant public sphere generate the collective authority they need to Write-to-Redress for the public sphere. By focusing on people who had material resources but no political power or representation, Zaeske (2002) argues that women who took part in the signature campaigns were helping compose a "collective subjectivity" (162). As the lists of signatures on the petitions grew, she argues, so did a codified "female collective," as handwritten names accumulated "for all to see the existence of . . . women who coalesced discursively by signifying their agreement" with the written words on the page (156).

For Zaeske, then, it is with the practice of gathering signatures and signing names that forms of discursive coalescence and codified collectives become possible. And this would have been even more so for incarcerees who wrote and coalesced out of damage inflicted upon their own bodies, generalized as "Japs." The visual accumulation of signed names of people recently "forced to experience themselves generically" became a means of transformation from negative (generic) to positive (collective). In other words, literacy became a means and a practice of collecting authority out of damage inflicted, a right that oppressed people share to publicly and collectively write back.

This literacy practice of collecting authority out of damage inflicted can be seen in several examples of the collective writing-to-redress I attended over the course of my research, where explicit references to damage wrought by mass incarceration suggest the ways in which these texts and activities had indeed "in the first instance" stemmed from destruction, dismantlement, deracination, or the prevention of humane modes of social formation. For example, much of what I found explicitly referenced the particular damages of the 1943 loyalty questionnaire or the 1944 reclassification of Nisei men as eligible for the draft. In the beginning of the incarceration period, though, most collective writing-to-redress referenced the more day-to-day damages of subpar living conditions. For example, Rita Takahashi Cates notes that the "women of Heart Mountain," the majority of whom hailed from Southern California, collectively wrote to their camp director to redress the fact that incarcerees had, by October 19, 1942, still not received long-promised winter clothing or cash allowances for such clothing. And yet, "all the women of this camp" insisted that this promise be "carried out effectively" as "severe snow weather" had already arrived and children were attending camp schools in "thin summer clothes," a "very serious problem on their health as well as their education" (quoted in Takahashi Cates 1980, 211–12).

Just one month later, another collective literacy event explicitly redressing daily life damage emerged in Heart Mountain when 3,000 incarcerees wrote to redress by signing onto a petition to remove the barbed wire fence surrounding their camp (Inouye 1998; Takahashi Cates 1980; Hansen 2002). Citing Roger Daniels, Takahashi Cates claims this number was roughly half the adult population at the time (Takahashi Cates 1980, 211–12), a remarkable figure given the explicit naming of damage within the petition. Collectively writing as "[w]e, the undersigned residents . . . composed of American citizens of Japanese ancestry, and, Japanese Nationals, individuals and jointly as a group," the incarcerees proclaimed the fence and guard towers to be "devoid of all . . . understanding, and principles of democracy." In addition, the signatories wrote, the fence and towers were "ridiculous in every respect" and "an insult to any free human being." If the fence remained, the petition continued, Heart Mountain "residents" would not be able to see their status as anything else but "prisoners of war in a concentration camp" (Heart Mountain Sentinel 1942).

But even with time, incarcerees continued to face enough damages of subpar living conditions that they continued to Write-to-Redress as a group. In January 1944, the "Ladies of Hunt Relocation Center" (Minidoka) wrote to the director of the WRA, Dillon Myer, to redress the lack of hot water in camp because of a labor struggle between the camp administration and the Nikkei boilermen. Careful not to lay blame at the feet of the striking workers, "the women and mothers of this project" argued that the damages they faced were unacceptable, as they had been "brought here . . . against [their] wishes and were guaranteed to lead a normal life, but . . . now, without hot water for bathing babies, washing and general cleaning," it had become impossible to do so. As such, the women wrote, they "demand[ed] hot water service at once" (Ladies of Hunt Relocation Center 1944).

Aside from the day-to-day damages that prevented incarcerees from leading "a normal life," the damages wrought by cross-camp crises also brought forth a number of collective writing-to-redress activities. In 1943, for example, several literacy events emerged with the "registration crisis" and its questionnaire purportedly designed to determine the loyalty of both citizen and noncitizen incarcerees (for a more detailed discussion of the registration period, see chapter 4), in part, to begin reaccepting Nisei volunteers into the armed forces. While I came across several accounts of writing-to-redress events performed by individuals (like rewriting some of the questions on the form), there were also events performed by collective groups who used writing to directly address the damages they faced.

In Topaz, a "resident committee" formed in direct response to the crisis, as each of the thirty-three blocks elected one representative to participate. According to the *Topaz Times* and Russell Bankston, sociologist for the Topaz Reports Division, nine members of the "committee of 33" were appointed to write a response; Bankston (1943) writes that they "refus[ed] to take time out even for supper." By 9:45 p.m., the draft of the resolution had been taken back to the blocks for approval, where general meetings were held and finished in such time that by 11:30 p.m. the subcommittee of nine had come back to the local administration with their final resolution to be teletyped to both Myer and Secretary of War Harry Stimson.

Arguing that incarcerees have "given [their] fullest cooperation," the first half of the resolution consists, in part, of a list of damages. Naming themselves as "citizens of the United States," the collective "we" of the text asserts that they have "temporarily surrendered many of the rights and privileges of citizenship" as well as "suffered losses of homes, properties, work, freedom of movement, [and] separation from friends." In addition, the text asserts, the collective "believe[s] some of these things . . . [to] constitute a violation of [their] civil rights" (quoted in Topaz Times 1943; Bankston 1943).[9]

This kind of language referencing a broader damage than that inhibiting the conduct of "normal" life would soon emerge again. A little less than one year after registration, the War Department announced the re-institution of the draft for Nisei men. While male American citizens of Japanese ancestry had, in the wake of Pearl Harbor, been reclassified as "aliens not acceptable to the armed forces" (Muller 2001, 41), these same men were now reclassified "on the same basis as other citizens" (Muller 2001, 64), thus making them susceptible to the Selective Service. Throughout the camps, the news appears to have been met with a kind of quiet resentment at first, but much of the writing-to-redress I found and learned of suggests that the news spawned a massive amount of written rhetorical activity. Within the two months immediately following the government's announcement, writing-to-redress the draft emerged in at least seven of the ten WRA camps, as incarcerees used writing to set right what seemed so blatantly wrong—telling a group of young citizens that had been held behind barbed wire for two years without charge that only one of their rights was being returned: the "right to be shot at" (Weglyn 1976, 136).

Notably, the damages recounted in several of these texts are broader than the immediate damage of the draft. For example, the newly formed Delegates of Manzanar Draft Age Citizens drafted a resolution complete with a cover letter to their camp director, Ralph Merrit, to redress the circumstances of the draft. In the letter, dated March 1, 1944, the delegates explained that they were not "unmindful of [their] duties" as "citizens" who must "show [their] loyalty to [their] country by acts and deeds" during a time of war, but they had already faced the damage of a "gauntlet of many bitter tests of loyalty—tests to which no other citizen group has been subjected in the history of these United States." Avoiding the naming of names, the delegates continued by referencing such "bitter tests" and their effects on the group's stance toward the United States:

> Buffetted [*sic*] by the vitriolic and unceasing attacks against us by self-seeking politicians, yellow journalists, hirelings of vested interests and pressure groups as well as being branded by uncalled for and unfounded remarks of our own military leaders, we admit that we have, at times, wondered whether the principles of democracy upon which our nation is founded are real and existent, or whether we are embracing and cherishing principles built upon the shifting sands of empty, meaningless words. (Delegates of Manzanar Draft Age Citizens 1944)

Even so, the delegates continued, "we still cling firmly to our faith in the fairplay, equal treatment and justice of the government." And given such a belief, the delegates reasoned in their closing, the damages of "certain bans and restrictions" as well as the "discriminatory rules and regulations imposed on [them] as a racial group" should be redressed.

With these examples, we can see the ways several groups of incarcerees generated a collective authority "[o]ut of . . . damage inflicted." In this way, these public literacy practices uphold JanMohamed and Lloyd's theory of "minority discourse," which posits that the "possibility of a collective subjectivity" always exists amidst the life conditions of people racialized as minorities, "forced to experience themselves generically" (JanMohamed and Lloyd 1990, 10). As people assigned the "negative, generic subject-position" of "enemy aliens," "prisoners of war," and/or "Japs" who would always be "Japs," Nikkei incarcerees transformed their public position as they wrote to redress the damages they faced into positive, collective subjectivities such as "all the women of this camp," "Ladies of Hunt Relocation Center," members of a "Mother's Society," and "residents composed of American citizens of Japanese ancestry and Japanese nationals . . . jointly, as a group." In doing so, they collected the authority to speak out of the negative damage inflicted upon them and transformed it into a positive and public collective authority to write.

But in order to more fully understand how Nikkei incarcerees collected the authority to publicly write-to-redress, we must consider additional ways in which their collective authority was, using Brandt and Clinton's term, multisourced. If some experiences worked to authorize incarceree collective authority by attempting to deny their right to live as full human beings, other experiences authorized a burgeoning public ethos by doing the opposite—encouraging the incarcerees to fully claim that right and, in doing so, encourage them to Write-to-Redress, "jointly, as a group." Such encouragement can be better understood by considering how collective authority is both sponsored from above and amassed from below.

Institutional Influences: Sponsoring Authority from Above

> Even within single institutions, the uses and networks of literacy crisscross through many domains, potentially exposing people to multiple sources of sponsoring power.
>
> —*Brandt*

> Accumulated layers of sponsoring influences—in families, workplaces, schools, memory—carry forms of literacy that have been shaped out of ideological and economic struggles of the past.
>
> —*Brandt*

With her now oft-cited article, "Sponsors of Literacy," Deborah Brandt theorizes literacy sponsorship as a way to understand "who or what underwrites occasions of literacy learning and use" (Brandt 1998, 166). In doing so, Brandt helps us see how "ideological freight" can be carried in acts of sponsorship, whether or not sponsored writers are consciously aware of such freight. But even as the sponsored just as often as not use literacy "pragmatically under the banner of other people's causes" (168), the discourses and ideologies of literacy sponsors continue to carry rhetorical authority whether writers like it or not.

As such, sponsorship remains a provocative analytical concept for understanding the ways people generate the authority to write (Goldblatt 1995). But to understand how sponsorship can serve the genesis of a *collective* authority, we need to peel back what Brandt would call the "accumulated layers of sponsoring influences" at play within the single institution of camp. From there, we should be better able to attend to the ways "uses and networks of literacy crisscross[ed]" during mass incarceration and enabled Nikkei incarcerees to collect the authority to write back.

"[F]or the Principles of American Democracy": Collecting Authority from Americanization

Having grown up as the children of immigrants during the 1920s and 1930s, most of the incarcerated Nisei would have been immersed in the ideology of the Americanization movement in public schools. According to David Yoo, the movement in California, where most incarcerees would have originally lived, provided educators with "a rhetorical framework for those who worked with immigrants. Some general characteristics of Americanization included staunch support for democracy, representative government, law and order, capitalism, general health . . . and command of the English language. Public schools were a key component of Americanization, the aim of which was to transform immigrants into patriotic, loyal and intelligent citizens of the Republic" (Yoo 2000, 22). According to the *Los Angeles School Journal*, by 1925 most children of immigrants in California had already become to a "considerable extent Americanized," having "placed upon them the imprint of American citizenship" in their "desire to live as Americans" (Shafer 1925, 10). Whether this was true or not, we can certainly imagine that the discourse of American citizenship and civics education, including discussions on the US Constitution, was highly prevalent in public schools (Olneck 1989). As such, it would have been readily available to most Nisei children of the time.

Interestingly enough, in addition to their Americanist experiences in the public schools, the Nisei along the West Coast may have also received a heavy dose of Americanization through Japanese-language schools, which almost every Nisei child attended during this time period. Frequently under attack by xenophobic organizations along the West Coast, the Japanese language schools were designed by the Issei leaders as a way to teach Japanese language to the second generation and instill in them cultural values deemed necessary to strengthen and maintain ethnic ties. While leaders in the community differed as to how much the schools should teach values associated with the militarism of the then Japanese empire (Azuma 2005), they also found themselves confronted with two ongoing characteristics of the American empire: white supremacy and American chauvinism. By 1921 the state legislature of California had passed laws to govern these non-state-funded community institutions, including those that would "regulate the operation of schools, the certification of teachers, and the content of instructional materials . . . To be certified to teach in a school, all teachers had to pass a state examination in

English competency (reading, writing, and speaking) as well as in American history and institutions in English. All textbooks and curricula had to be approved by the Superintendent of Public Instruction" (Ichioka 1988, 207).

By the mid-1920s, in response to the growing institutionalization of anti-Japanese racism, the language schools had revised their stated goals to be "[b]ased on the spirit of American public schools," with their "purpose" being more to "supplement good civic education'" (Ichioka 1988, 207). In other words, the atmosphere of Americanism and its discourse had been present on some level in both types of schooling available to future Nisei participants in camp literacy practices, both of which may have added another kind of authorization to publicly Write-to-Redress.

As "one layer" of what Brandt would call a "sponsoring influence," this kind of Americanist discourse can be seen throughout collective writing-to-redress. Notably dominant in the writing of the Heart Mountain Fair Play Committee, the central manifesto of which will be discussed later in this chapter, the themes of Americanization are present in almost all of the writing-to-redress the draft or the concurrent announcement of segregated units that I attended. Drawing heavily on an explicit rhetoric of citizenship, several texts seem reliant on a collective authority that is, in part, generated by explicit references to the authors' legal status within the United States. The Manzanar resolution, we see right away, is from the "Delegates of Manzanar Draft Age *Citizens*." In Gila River, the 620 "undersigned" petitioning for "equal privileges" within the military are "American citizens of Japanese ancestry" (Gila News-Courier 1944; Omura 1944a). And in Poston, a resolution passed unanimously by 1,000 Nisei begins with "We, citizens of the United States of America of Japanese Ancestry."

Even the mothers of the Nisei, all of whom were denied naturalization rights and thus considered "enemy aliens" during World War II, collected authority from discourses of American citizenship. For example, the mothers of Minidoka explicitly referred to themselves not as aliens but as "parents of American citizens" in order to be heard by President and Mrs. Franklin Roosevelt, to whom they addressed their writing. Similarly, when over 1,000 Issei women from Topaz wrote to the president to request the "restoration" of civil rights for their sons fighting in the military, they referred to themselves as "mothers of American citizens of Japanese descent" (Mothers of Topaz 1944).

As for the sons of the mothers in Topaz, their writing-to-redress also gathered some of their collective authority from the discourses of Americanization. In their "Recommendations of Topaz Citizens for the Principles of American Democracy," they responded to the proposed formation of all-Nisei military units by opening with a lengthy epigraph that they cite as being from Abraham Lincoln's Gettysburg Address, while the main text begins by introducing a recent "public statement directed to the Sec'y of War Stimson" in which "President Roosevelt expressed his views." With this explicit reference to the highest-ranked leader of the country, the "Topaz Citizens" continue their "recommendations" by first including four paragraphs of text from Roosevelt's statement, emphasizing with underlined text a phrase that repeats in several writing-to-redress texts: "The principle on which this country was founded and by which it has always been governed is that Americanism is a matter of the mind and heart; Americanism is not, and never was a matter of race or ancestry." While the text continues by recounting numerous ways "the nisei, Americans citizens of Japanese descent, have shown their loyalty by complying with all government regulation," the document closes by stating that the "Topaz Citizens Committee is opposed to the discriminatory segregation of all Japanese American draftees" and recommends that all military segregation should end. But with their final words, the committee reestablishes their collective authority as stemming from an identification with the ideologies of Americanization: "Buddies, regardless of color or ancestry, made on the battle fields can best help to accomplish this great task that is before us—a task that is for a greater America" (Topaz Citizens for the Principles of American Democracy 1944, notation in original).

"Petitions may be circulated": Collecting Authority from the WRA

Aside from the sponsoring influence of an Americanization ideology, which, following Brandt, we might think of as a "distant" and "abstract" sponsor of literacy, incarcerees also collected authority from the War Relocation Authority, a sponsor that was more local and concrete. While WRA-sponsored newspapers, schools, adult English classes, and literary clubs provided sanctioned space to write, one could certainly argue that this "freedom within confinement" (Nakano 1990) merely served to uphold what Michael W. Apple and Lois Weis might consider a "legitimating function" in which the camp newspapers and schools help "generate consent from the governed" (Apple and Weis 1983, 5–6) by suggesting that camp was a fair and legitimate institution. However, at times, the WRA-sanctioned spaces indirectly enabled a collective writing-to-redress to emerge.

For example, according to the daughter of one of the mothers of Minidoka, the women who signed the petition-letter had originally been brought together in one of the Issei English classes (Aburano 2008). And in Heart Mountain, individuals including Paul Nakadate, Frank Emi, and Frank Inouye—all of whom played significant roles in subsequent collective writing-to-redress events—were able to practice and hone their writing-to-redress skills within the spaces assigned for letters to the editor in the WRA-sponsored *Heart Mountain Sentinel* (Nakadate 1944; Emi 1944; Inouye 1943).

In addition, in response to the growing discontent over the draft, the WRA issued a memo dated February 21, 1944 to all camp administrators stating, "every citizen of the United States has the right to petition for the correction of any grievances." Recovered in the files of Chica Sugino at JANM, the memo attempted to circumscribe the boundaries of future writing-to-redress petitions with explicit guidelines: "Petitions may be circulated, or the opinion of groups or individuals otherwise expressed, declaring the participants' loyalty to the United States, but requesting that the rights of persons of Japanese ancestry to complete freedom of movement including freedom to return to the West Coast or other rights, be restored before their young men of military age are drafted for military service" (War Relocation Authority 1944). While the full effect of this memo is unknown, it does seem likely that several groups of incarcerees collected at least some authority from this WRA authorization: over half of the writing-to-redress drafts I found in my research are marked with a date that comes after that which appears on the memo.

"Under the protection of the Japanese flag": Collecting Authority from Countervailing Institutions

US-based sponsors were not the only institutions and ideologies from which incarcerees were able to generate a collective authority. As Eli Goldblatt argues in his discussion of marginalized writers and authority, "To write well is to accept a challenge to participate in the institution sponsoring the writing, even if that institution resists the writer's contribution" (Goldblatt 1995, 27). When the writers are the ones choosing to resist, they can only "succeed," Goldblatt continues, "when they gain the backing of a sizable countervailing institution" (34). While the relative "success" of writing-to-redress is less important here, Goldblatt's point about the backing of a counter sponsor is. For many Isseis writing to redress, critical forms of sponsorship were provided by non-US institutions and ideologies, especially the Spanish consul and Japanese nationalism.

According to Michi Weglyn, in January 1943, after several of the Issei men held by the FBI were released from the Department of Justice camps into the WRA camps where their families were being held, "it became widespread knowledge that interned nationals could make their grievances known to the Japanese Government" by addressing the Spanish consul. Writing to the Spanish consul, a kind of "neutral" audience, would eventually become a common strategy by any Issei writing-to-redress, as many hoped they would be better heard via this avenue. According to Weglyn, though, it was not until this information became known to a broader range of Issei in the WRA camps that it even "occurred to [them] . . . that protests could be made with any degree of success." It was in this context that an unknown number of "concerned issei" in Topaz collected the authority to write to the countervailing institution of the Spanish Consul on February 19, 1943 to redress their living conditions, salaries, and the food available for children, all on the basis of "universal principles of health and morals" (Weglyn 1976, 120).

By 1944 many more incarcerees must have learned of this countervailing sponsor. According to the *Rocky Shimpo*, in March the "Heart Mtn Mothers" wrote to "Protest Draft Procedure" and asked the Consul to "take immediate steps to have 'the United States government desist from further efforts to induct any member of this Fair Play Committee.'" Contending that many of their sons were still minors, the women argued their citizenship status was still in question since the guardians of the young men, including the mothers themselves, were nationals of Japan. As legal guardians, the mothers declared that until their sons' status had been "properly established," they would "withhold" the "sanction" they claimed was necessary for the United States to proceed with the draft (Omura 1944b).

These acts of collecting authority from the Spanish consul seem to have been, for some time, in full effect in Tule Lake, at least according to accounts recollected by Weglyn. On January 5, 1944, for example, a collection of "underground activists" sent a series of two letters to the Spanish consul regarding fellow Kibei being held in the camp stockade who were all on hunger strike. writing-to-redress with great formality, they addressed the Consul as "Excellency," as they opened their first letter with a request to be heard: "May we be as selfish as to request your Excellency's attention concerning the incident at Tule Lake Center, Newell, California." Continuing, the activists outlined the current circumstances of damage:

> At present more than 200 Japanese, including our nine representatives and delegates of the Negotiation Committee, are confined in the army barracks. Furthermore:
>
> 1. Japanese people who are detained in the stockade are being inhumanly treated from the military authority.
> 2. The food and coal situation of the people held in custody in the army guard house is very acute.
> 3. The army is ordering Japanese held in custody to forced labor at the point of a gun.
> 4. There have been cases where Japanese in custody received brutal beating and serous injury without any reason . . .
>
> For the reasons above, all the two hundred people held in custody have gone on a hunger strike since January 1, 1944 . . . (quoted in Weglyn 1976, 169)

"Consequently," the activists asked by continuing formalities, "may we request of your Excellency two favors, namely: 1. To report to the Japanese government the facts mentioned above . . . 2. [To investigate] the lives and health conditions [of the prisoners]."

Through the above examples we can see how the Spanish consul served as a concrete countervailing institution via which incarcerees, especially those whose legal status was more aligned with Japan, could Write-to-Redress. In addition to collecting authority from this concrete institution, several incarcerees also generated a collective authority out of appeals to a more abstract sponsor: the ideology of Japanese nationalism.

Some of the more strident appeals to Japanese nationalism can be found in the writings of Joseph Kurihara, a Nisei World War I veteran who had tried to reenlist after Pearl Harbor only to be turned away. Over the course of Kurihara's writing-to-redress, which recounts damage after damage performed by agents of the US government, his increasingly nationalist tone, while potentially disturbing to some, becomes understandable in context. As he wrote in an essay, rhetorically unheard at that time, submitted to the *Saturday Evening Post*:

> In the face of what has been done to us must we continue to submit ourselves to further insults? No! Then let us proclaim ourselves Japs. Yes, Japs! I repeat, "what is there for to be ashamed of being a Jap?" To be born as a Jap is the greatest blessing God has bestowed on us. To live as Jap is the greatest pride we can enjoy in life. And to die a Jap under the protection of the Japanese flag, which has weathered through many national storms without a defeat for 2600 years is the greatest honor we can ever hope to cherish. I in the name of the Niseis proclaim ourselves Japs, 100 per cent Japs, now, tomorrow and forever. (Kurihara 1943b, 6)

While Kurihara's individually authored essay does not provide an example of collective authority as I have been using the term, it does offer a glimpse into the ways Japanese nationalism could serve as a kind of countervailing authority that could be collected by incarcerees who had grown incensed at the accumulating damages or "insults." As such, Kurihara's writing offers a discursive glimpse into the literacy sponsorship provided by ideologies of an enemy or counter force. In addition, the text can help us imagine other public and collective writing-to-redress, the activities of which we learn about but the texts of which we never actually see.

One example is the activities and texts that surrounded the mass petitions of the *Saikakuri Seigan*, or "resegregationists." This nationalist movement emerged in Tule Lake, where the government had segregated all incarcerees they deemed disloyal during the registration period, regardless of incarcerees' true feelings about Japan or the United States. According to Weglyn, by 1944 thousands of Tule Lake incarcerees, many of them members of families headed by Issei or Kibei,[10] had developed the attitude that it would be better to return to Japan than stay in a country so hostile to the Nikkei. After the anti-draft movement started to dissipate, several Kibei Saikakuri Seigan "agitated and petitioned constantly for the fulfillment of a more complete segregation which would physically separate them from those whom they suspected of stool-pigeon activities, the pro-American loyals," in preparation for their now-desired return to Japan (Weglyn 1976, 230). On May 30, 1944, one petition was submitted with 6,500 names, but by September another had garnered 10,000 signatures out of a camp population of 18,734 (Myer 1971, 315). While Weglyn cautions that many "signed out of fear of being stigmatized as an anti-segregationist" or under the pretense that signing would simply earn one priority in taking part in a prisoner exchange with Japan (Weglyn 1976, 317n2), the son of one of the resegregationist leaders, Tom Akashi, maintains that the petition signed by 6,500 did include the request for a "revival of the exchange . . . program." When the first petition failed, Akashi says the organizers shifted their energies and created a "young men's organization" called *Sokoku Kikoku Kenkyu Dan* (Young Men's Association for the Study of the Motherland), which focused on "Japanese culture, the language, [all] to get the body and mind in the frame of going to . . . live in Japan," and by the time September came, "ten thousand people supported the idea of resegregation" (Akashi 2004). While it is difficult to determine if and how many incarcerees may have signed out of fear or under false pretenses, the differences in signature numbers between May and September is striking. And if Akashi is correct, then incarcerees were building the collective authority they needed for the petition, and they were doing so out of a deepening of the cultural nationalist activity put forth by the Sokoku Kikoku Kenkyu Dan.[11]

From all of these sponsors—Americanization campaigns, the War Relocation Authority, and countervailing institutions—incarcerees collected authority from above to write-to-redress and respond to the collective damage set forth by forced removal and mass incarceration. However, while damage and sponsorship are helpful categories in analyzing the multisources of collective authority, both concepts remain applicable to individually authored texts. That is, these analytical concepts alone do not provide a lens by which we might understand how incarcerees generated authority *together*. It is just such a lens, one that focuses on the ways writing-to-redress is collectively authorized from below, that makes up the discussion that follows.

If We Nisei Get Together: Amassing Authority from Below

> You cannot do anything unless it is combined with everybody's strength. That's why you must be grateful for everyone's effort . . . There are many

people who think only of themselves. We must help one another and be grateful for their efforts or happiness will not come to us.

—*Michiko Tanaka, in Kikumura and Tanaka*

Together, damage and sponsorship help us see the ways that incarcerees may have collected authority out of the tension between suppressing and enabling sources of authority, sources that all come from above. In other words, both damage and sponsorship originate with "more powerful others." However, it is important to understand that writing-to-redress also grows out of collective authority generated from below. One source of the multi-sourced authority behind collective acts and texts of writing-to-redress came from the incarcerees themselves, as they organized to redress the wrongs inflicted upon them. To be clear, I do not simply mean individual incarcerees added together. Rather, I'm arguing that through a practice of mass organizing,[12] a synergy developed, and this synergy helped incarcerees develop a more group-based authority. This synergy, which can develop among any group organizing to redress anything, I call *amassed authority*.

To further illustrate this concept, let me return to Eli Goldblatt. Goldblatt (1995, 27) argues that the generation of authority in writing stems from a willingness to "participate" or "identif[y] with institutions that sponsor writing" (4).[13] But he also acknowledges that authority can develop when authors who write to resist "the common drift" "gain the backing of a countervailing institution" (34). Goldblatt's wording here—"gain the backing"—resonated with some of my findings. So did the assertions of Lynne Tirrell, who echoes Goldblatt when she argues that a politically marginalized rhetor cannot assume "semantic authority all by oneself" because "one needs community to *back one up*" (Tirrell 1993, 16). What Tirrell and Goldblatt assert, then, is the importance of *backing* when it comes to those writing with less power than those being addressed. As such, we might think of the ways writers collectively have each other's back when they participate in a given literacy event, especially when they Write-to-Redress the bad conditions of their lives.

These notions of authority as tied to a collective body that has each member's back, also recalls the socially interdependent vision of the concept laid out by Peter Mortensen and Gesa Kirsch. Drawing upon work by Nel Noddings, Mortensen and Kirsch (1993, 565) argue for seeing discursive authority as a type of social "caring, stemming from a ethic of 'taking care of' an obligation to another."

It is these notions of collective interdependence, of having one's back and taking care of obligations to one another, that struck me as suggestive for the ways Nikkei incarcerees collected the authority to Write-to-Redress in public, without solely relying on identification with WRA-sponsored institutions.[14] While it is important not to culturally essentialize incarceree writers, several Japanese American studies scholars have commented on the collective or group "orientation" of the Nikkei community (Kitano 1976; Mass 2002; Kikumura and Tanaka 1981; Nakano 1990), as well as the persistence of cultural values like reciprocity and *giri*, which Nakano (1990, 37) glosses as "a sense of duty or obligation" that "encourag[es] continuous interaction between people."[15] Within the Nikkei community there are already a number of ethoi (including gaman) related to social interdependence, ethoi that could have informed the ways incarcerees generated a collective authority.

As such, instead of seeing the participants of collective writing-to-redress as "isolated individual egos" performing an "ego-function," as has been common in previous analyses of "protest rhetoric" (Gregg 1971; Mao 2006), I suggest that through the process of organizing, participants were coming to see themselves as a collective. In other words, incarcerees writing-to-redress together saw themselves as an interdependent mass that not only shared wrongs committed against them but were committed to having each other's back and taking care of obligations to one another during the given literacy event.

In this way, it is my contention that in addition to collecting authority out of damage inflicted and from sponsoring influences, the participants of collective writing-to-redress also consciously collected authority *from each other*. That is, incarcerees who composed and drafted together, circulating and signing petitions, or contributed their labor and efforts to publicize writing-to-redress, were synergistically *amassing authority*.[16]

This synergy can perhaps best be seen in the collective writing-to-redress that emerged during mass protest movements. As Brandt (2001, 137) noted in her study *Literacy in American Lives*, "mass movements [can] sponsor literacy" in that "a sustained period of well-publicized civil rights protest" can "disseminate into public consciousness various formats and stances to structure the release into anger and the exercise of rights and self-determination." But while Brandt uses the verb *sponsor* here, in line with her analytical concept, I would argue that since her own definition presumes that "more powerful others" control the access to literacy (Brandt and Clinton 2002, 349), mass movements made up of *less* powerful others are, instead, serving as a conduit for amassed authority.

For example, in November 1942, 2,500 incarcerees protested the arrest of two men accused of beating another in Poston. According to Gary Okihiro (1973), demands for the men's release were read to the crowd, an action immediately followed by the collaborative composing of a written resolution demanding the immediate release and dropping of all charges. One month later, this collective writing-to-redress was followed with a similar event in Manzanar, when mess hall chef Harry Ueno was arrested for the beating of a JACL leader. To this day, many suspect Ueno was framed, as he had been both organizing a mess hall workers union and investigating the pilfering of food meant for incarcerees by the administration (Ueno et al. 1986).[17] When Ueno was arrested, somewhere between 3,000 and 4,000 people protested, and subsequently, a committee of five representatives wrote up a list of demands, including the unconditional release of Ueno and the investigation by the Spanish consul into the general conditions of camp (Okihiro 1973). And according to Weglyn, in November 1943, 5,000 incarcerees protested the "neglect, incompetence and corruption" that had become the norm in Tule Lake, as they drew up a list of eighteen demands for an "immediate redress of grievances," including increased food allowances, the creation of an incarceree self-governing body, and the resignation of the camp director and other administrative staff, all of whom "harbor[ed] feelings of racial superiority" (Weglyn 1976, 162).

While it is not clear exactly how many took part in the collaborative writing of these particular demands and resolutions, it seems safe to say that regardless of how many hands touched the paper, these mass movements meant that 2,500, 3,000–4,000 and 5,000 incarcerees participated in these collective writing-to-redress events. As such, the literal authors must have felt that masses of fellow less powerful others had their backs. And out of such a felt sense of mass community backing, collective authority seemed to amass for incarcerees to commit their collective demands to paper, as they wrote to redress jointly, as a group.

Aside from these movements, and the petitions of the resegregationists mentioned earlier, few other public writing-to-redress events I learned about involved such dramatic numbers. But as I rhetorically attended my data, I was still struck by the numbers that *were* recorded, numbers that fed my critical imagination regarding the amassing of authority. As previously mentioned, the Heart Mountain anti-fence petitions garnered 3,000 signatures, or half the adult population of the camp (Takahashi Cates 1980, 211–12). And after the announcement of the draft, resolutions were either signed or passed by 1,141 mothers in Topaz (Topaz Times 1944), a "Mass Meeting" of 1,000 Poston Nisei (that will be discussed later in this section), 620 American Citizens of Japanese Ancestry in Gila (Omura 1944a), and 119 members of the Poston Women's Club (Poston Women's Club 1944). Even with conservative estimates, these figures add up to roughly 20 percent of the total population of incarcerees over the age of fifteen.[18] With these types of numbers, it is hard to imagine that collective authority was not amassing via the practice of such writing-to-redress events. For, like the women participants in the nineteenth-century petitions discussed by Zaeske (2002), these large numbers of incarcerees were also "coalesc[ing] discursively," (156) and in doing so, they too "transformed from isolated individuals [in]to political actors" (150). And, as they vocalized their votes in the mess halls or signed their names on the page, these amassing incarcerees must have generated a felt sense of backing as they came to more clearly see themselves "in relationship" to one another (Patricia Waugh quoted in Zaeske 2002, 162).

So the same must have been true for smaller groups of participants in collective writing-to-redress, who also wrote to set right what was wrong or to relieve suffering. For example, in March 1943, seven Heart Mountain incarcerees attended to their obligations to the community by initiating their own research and completing a report on the effects of mess hall food on incarceree health. According to Takahashi Cates, among the participants in this literacy event were two doctors and three hospital staff who added their authority to that which had amassed as the research was being conducted. By the time the group submitted their final report to the camp administration (that had never asked for such a report), these new authorities on camp health were able to incorporate statistics that drew explicit connections between the inadequacies of what was being served and the "general health of children" or what is even minimally "suited" for "diabetics," "stomach" or "hypertension patients," and "nursing mothers" (quoted in Takahashi Cates 1980, 208).

At times, small groups that had amassed their authority to Write-to-Redress could, in turn, create a kind of symbolic backing to other less powerful others. During the registration period, for example, thirty-five young Nisei men, the majority of whom were seventeen or eighteen years old, marched into the Tule Lake administration building and handed over their collective writing-to-redress, described by Weglyn as "a protest letter stating that they had no intention of registering 'for Selective Service,' but that they would sign 'any time' for repatriation." The young men were subsequently arrested for their actions, a decision camp administrators made, Weglyn writes, "with Washington's approval" to serve "as an object lesson for all who would persist in defiance" (Weglyn 1976, 147). According to one observer, a Nisei high school teacher who had previously supported registration efforts but ended up being placed in isolation "for refusing to register in support of the youth" (147), the young men were "apprehended by an army of soldiers equipped with light machine guns, tear gas bombs and fixed bayonets" out in the open such that other incarcerees, including "little kid brothers and sisters," turned witness to a mass "capture of American-citizen niseis by American soldiers." Continuing in his written statement for the Tule Lake Community Analysis report, the teacher explained his stance and the stance of others: "To the Japanese mind the army's provocation was an indignity and a challenge. So they [more incarcerees] accepted the challenge and all those having conviction and courage flatly refused to register, taking the similar stand as the thirty-five young boy prisoners" (unnamed teacher quoted in Weglyn 1976, 148). As such, the less powerful young men who were arrested had effectively amassed authority among themselves to Write-to-Redress registration as well as among additional less powerful others, who courageously followed their arrests with a similar resistance, amassing further collective authority.[19]

Stories such as these serve as important examples of both large and small groups amassing the authority they need to Write-to-Redress. However, their use can also inadvertently paint an overly utopian picture of collaborative writing-to-redress, where less powerful others always agreed, always had each other's back, and always attended to their obligations to one another. Of course, this was probably not so. In fact, I would argue that amassed authority, as I use it, is not an uncritical celebration of homogenized groups of writers but rather a critically romantic embrace of literacy events, where participants came to see themselves in relationship with each other such that they could formulate a public text together. Many such events were probably filled with struggle. Indeed, both oral histories of former incarcerees and existing ethnographies of camp suggest they were. To better illustrate how such contentious circumstances can still generate amassed authority, let me turn to the writing-to-redress that emerged in the 1945 All Center Conference.

The All Center Conference was convened in response to the WRA's announcement in late 1944 that all WRA camps (excluding Tule Lake) would be closed by the end of 1945. Despite incarceree feelings about having been rounded up in the first place, this news was met with great concern. As Lane Ryo Hirabayashi (in Nishimoto 1995, 164) explains, while the incarcerated community "did not necessarily oppose the idea of moving back out into the larger society, they were deeply concerned about their safety and their future." In addition, several community-minded incarcerees knew that many Issei and older Nisei "had been financially and sometimes psychologically broken and thus were unable to move back into the larger society," especially given the tiny WRA pittance of "twenty-five dollars and a free train ticket to one's 'point of origin' in the United States" (165). With these concerns, delegates from seven of the ten WRA camps agreed to meet in February 1945 and craft a collective response to what was about to become yet another forced relocation.

The final document itself can be summarized as asking for consideration of three points: "monetary reparations for losses and damages"; "special support for the elderly and needy"; and "full guarantee of the rights and safety of individuals" (Nishimoto 1995, 165). However, according to Nisei anthropologist Richard Nishimoto, whose ethnographic writings make up the focus of Hirabayashi's study, a struggle over wording ensued between Nisei and Issei representatives at the conference, resulting in two documents that contained roughly the same content but were draped in two different tones.

Both versions began with a letter format laying out the history of how the Nikkei came to live in the camps and a summary of the "general opinion among residents" that "the majority" are "not in a position to make plans" to relocate or return to their West Coast homes (All Center Conference quoted in Nishimoto 1995, 199). Closing their opening portion of the document, the delegates refer to their authority to write as being amassed both from "seven relocation centers" and their need to take care of obligations to their community: "mindful of our grave responsibility to do our utmost for the best welfare of 75,000 people" (All Center Conference quoted in Nishimoto 1995, 200).[20] Asking that the camps remain open "for the duration of the war and for some time thereafter as may be needed," the letter closes by introducing the "facts and recommendations" that follow. It is in these facts and recommendations that we begin to see more pronounced differences between an English version of the document, which was submitted to government officials, and a Japanese version of the document, which was the version first composed and agreed upon by the Issei delegates at the conference. According to Nishimoto's report, Yoshitaro Katow, one of the Nisei delegates from Poston, the subcommittee that translated the document into English felt that some of the original requests were "foolhardy and irrational," unfit for US government officials. As such, they "deleted all the objectionable points without the knowledge of other members of the conference," so the Issei delegates never knew that they "changed the content in translation." For example, Katow told Nishimoto that they "changed the word 'demands' in the Japanese original to 'petition' and 'recommendations,'" arguing that the Issei did not understand the "seriousness" of making demands upon the government (Katow quoted in Nishimoto 1995, 191).

Similar changes can be seen across the two documents included in Nishimoto's report, where Nishimoto translated the Japanese version for his English-language supervisor. For example, in the second "fact" that precedes the demands/recommendations, the Japanese version apparently read, "There has been a *complete* destruction of financial foundations," while the English-language version tones this statement down with "an *almost* complete destruction." In the eighth "fact," the Japanese version pointedly states that because most Buddhist priests are "excluded from the West Coast," "[t]here is *no* freedom of religion," while this final line is nonexistent in the English version, which simply states that Buddhism "has a substantial following" so "members . . . *prefer to remain* where the religion centers" (quoted in Nishimoto 1995, 202).

As for the list of demands/recommendations, the differences between the original and the English-language translation/revision are ones between a collective voice of those who deserve "proper restitution" because they have been wronged and a collective voice requesting "adequate government compensation" (quoted in Nishimoto 1995, 205). For example, in the fifth recommendation/demand, the English version recommends "[t]hat the WRA *make every effort* to obtain a return of property for evacuees, who due to evacuation and consequent inability to maintain installment payments, have lost the same." But the Japanese original *"demands[s] that aid be given* to the efforts to reestablish the right to the property which [h]as been lost" (quoted in Nishimoto 1995, 203). In the seventh recommendation/demand, the English version recommends "[t]hat the WRA *establish adequate staffed offices* in important areas," while in Japanese, the document directly demanded "[t]hat the WRA *establish branch offices* in important areas" (quoted in Nishimoto 1995, 204).

It is difficult to discern which collective voice more accurately represented the feelings of the collective body of incarcerees. We do know that the English version was sent to government officials, but the Japanese version was read to the Poston Community Council upon the delegates' return from the conference. As such, I suspect the Japanese version had a little more support. Regardless, neither recommendations nor demands were met by the WRA, news that Nishimoto reports came as little surprise to the community (Nishimoto 1995, 226).

Whether or not the All Center Conference was rhetorically heard, it is still clear that conference delegates had amassed the authority to Write-to-Redress their second relocation. Despite any disagreements that lay behind its creation and circulation, this document emerged, Hirabayashi argues, because of a "popular mass movement." As such, we need to see it as the "collective empowerment" of a disenfranchised community "able and willing to identify the federal government as the source of its original problem" and hold it "accountable for losses as well as for the protection of individual constitutional and human rights" (L. Hirabayashi 1998, 177). And all before incarcerees had even left camp. For these reasons alone, the document remains remarkable, no matter which version is under discussion.

But the rhetorical struggles over the All Center Conference resolution remind us that just because authority has been amassed—that is, collected from a community of people taking part in a given literacy event who both attend to their obligations to one another and have each other's back—does not automatically mean the birth of a "linguistic utopia" (Pratt 1987) or collaborative consensus (Trimbur 1989). On the contrary, writers working together may in fact have very different rhetorical priorities that need struggling over (or, from the perspective of the All Center Conference translation committee, to be edited out). Writers crafting their words together or signifying their collective agreement via signatures or collectively electing a committee to channel a collective voice will always have a wide range of varying opinions on the rhetorical details of how to best use writing to set things right or relieve suffering. But as these same writers struggle through their wide and jostling opinions, we must remember the importance of *deciding* to Write-to-Redress at all, and to do so as a group. That is, from the standpoint of amassing authority, the significance is less about the stated-goal success of any given rhetorical performance and more about the energy of "collective empowerment" that amasses as a collective literacy event unfolds. When a group or community begins to take care of their obligations to one another and have each other's back, we are witnessing the creation of a powerful collective authority, so needed to redress the wrongs in all of our collective lives.

Through the analytical lenses of damage, sponsorship, and amassing, I have argued that groups of writers struggle with the conditions of their lives in order to generate the authority to publicly and collectively Write-to-Redress. For any given rhetorical moment we navigate between and across competing processes that crisscross and accumulate in our lives. Some of these processes, like sponsorship and amassing, encourage us to rhetorically act; others, like any form of damage, discourage us. Amidst these tensions, we may or may not decide to collectively write, or we may write in some moments and not others. To illustrate the ways this struggle can provide the energy, and a kind of permission or authorization, to rhetorically act, I will turn to the extended example of the Heart Mountain Fair Play Committee. Through their story and an analysis of their writing-to-redress, we can see the ways damage, sponsorship, and amassing combine to generate an explicitly resistant collective authority.

THE HEART MOUNTAIN FAIR PLAY COMMITTEE: THE GENESIS OF A RESISTANT COLLECTIVE AUTHORITY

> To say that the War department's announcement last week opening selective service to Japanese Americans brought instant joy to the hearts of all draft-age men would be misleading and inaccurate.
>
> Many have waited hopefully for selective service to be opened. Others have hoped that it wouldn't; that it somehow would miss them and allow them

> to continue their pointless, purposeless lives behind the fences of relocation centers . . .
>
> Issues will provoke some to point out "why should their parents be confined behind barbed wire while the parents of other soldiers are free to go where and as they please. Why, since they may ultimately face the supreme sacrifice for this nation, their parents can't return to their former homes." The questions will be endless.
>
> Endless questions against the inevitability of the draft are senseless. The draft is here and welcome . . .
>
> —*Editorial, Heart Mountain Sentinel*

In Heart Mountain, the 1944 announcement of the draft was circulated on January 22 via radio and camp newspapers, including the *Heart Mountain Sentinel*, which served a population of approximately 10,000 incarcerees. The *Sentinel*'s contradictory claims, seen in the above epigraph, were made within a week of the announcement. However, questions about the draft were not "senseless," nor was the draft as "welcome" as the WRA-sponsored paper tried to proclaim. Less than three weeks after the War Department made its announcement, a committee of male, mostly Nisei, Heart Mountain residents, who would later describe themselves as a group "organized to inject justice in all the problems pertaining to our evacuation, concentration, detention and pauperization" (Fair Play Committee 1944), publicly emerged and began to speak out against the draft. These men called themselves the Heart Mountain Fair Play Committee (FPC) and went on to organize and articulate the only known collective Japanese American draft resistance during the World War II incarceration period.[21]

THE EMERGENCE OF THE HEART MOUNTAIN FAIR PLAY COMMITTEE

The year before the draft was announced, Kiyoshi Okamoto, a fifty-four-year-old Nisei who had challenged many WRA policies since the beginning of the incarceration period, began giving talks on the Constitution to whoever would listen, calling himself the "Fair Play Committee of One." One night, after an open debate with Nobu Kawai, one of the editors of the *Heart Mountain Sentinel*, on whether or not people should answer the infamous loyalty questionnaire with qualifications,[22] several younger Nisei, including Frank Emi, Paul Nakadate, and Isamu Horino, sought him out for weekly discussions. As historian Eric Muller (2001, 77) writes, these "younger men were drawn to Okamoto, seeing him as a visionary and a constitutional scholar, [even though] Okamoto had no legal training and developed his rather elaborate and some idiosyncratic views on the Bill of Rights and the Constitution entirely from his own study."

While the younger Nisei admired Okamoto for his righteous zeal in the face of oppression, the WRA and some *Sentinel* staff often portrayed him as "an 'intellectual hobo' and a 'latrine lawyer,' a man who was 'over-radical, unreasonable, irresponsible, and verbose'" (Muller 2001, 77). While much of this perception can be assumed to stem from the political anxiety that Okamoto must have instilled in WRA authorities, former FPC members also remember him as being in love with "salty expressions" (Emi 1998). Regardless, many of the draft-age Nisei in Heart Mountain were taken with his "great passion, creativity, and willingness to speak bluntly" (Muller 2001, 77). As former Heart Mountain resistor Mits Koshiyama (2001) put it, "I heard he had coarse language, but he was eloquent in preparing people to understand and study what the government was doing."

Some camp historians contend that this preparation would not have gone anywhere had a concrete issue not emerged while the FPC was holding their discussions (Nelson 1976, 119). But after the draft was announced, over the course of a week, the FPC transformed from a small study group to "a formal and militant resistance movement" (121) authorized by a sizeable number of both Issei and Nisei incarcerees. According to historian Douglas Nelson, "The change came on the evening of January 26, at a public meeting attended by almost 300 evacuees. The group voted to officially dedicate the Fair Play Committee to the clarification of 'certain issues raised by the decision to draft the Nisei'" (121).

Over the course of the next two months, the FPC responded to practically nightly invitations for standing-room-only talks across camp (Emi 2002, 53) and open public forums where their position was discussed and honed among audiences as large as 400 Issei and Nisei, including a dues-paying membership that grew to 275 young men. For those who could not attend the meetings, or perhaps felt too nervous to do so, the FPC also issued a total of three mimeographed bulletins of their evolving position, posting them on the outside walls of barracks, latrines, and the mess hall. It is in their third and final bulletin, "All for One, One for All" (appendix A), where we can see the FPC's conscious resistance fully articulated.

Opening their one-page manifesto with two epigraphs from the Bill of Rights, the document moves on to declare that the Nisei have been "complacent" and "too inarticulate" and that the time for "decisive action" is "NOW!" Following a sweeping, detailed catalog of the ways the rights of Japanese Americans have been violated thus far, the FPC declares the draft to be the proverbial straw that broke the camel's back. It is then that the group openly refuses to go to war while the Japanese American community is still incarcerated en masse:

> [U]ntil we are restored all our rights, all discriminatory features of the Selective Service abolished, and measures are taken to remedy the past injustices thru Judicial pronouncement or Congressional act, we feel that the present program of drafting us from this concentration camp is unjust, unconstitutional, and against all principles of civilized usage. Therefore, WE MEMBERS OF THE FAIR PLAY COMMITTEE HEREBY REFUSE TO GO TO THE PHYSICAL EXAMINATION OR TO THE INDUCTION IF OR WHEN WE ARE CALLED IN ORDER TO CONTEST THE ISSUE.

Even though it followed this paragraph by declaring that members were "all loyal Americans fighting for JUSTICE AND DEMOCRACY RIGHT HERE AT HOME," it was this bulletin, and this exact wording, that eventually landed the seven-man steering committee of the FPC in prison. While sixty-three other FPC-member resisters were arrested for refusing induction, the FPC leadership was arrested, tried, and convicted for "conspiracy to counsel Heart Mountain's draft-age Nisei to evade the draft" (Muller 2001, 114). In other words, it is because of this final bulletin, the focus of this section, that the FPC leadership was convicted for their rhetorical actions.

THE MULTISOURCES OF THE FPC'S COLLECTIVE AUTHORITY

Damage

To understand the Fair Play Committee's emergence as rhetorical actors, and the simultaneous construction of their resistant ethos "amid disempowering forces," I want to first recall the role oppression plays in both authoring and authorizing writing-to-redress. First and foremost, "minority discourse," Abdul JanMohamed and David Lloyd explain, is a "product of damage." Both local and distant agents can perpetuate that damage and discourage us from claiming or locating any rhetorical authority within ourselves or each other. Locally, in Heart Mountain itself, the Fair Play Committee experienced one of those agents of "damage" to be the WRA-sponsored paper the *Heart Mountain Sentinel*.

One week after the FPC issued its third and final bulletin, the *Sentinel* issued a front-page editorial, "Our Cards on the Table," accusing the FPC of "deluding" Nisei youth by drawing the "unsuspecting into a tangle of intrigue" (Abe 1944). The following week, FPC Vice President Paul Nakadate accused the *Sentinel* of painting a distorted picture of the amount of support that the draft did or did not have throughout camp and the FPC's position itself. In doing so, Nakadate explicitly questioned the *Sentinel*'s allegiances: "With the FPC in demand for nightly educational bookings at the request of the Block, the Sentinel could have very easily learned the true stand of the organization . . . If the Sentinel is going to be the Sentinel of this camp I should like it to have it come out clean and straight. Why cannot the outside public know of our genuine feeling instead of putting an artificial front in accordance with WRA policy" (Nakadate 1944).

The *Heart Mountain Sentinel* did seem to be serving as a medium by which a pro-WRA policy position could be fostered, though former editors have more recently denied this accusation (Hosokawa 1998). Whether or not the WRA-sponsored *Sentinel* stayed consistent with WRA newspaper policy to "provide a medium through which WRA can direct public opinion within the evacuee group, and stimulate reactions and attitudes desirable for the maintenance of a high morale" (quoted in Mizuno 2001, 507) is less important for the purposes of this chapter as is the reality that the FPC perceived that the *Sentinel* was doing so. And given the tone and attitudes professed in earlier articles and editorials leading up to the FPC's public emergence of their resistant rhetoric, their perception is more than understandable.

The week after the announcement of the draft and a month before the FPC issued their third bulletin, the *Sentinel* ran a front-page story profiling a young Nisei, a former "newshound for the Sentinel" who had volunteered for the military even amidst his conflicted feelings about serving while his community lived behind barbed wire. Engaging a kind of proto model minority rhetoric, the *Sentinel* began its tale of honor: "One of the most striking proofs that America has met with success in teaching its people loyalty to democratic traditions is found, we believe, in the Japanese American evacuees whose faith in American democracy remains solid and real despite the rankling injustice of evacuation" (Kitasako 1944, 1).

Continuing, the *Sentinel* acknowledged the hardship and the confusion the Nisei faced as they navigated their decision:

> The economic losses cut deep, but equally as painful was the severe beating his faith in American democracy suffered. To a youth who had been nourished on the tenets of democracy, evacuation was something which threw him way off. He found it hard to get his bearings. Things happened too fast, too crazily, too un-Americanly.
>
> Where was the sanctity of United States citizenship, where was the justice of American democracy? Was it all talk after all?
>
> It was disappointing, heartbreaking. America had rudely let him down.
>
> But in the cool light of second thought, he realized the futility of protesting. He rationalized, and decided to fall in line with what the government wanted evacuees to believe: that evacuation was a military necessity.
>
> "You can't buck the army. It's [*sic*] word is final. But I'll always feel that evacuation was not fair."
>
> But the healing salve of time went to work on his wounds, and as the months went tumbling by, even amid the penal atmosphere of this camp, his battered faith was patched up almost as good as new . . . (Kitasako 1944, 1, 5)
>
> "It takes a maximum of faith to volunteer after you've been stuck into a camp like this, and in face of that sentiment," he said. "But if you want to be an American, you have to show it, and the best way to prove it is to offer your life for your country." (Kitasako 1944, 5)

With this article, the *Sentinel* seems to address the "endless questions" they anticipate the Nisei having in their editorial the week before. But the answer was simple: faith in American democracy is best shown by offering your life for your country, certainly not by protesting what everyone, even the staff of the *Sentinel*, seemed to agree was an injustice. With this kind of tacit silencing of dissent—"if you want to be an American"—the *Sentinel* perpetuated the idea that Japanese Americans should just accept the realities of their oppressive situation.

It is important to note, though, that the *Sentinel* was only a local incarnation of government policies put forth by the WRA and the Office of War Information (Mizuno 2001). The true oppressive culprit here was not the *Sentinel* but the US government, with its history and contemporary reality of institutionalized racism toward the Nikkei and other people racialized within the United States as "minorities." After all, this entire situation took place during a time of war, when racialized animosity was heightened toward people of Japanese ancestry, no matter what they professed the best response to be. Just eleven months before the draft announcement, the head of the Western Defense Command, General John DeWitt, uttered before Congress, "A Jap's a Jap . . . There is no way to determine their loyalty . . . It makes no difference whether he is an American citizen; theoretically he is still a Japanese and you can't change him" (quoted in Niiya and JANM 2001, 66). And the previous year, right before the announcement of the forced removal, the *Los Angeles Times*, which served an area of California where Heart Mountain Nisei had grown up, had written a similar argument on their editorial page:

> A viper is nonetheless a viper wherever the egg is hatched . . . So, a Japanese American born of Japanese parents, nurtured upon Japanese traditions, living in a transplanted Japanese atmosphere and thoroughly inoculated with Japanese . . . ideals, notwithstanding his normal brand of accidental citizenship almost inevitably and with the rarest exceptions grows up to be Japanese, and not an American in his . . . ideas, and is . . . menacing . . . unless . . . hamstrung. Thus, while it might cause injustice to a few to treat them all as potential enemies . . . I cannot escape the conclusion . . . that such treatment . . . should be accorded to each and all of them while we are at war with their race. (quoted in Niiya and JANM 2001, 59)

Publicly, Nikkei loyalty to the United States was continually questioned, regardless of the fact that a twenty-five-page government report had been conducted a month before the attacks on Pearl Harbor and circulated among high officials of the State and War Departments prior to the incarceration decision, concluding that "there was no Japanese problem" in regard to loyalty (Weglyn 1976, ch. 1). While the Nikkei community was unaware of the report at the time, it was aware of the absurdity of the mass suspicion and the effects of the racist hysteria it continued to face even inside the camps.

Given this historical context, some might find the "advice" of the *Sentinel* editors to be reasonable. All of these processes do seem to discourage Japanese Americans from acting in any explicit form of public opposition, especially if the cultural norms of shikataganai (it can't be helped) and gaman were as prevalent in the community at this time. But when a newspaper that is sponsored by one's oppressors baits its readers' allegiances ("if you want to be an American"), declares the "endless questions" of the draft as "senseless," and portrays those that do question the draft as manipulative provocateurs, it does seem as if the editorial staff has become conscious or unconscious agents of the damage being inflicted. And despite all implicit and explicit warnings, the FPC was not going to remain "complacent" or "inarticulate"; instead, it would move to actively respond to these types of silencing processes designed to discourage them from engaging in a rhetoric of resistance via local and distant agents.

Well-aware of the *Sentinel*'s local position on the draft, the FPC knew part of what was at stake in organizing an effective movement was their disagreements with the WRA-sponsored editorial staff as to the nature of true American behavior—that is, what being a "loyal" American entailed. Anticipating their detractors, the FPC explicitly addressed the issue in the second half of their manifesto:

> We are not being disloyal. We are not evading the draft. We are all loyal Americans fighting for JUSTICE AND DEMOCRACY RIGHT HERE AT HOME. So, restore our rights as such, rectify the injustices of evacuation, of the concentration, of the detention, and of the pauperization as such. In short, treat us in accordance with the principles of the Constitution.
>
> If what we are voicing is wrong, if what we ask is disloyal, if what we think is unpatriotic, then Abraham Lincoln, one of our greatest American President was also guilty as such, for he said, "If by the mere force of numbers a majority should deprive a minority on any Constitutional right, it might in a moral point of view justify a revolution."

Calling upon "the principles of the Constitution" and the denial of "[c]onstitutional right[s]," the FPC denied the disloyalty of which they knew they would be accused. In this way, the FPC's resistant rhetoric can be seen as authorized, or called forth, in part, by the rhetorical processes of the *Sentinel*, which had encouraged Nisei to emerge from their "questioning" with a "maximum of faith" in American democracy and with the willingness to "offer [their] li[ves] for [their] country." This local position simply incensed most of the FPC.

While it is important not to oversimplify any characterization of the *Sentinel* staff as WRA "dupes," it is important to see how the positions set forth by the *Sentinel* were connected to distant and more global forces. As I argued earlier, large-scale oppression can also work to authorize an oppressed group of people to claim their rhetorical agency, as JanMohamed and Lloyd explain through their earlier mentioned theory of "minority discourse":

> Out of the damage inflicted on minority cultures . . . emerges the possibility of a collective subjectivity formed in practice rather than contemplation. (JanMohamed and Lloyd 1990, 9)

> [T]he collective nature of all minority discourse also derives from the fact that minority individuals are always treated and forced to experience themselves generically. Coerced into a negative, generic subject-position, the oppressed individual responds by transforming that position into a positive, collective one. (JanMohamed and Lloyd 1990, 10)

Reading the FPC bulletin through JanMohamed and Lloyd, we can see such a transformation in the first half of the text. Here, the FPC testifies to its given "negative, generic subject-position" of a collection of oppressed "one hundred and ten thousand innocent" individuals who, as it recounts, "were kicked out of their homes, literally uprooted from where they have lived for the greater part of their life, and herded like dangerous criminals into concentration camps with barbed wire fences and military police guarding it"; it then transforms that position into a "positive, collective one" in the "practice" of its collective writing-to-redress:

> *We, the Nisei* have been complacent and too inarticulate to the unconstitutional acts that we were subjected to. If ever there was a time or cause for decisive action, IT IS NOW!
>
> *We, the members of the FPC* are not afraid to go war—we are not afraid to risk our lives for our country. We would gladly sacrifice our lives to protect and uphold the principles and ideals of our country as set forth in the Constitution and the Bill of Rights, for on its inviolability depends the free-

> dom, liberty, justice, and protection of all people *including Japanese-Americans and all other minority groups* . . . unless such actions are opposed NOW, and steps taken to remedy such injustices and discriminations IMMEDIATELY, *the future of all minorities* and the future of this democratic nation is in danger. (notations in original)

As one part of a body of people "forced to experience themselves generically," the FPC claims its coauthorized ethos on the grounds of that experience, employing repetition to build a sense of indignation as the particularities of both the authors' and intended audience's oppression is recounted: "Without any hearings, without due process of law as guaranteed by the Constitution and Bill of Rights, without any charges filed against us, without any evidence of wrongdoing on our part." This indignation then erupts into the use of all capital letters, rhetorically symbolizing the FPC's collective rage, with which, hopefully, the audience now identifies: "AND THEN, WITHOUT RECTIFICATION OF THE INJUSTICES COMMITTED AGAINST US NOR WITHOUT RESTORATION OF OUR RIGHTS AS GUARANTEED BY THE CONSTITUTION, WE ARE ORDERED TO JOIN THE ARMY THRU DISCRIMINATORY PROCEDURES INTO A SEGREGATED COMBAT UNIT!" Thus, in this passage, the FPC is able to rhetorically claim its experiences with racialized oppression and "[o]ut of the damage inflicted" and authorize its members to claim their rhetorical agency to resist through the written word.

In order to more fully understand how the FPC did this, though, we must consider the additional multisources of its collective authority. If some experiences functioned as negative generic damage out of which the committee could transform into a positive collective, other experiences functioned as positive encouragement—both from above by more powerful others, and from below, by less powerful others. As such, the FPC both collected authority from movements created by distant sponsors and amassed authority from the synergy created by local incarcerees.

Sponsorship

As Nisei growing up in California during the 1920s and 1930s, the majority of the FPC leadership would have been immersed in the ideology of the

Americanization movement. As such, the atmosphere of Americanism and its discourse would have been readily available to the future FPC Nisei, adding another resource to their growing collective authority to Write-to-Redress.

This kind of Americanist discourse can be seen throughout the FPC bulletin. The first thing Heart Mountain residents would have read in the FPC's third and final bulletin are two epigraphs from the Bill of Rights:

> No person shall be deprived of life, liberty, or property, without due process of law, nor private property be taken for public use without just compensation. (US Const. art. 1)

> Neither slavery nor involuntary servitude, except as punishment for crime whereof the party shall have been duly convicted, shall exist within the United States, or any place subject to their jurisdiction." (US Const. art. 13).

Continuing through the one-page mimeographed manifesto, readers would have encountered at least seven different references to the Constitution, the Bill of Rights, "constitutionality," or "unconstitutionality," including explicit reference to the ways in which the current Japanese American circumstances violate the supposed highest law of the land:

> Without any hearings, without due process of law as guaranteed by the Constitution and Bill of Rights, without any charges filed against us, without any evidence of wrongdoing on our part, one hundred and ten thousand innocent people were kicked out of their homes . . .

> WITHOUT RESTORATION OF OUR RIGHTS AS GUARANTEED BY THE CONSTITUTION, WE ARE ORDERED TO JOIN THE ARMY . . .
>
> we feel that the present program of drafting us from this concentration camp is unjust, unconstitutional . . .

In addition to the constitutional references threaded throughout the bulletin, another aspect of Americanist discourse appears with the invocation of Abraham Lincoln in the fifth paragraph—one discussed earlier in relation to the FPC's rhetorical move to appeal to the principles of the Constitution:

> If what we are voicing is wrong, if what we ask is disloyal, if what we think is unpatriotic, then Abraham Lincoln, one of our greatest American President

was also guilty as such, for he said, "If by the mere force of numbers a majority should deprive a minority on any Constitutional right, it might in a moral point of view justify a revolution."

Clearly drawing upon Lincoln's stature as an iconic emancipator of slaves, the FPC seems to draw upon Lincoln's name and words not as a kind of legal authorization, as it does with references to the Constitution, but as a kind of moral authorization to resist when rights are clearly being denied. Whether or not Lincoln can truly be considered a "great" American president (and whether or not the FPC truly believed this to be so) matters less than the fact that the FPC knew that within the rhetorical framework of Americanization, he was considered a great American president, having read about him in textbooks used in either US public or Japanese-language schools.[23] Because the FPC knew that Lincoln was held in such regard within Americanist mythology, his name provided additional sponsorship to generate the collective authority to write its manifesto.

Amassing

In addition to the more "distant" authorizing process of Americanization, designed and executed by more powerful others, less powerful others also helped to enable the FPC's collective authority. Through the course of this movement, fellow Heart Mountain incarcerees began to see themselves in relationship and back each other up and tend to their obligations to one another. For example, each of the 275 Nisei members of the committee paid $2 in dues, which was used to buy ink and paper for the mimeographed bulletins (Emi 1998). Additional financial support and authorization came from residents who were not officially members of the committee but who seemed to at least secretly believe in its cause. Guntaro Kubota, the lone Issei on the steering committee, was responsible for drumming up Issei support, providing translation at all meetings and for all bulletins. His wife, Gloria, later described how important Issei sponsorship was: "[T]hat's the only way they can make the money, raise the money, 'cause the Isseis have the money, the Niseis, they're young . . . they didn't have any money." And after listening to Guntaro, many Issei did authorize the committee's rhetorical and material actions. As Gloria Kubota explained, the FPC and her husband, "got quite a

FIGURE 5.1. Frank Emi (right) and an FPC supporter during the draft resistance movement in Heart Mountain, WY. (Photographer unknown, 1944, Frank Abe Collection, Densho.)

few people, older ladies to follow him around and donate, and it was really cute how some of these old people . . . the ones that believed in him, they just followed him around . . . there were thirty blocks in our Heart Mountain, and it used to be cold but he'd go all over and they'd follow him around. Some people brought all the cash that they had and they'd give it to him" (Kubota 1993).

Female relatives of the FPC leadership also served as backing for the resistance. As Gwendolyn Pough and Terese Monberg have argued, we would do well to extend our inquiries not only toward the ways women have assumed a "presence" in the public sphere, but also toward their "roles in shaping that sphere." In other words, Pough and Monberg argue, we need to understand how women have "enabled" the rhetorical performances of their communities (Pough quoted in Monberg 2008, 87).

For the FPC, this shaping performed by women can be seen through the labor of Gloria Kubota and Frank Emi's sister, Kaoru Emi. According to Frank Chin, Kubota helped hide FPC documents in her laundry basket.

As the FBI searched her room for FPC materials, Kubota quietly ironed her family's clothes, "tak[ing] her time . . . as the FBI engage[d] her in conversation." Careful not to "expose the documents at the bottom of the basket," Kubota remained calm as "the FBI linger[ed]" and then finally left her room (Chin 2002, 449). And according to both Frank Emi and Frank Chin, Kaoru Emi contributed literacy skills to the FPC cause. Taking notes at talks given by Nobu Kawai for the JACL so "he would not be misquoted," Kaoru was helping enable the FPC to compose its public responses (Chin 2002, 415), and since she was faster than Frank at typing, she also typed various materials for the committee (Emi 2008), adding her labor to the amassing of collective authority taking part in the public sphere of camp.

In addition to sisters and spouses, a few Nikkei individuals outside of camp also helped amass authority. During the draft resistance movement, James Omura, the editor of the Denver-based bilingual Nikkei newspaper *Rocky Shimpo*, helped amass authority both within Heart Mountain and across other camps. As noted earlier, Omura had already taken a public stand against "evacuation," directly connecting it to "Hitler's mistreatement [*sic*] of Jews" (quoted in Hansen 2002, 99),[24] and was thus known by the more conservative community leaders as unaccommodating when it came to the slew of racial injustice the government had already heaped upon the Nikkei community. Omura's one-page English-language section of the *Rocky Shimpo* actively reported on the writings of the FPC.

While we might be tempted to see Omura and the *Rocky Shimpo* as sponsors of writing-to-redress, given the status and resources of the paper, it is important to understand that Omura was on the outs with the more politically powerful JACL that actively editorialized against Omura's writing (Chin 2002, 394–95). Nonetheless, the less powerful Omura continued to report and editorialize, serving as a key conduit for the collective authority amassing within and across camps. For example, the *Rocky Shimpo*, whose sales and subscriptions during this period "dramatically increased" (Hansen 2002, 100), was one of the few sources spreading positive coverage of the FPC across the camps.[25] Within Heart Mountain itself, the paper enabled FPC leaders to learn about writing-to-redress activities that predated their own, like those in Poston (Emi 2008). And at least one former Heart Mountain resister, Mits Koshiyama, says that Omura's paper kept him informed about FPC meetings in his own camp, since he was, at the time, "more interested in [being] with my buddies" than attending the political gatherings himself (Chin 2002, 401). In all these ways, even as he helped sponsor the FPC from above, James Omura also helped the FPC amass authority from below.

But aside from authority amassed from dues-paying members, women relatives, and *Rocky Shimpo* editor Omura, there was also the growing collective synergy amassing at public meetings. By several accounts, approximately 400 people were present at the meeting where the decision to explicitly refuse to go was decided. While some say 99 percent voted for it, others say everyone did (Emi 1998; Nelson 1976, 122). Regardless, the FPC leadership afterwards certainly would have felt authorized to incorporate explicitly resistant wording into "One for All, All for One," and they certainly would have felt authorized to claim a collective authority to say "We, Nisei . . ." and distribute their resistant rhetoric throughout Heart Mountain, the prison home in which their authority amassed to Write-to-Redress.

COLLECTIVE AUTHORITY AS HISTORICAL LOCATION

In some of her early work on the "politics of place," Nedra Reynolds (1993, 333) suggested the possibility of considering "ethos as location": "Ethos in fact, occurs in the 'between' . . . as writers struggle to identify their own positions at the intersections of various communities and attempt to establish authority for themselves and their claims." Following Reynolds, we can see how the FPC's construction of a collectively resistant ethos took place at the intersection of both various communities and of several processes discussed above. But in addition to these "discouraging" and "encouraging" authorizations, I'd like to extend Reynolds's point here (as well as echo recent work by Min-Zhan Lu and Bruce Horner) and suggest that in considering the construction of a collective *ethos*, or a collective authority, location matters in terms of both space and *time*: historical location matters (Lu and Horner 2013).

In writing about Asian American literacy narratives, Morris Young describes the genre as an engagement in a metaphorical "rhetoric of citizenship" in response to the ongoing anti-Asian racism within the United States that constructs anyone of Asian ancestry as being a "perpetual foreigner," no matter how many generations their family has lived within the United States. For Japanese Americans during World War II, this construction was foregrounded in the racist rhetoric of military leaders and the mainstream press and materialized in the mass incarceration of all West Coast Nikkei, citizen and noncitizen alike. As a group, people of Japanese ancestry were continuously questioned as to whether they could be truly American (read, *human*) with "faces of the enemy" (Hayashi 1992). For some Japanese Americans, being a loyal American meant "cooperating" with the WRA and all government policies; for the FPC, being a loyal American meant calling upon the discourse of the American constitution and of the Americanist ideologies in which most of them had been schooled, thus exposing the racist hypocrisy of Americanist discourse at the time.

And in ages of anti-immigrant rhetoric and legislation, especially those that bring us the mass incarceration of both citizens and noncitizens, many Asian Americans may consider a "rhetoric of citizenship" to simply symbolize the right to be treated as an equal human being. This was the rhetoric of the Americanist curriculum most Nisei had learned in school. And this was the "master's house" that they knew, the one where they lived. And these were the tools, the "codes of power" that they had.

But what remains true with the use of all codes of power remains true with the use of Americanist discourse: the relations of power tend to be reified and stay intact. After all, much public writing-to-redress had to call upon discourses, ideologies, and rhetorics (or, as Eli Goldblatt might put it, "sponsoring institutions") that either implicitly or explicitly upheld systems of oppression. Writing that redressed living conditions in some ways justified the forced relocation, implicitly suggesting that if the barbed wire had *not* been in place or if winter clothes *had been provided*, then being legally barred from the West Coast would not be so bad. Writing that called for a "self-governing body" or a new camp director, as did some of the pieces of literacy that arose out of mass protests, implicitly suggested that with different, more benevolent leadership, being held against one's will without any form of due process would be acceptable.

And, like the FPC's manifesto, much of the writing that redressed registration and the draft called upon a rhetoric of US citizenship and/or other Americanist discourses, the ideologies of which have problematic implications for other human beings. As Kandace Chuh asserts, "By claiming ownership of US national identity, Asian Americanists must also then claim responsibility for the cultural and material imperialism of this nation" (Chuh 2001, 278). In other words, when we appeal to Americanist ideologies, all of us born with US citizenship, despite any antiracist intentions we have, inherit the legacies (become the benefactors) of things done in our name, whether it has been recognized as our name or not.

Of course, this is not to argue that the FPC or other participants in writing-to-redress were wholeheartedly guilty of imperialist design via their reliance on a discourse of Americanization (or Japanese nationalism, for that matter). On the contrary, there is no question in my mind that the FPC was asserting its rhetorical agency to resist racist oppression, *especially given its exact historical location*. After all, incarcerees often put themselves at risk when they enacted their collective agency to Write-to-Redress. But I am also reminded of Perry Anderson (1980, 18), who noted that the term *agent* "possess[es] two opposites connotations. It signifies at once active initiator and passive instrument." Or, as Brandt and Clinton (2002, 350) so ominously assert, "When we use literacy, we also get used." Of this duplicitous potential, whenever we make a claim on our rhetorical agency—even if it is, in that moment, designed to resist—we should always be aware. This is the complicated path we continue to walk, even today, as we find ourselves at the intersections of many processes working to enable and disable our sense of authority to speak and write.

However, for the FPC and other collective groups composing writing-to-redress, their genesis of a collective authority in a time of mass incarceration, we must understand that the most pressing contradiction was the absurdity, the *audacity*, of the US government to strip a group of humans of the rights they had been taught all their lives were *inalienable*, force them into so-called relocation camps, surround them with barbed wire and armed guards, tell them they would send them to war, and after three years of enduring this treatment, force everyone to return to hostile environments with little more than a train ticket. It is this historical location, this location of *damage*, this intersection of a wild mix of various and jostling sponsorships, or literacy authorizations, that we must understand the formation of the collective authority that brought forth much public writing-to-redress.

But we must also recall the ways authority can amass from any number of participants in a given literacy event of writing-to-redress. That is, when writers find themselves in a location of damage, so "emerges the possibility of their collective subjectivity" that can be "formed in the practice" (JanMohamed and Lloyd 1990, 9) of what I call collective writing-to-redress. In such public forms of writing designed to "intervene in society" (Wells 1996,

329), incarcerated Nikkei attended to their obligations to one another in the face of mass oppression. These incarceree writers came to have each other's back, and in doing so, amassed the authority they needed from each other to Write-to-Redress, "transforming" a "negative, generic subject-position" of "enemy alien" or "Japanese" or "prisoner" into a "positive, collective" subject-position of an oppressed but empowered mass of community members writing to be publicly heard (JanMohamed and Lloyd 1990, 10).

In all of these ways, out of damage and sponsorship and the synergy created by amassing, Nikkei incarcerees collected authority from a wide range of people, discourses, ideologies, and moments in history. In this way, much public writing-to-redress suggests that despite common perceptions of the incarcerated Nikkei masses, many people were quite, as Kazu Iijima put it in her interview, "angry," so much so that "everyone wanted to put in a word" (Omatsu 1986–1987, 93). While the material evidence and memories of some of these literacy events may be as "lost in the wind" as the anti-evacuation statement Iijima discussed, much text and memory remains in oral histories, community and university-based archives, and between the lines of inter- and cross-disciplinary scholarship on camp. Some of it has been collected here, but there is no doubt in my mind that more remains for our rhetorical attendance. With the authority amassed by the writing discussed in this chapter, combined with the damage of a paucity of scholarship on Asian American rhetorical/literacy history and the sponsorship of comp/rhet's disciplinary embrace of diversity, I can only hope we will rhetorically and collectively stretch our minds toward and then follow those public texts of writing-to-redress by putting in a few words of our own.

Notes

1. Yasui, Hirabayashi, and Korematsu were three Nisei men who publicly resisted various aspects of the mass evacuation orders prior to the community's forced removal. In March 1942, Yasui, a Portland-area lawyer, purposefully broke the pre-evacuation curfew that only applied to the Nikkei in attempts to legally challenge the law. Hirabayashi, a University of Washington student, explicitly resisted the "exclusion order" itself by marching into the FBI in May 1942 with a four-page statement titled "Why I Refused to Register for Evacuation." Korematsu,

an Oakland-area welder, attempted to conceal his ethnic identity in March 1942 by undergoing plastic surgery and marrying his Caucasian fiancée but was subsequently arrested when he did not report to his assigned assembly center with his parents and brothers. The three men were part of the landmark Supreme Court case regarding the constitutionality of mass incarceration first tried in 1943 but decided in favor of the government. These three cases became the "coram nobis" cases of the 1980s, for which Aiko Herzig-Yoshinaga recovered key evidence that eventually helped vindicate the three men (Niiya and JANM 2001, 422, 194, 251, 145).

2. Iijima was also the eventual cofounder of Asian Americans for Action, the organization that brought Aiko Herzig-Yoshinaga into political life.

3. According to Robert Maeda, the artist Isamu Noguchi submitted an essay titled "I Become a Nisei" to the *Reader's Digest* sometime in October 1942; the essay, which spoke of his feelings about being in camp—"[s]ometimes an indescribable longing for freedom comes over me"—was never published (Maeda 2001, 161–62). In addition, on November 2, 1943, incarcerated WWI vet Joseph Kurihara submitted his essay "Niseis and the Government" to the *Saturday Evening Post*, complete with a cover letter qualifying the essay's tone: "Since it speaks of facts, it hurts, but if the American people are fair-minded, of which I am sure they are, I believe they'll understand why so many of us have turned against the country" (Kurihara 1943a).

4. Reports of incarcerees rewriting or qualifying yes/no answers on the questionnaire are mostly available in the memoirs of Frank Emi (2002, 52) and Toyo Suyemoto (2007, 147), as well as in the video histories of Mits Koshiyama and Bill Nishimura on the Densho website.

5. By public, here I mean intended for circulation within a given camp or beyond the barbed wire. As Susan Wells (1996, 335) notes, we might better understand "publicity" as simply a "constructed . . . relation of readers to writers." For my purposes, then, I mean how the writers attempted to construct that relation as they wrote and distributed their texts.

6. Closer to my interest in collective agency is historical scholarship on petitions, some of which will be discussed later in this chapter. In addition, Lu-Ming Mao (2006, 126) offers a discussion of how members of a Chinese American community collectively used language to "reclaim their agency and . . . redefine the existing relationship of power" when confronted with a racist act. However, Mao's discussion stays close to the discourse within texts of this event, so we do not get a sense of how the rhetorical performances (some of which were written and some of which were spoken) might have been shaped by the collective agency of their participants.

7. In fact, as Nedra Reynolds (1993) has argued, rhetorical authority can often emerge and grow out of the political margins, though whether that authority

will be recognized by those in the political "center" remains a contested issue (Pittman 2006).

8. "Minority discourse is in this respect a mode of ideology in the sense in which Marx in 'On the Jewish Question' describes religion—at once the sublimation and the expression of misery—but with the critical difference that in the case of minority forms even the sublimation of misery needs to be understood as primarily a strategy for survival, for the preservation in some form or other of cultural identity, and for political critique" (JanMohamed and Lloyd 1990, 5, emphasis in original).

9. According to Russell Bankston, this resolution was rejected by a good number of incarcerees, but the contemporary encyclopedia of Japanese American history published by JANM notes that Topaz was one of the only camps that had "an organized protest against the registration questionnaire, in which a petition was circulated demanding the restoration of rights as a prerequisite for registration" (Niiya and JANM 2001, 390).

10. Kibei were born in the United States but/and educated in Japan. As such, in discussions of the wartime Nikkei community, they are often discussed as a distinct cultural group.

11. I want to be careful not to romanticize this movement, which I still know little about. Given Japan's status as an imperial power during these years, and its alignment with Hitler's Germany and Mussolini's Italy, it is quite likely that the movement had fascist under- and over-tones, as has been suggested by a number of camp scholars. But any pulls toward fascist nationalism within the US Nikkei community cannot be understood apart from the pushes of US racism, including mass incarceration. As such, to dismiss such a movement as simply fascist or rightist ignores the complex crisscross of accumulated sponsorship to which Nikkei incarcerees had access.

12. As noted earlier, JanMohamed and Lloyd (1990, 9) suggest that "the possibility of collective subjectivity" is "formed in practice rather than contemplation."

13. Goldblatt argues that authority is similar to the rhetorical concept of ethos in that both deal with an individual author/rhetor's "personal and social relationship with a culture." However, for Goldblatt, the term *authority* better highlights "the power transaction implicit in the writing situation" (Goldblatt 1995, 41).

14. This is not to say that incarcerees did not call upon the discourses of some prevailing (and countervailing) institutions as they wrote toward their intended audiences, as was clear earlier. It is only to argue that the decision to sit down to use writing-to-redress often precedes any discursive choices that writers may make; and to understand the authority writers collect to do so means we must develop a sense of authority that is broader that what can be found in the exact words of the text.

15. Nakano adds that the ideal of "giri ninjo" was particularly salient for the Issei, which, she writes, "encompasses a range of meaning relating to carrying out reciprocal obligations and responsibilities accompanied by 'heart.'" (Nakano 1990, 37). Weglyn (1976, 40–41) reports that the US government had made note of this cultural ethos of obligation in their pre-incarceration Munson Report.

16. My use of *amassing* is different from Deborah Brandt's *accumulating*, or the "piling up" or "amalgamation" of literacy practices that readers and writers draw upon to negotiate the conditions of their lives (Brandt 1995, 2001). Instead, amassing refers to the ways writers draw upon the synergy that's created as a collective literacy event unfolds, a synergy that is dependent upon a mass of people consciously interacting in order to publicly write as a way of "interven[ing] in society" (Wells 1996, 329).

17. While many of Ueno's papers are held in the UCLA and Stanford archives, a great many documents related to this incident, including writing-to-redress texts penned by Ueno himself, are reproduced in the appendices of his interview, available in book form as Manzanar Martyr (Ueno et al. 1986). Also related to this incident are the individually authored writing-to-redress texts of Joseph Kurihara, whose papers can be found, in part, at the JANM and in the JERS collection at UC Berkeley's Bancroft Library.

18. Assuming there was some overlap in who took part in a given camp's writing-to-redress activities, I came to this number by adding all of the lowest estimated figures of participants in a given literacy event: 6,500 on the Tule Lake resegregationist petitions; 2,500 and 3,000, respectively, in the Poston and Manzanar mass protests; 3,000 names on the anti-fence petition in Heart Mountain; 1,100 signatures of Issei women in Topaz; and 620 on the resolution from Gila. These figures add up to 16,720 incarcerees out of a 1943 total of 85,432 incarcerees over age fifteen. If the total adult population was restricted to those age twenty and over, the figure of those involved in writing-to-redress activities jumps to 24 percent (Myer 1971, 334).

19. This is not to say that a mass resistance to registration took place in Tule Lake. On the contrary, as Weglyn reports, the military's actions had the mass effect of "breaking up" any additional collective resistance "as terrified evacuees began rushing to register." However, according to Weglyn, "an inflamed, organized backlash to the Army violence" soon followed the arrests, suggesting that while resistance to registration may have been thwarted, resistance to the WRA in general had not (Weglyn 1976, 148). See chapter 8 in Weglyn for a full account of the registration period in Tule Lake.

20. Neither Tule Lake nor the Department of Justice camps, with their respective populations of 18,789 (Niiya and JANM 2001, 395) and 17,500 (Kashima 2003, 125), were scheduled to be closed at this time; thus, the number of incarcerees referred

to here is significantly lower than the total number given earlier of over 110,000 incarcerees.

21. While earlier portions of this chapter demonstrate that writing-to-redress the draft emerged in most of the WRA camps, the FPC was the only group to explicitly refuse induction. Individual acts of draft resistance (refusals of induction) also took place at camps such as Tule Lake and Minidoka but not in the same collectively organized manner as it did in Heart Mountain. For additional information, see work by Arthur A. Hansen and Eric L. Muller.

22. Most FPC members had answered yes to both questions 27 and 28, but many had written in qualifications to their answers, saying they would fight only if their present circumstances were changed.

23. Compilers and translators of a textbook approved by the California State superintendent in 1923 for the state's Japanese-language schools prominently featured "[s]tories about George Washington, Abraham Lincoln, Betsy Ross and other American figures" (Ichioka 1988, 210).

24. The full text of Omura's speech, an incredible piece of righteous rhetoric in itself, is available in Ripples of Hope: Great American Civil Rights Speeches (Gottheimer 2003, 178–81).

25. As Nisei anthropologist James Sakoda reported, the Mother's Society of Minidoka (whose writing is the focus of chapter 6) used articles about the FPC, most likely from the *Rocky Shimpo*, to try and persuade their sons to take similar action (Sakoda 1944, 77–78, frame 398).

6

ANOTHER EARNEST PETITION

ReWriting Mothers of Minidoka

All of the protestors and collaborators . . . were men, while women were typically limited to supporting roles.

—*Kurashige (2001)*

[A]ll the Issei women [may have] appear[ed] . . . submissive . . . [but] I tell you, they were iron-fisted.

—*Aburano (2008)*

At secret block meetings held throughout [Minidoka], Issei and Nisei alike conferred in hushed tones about the injustice of the government's demand and the sacrifice it would entail. The Minidokans, however, stayed true to their peaceful reputation and, at least initially, kept their dissatisfaction to themselves.

—*Muller (2001)*

DOI: 10.5876/9781607324010.c006

While the multisource interplay of damage, sponsorship, and amassing enabled the rhetorical authority claimed with the FPC's manifesto, in order to redress some of the myths of incarceration, it is important to remember that the announcement of the draft spawned a large amount of rhetorical activity even beyond Heart Mountain. As noted in chapter 4, within two months of the Selective Service announcement, collectively authored public responses emerged in at least seven of the ten WRA camps. Notably, the earliest of these responses to the draft were authored by groups of Issei mothers. In other words, despite previous scholarship on the dearth of women's resistance in camp, my own re-collecting activities suggest that the first public, collective statements to even question the draft were written by noncitizen women.

In this chapter I want to focus on one such statement, a letter-petition written and signed by over 100 Issei women. Calling themselves the Mother's Society of Minidoka (1944), these mothers of draft-age citizens were prevented from becoming citizens themselves due to racist naturalization laws in place during the time. As such, during World War II, the majority of the mothers in this society were considered enemy aliens. Given their status, and thus the absence of a legal right to petition the government (Okawa 2011, 55), the mothers' rhetorical actions were quite bold. They not only made a decision to use writing to redress the wrongs of Selective Service, they also *rewrote* to redress the initial letter-petition penned *for* them by a male citizen lawyer, a document they deemed "too weak." Such actions suggest that the women of Minidoka were far from just "supportive," "submissive," or "hushed" when it came to public protest. Instead, the rewriting-to-redress actions in which they engaged suggests that these women were careful, thoughtful, and strategic about their public use of language, which has gone the way of many public acts of writing-to-redress—rhetorically unheard.

SUPPORTING, SUBMISSIVE, HUSHED: REGARDING THE RHETORICALLY UNHEARD WOMEN OF CAMP

As many feminist rhetoric scholars have argued, due to longtime patriarchal influences on the ways we come to know rhetorical acts (i.e., a "tradition of vocal, virile, public—and therefore, privileged—men" [Glenn 1997, 1]), in order to fully "hear" or attend to the history of women's rhetorical uses of literacy, we need to be "strategic" in our "contemplation" of information and "critically imagine" what took place in the gaps of our knowledge (Royster and Kirsch 2012).

For me, that has meant *rhetorically attending* my materials and sources, a methodological orientation explained in chapter 1. Since I was less interested in whether or not writing performed in camp made it to the public eye or performed a public action, I did not begin my research in the National Archives or in WRA-sponsored camp newspapers. Instead, I wanted to know how incarcerees *used* writing—as a tool to both talk back to and emotionally survive the experience of mass incarceration. As discussed earlier, this orientation was strategic because I wanted to attend to longtime stereotypes of incarcerated Nikkei as culturally passive and accepting of their oppression. But I was also interested in the *meaning* of such writing (both the activity of those rhetorical uses and the texts produced) for more contemporary generations. It seems to *matter* to contemporary activists and descendants of camp survivors that incarcerees wrote-to-redress, regardless of the immediate results.

While I discuss this contemporary significance of writing-to-redress more in-depth in chapter 7, I raise the point here of how much the writing (both the activity and the texts) matters to Nikkei activists today because this research interest helped orient my reading of the first source for this chapter, *Lost and Found* by Karen L. Ishizuka.

Ishizuka's book, the subtitle of which is "Reclaiming the Japanese American Incarceration," narrates the experience of organizing the JANM's 1994 exhibit "America's Concentration Camps: Remembering the Japanese American Experience." Emphasizing the ways the community became the curator of the exhibit, Ishizuka shares a number of stories about the ways items were gathered and received. One such story is that of a letter signed by the mothers of Minidoka. Claiming that it was "one of the most astounding documents" donated to the museum, Ishizuka described it as "a two-page typed written letter to President Franklin D. Roosevelt from an organization called the Mother's Society of Minidoka," and that it "ask[ed] that the drafting of Japanese American men be suspended until their civil rights were reinstated." She wrote that, in addition to challenging stereotypes, the letter exemplified extraordinary "grit and gumption to speak out against what . . . was wrong and to appeal to the highest authority" (Ishizuka 2006, 176). I was immediately taken with Ishizuka's three-paragraph discussion of the document, although she never fully reproduced the letter or its text in full. The letter did indeed sound astounding, but I was also genuinely moved by the writer's description and interpretation of its significance. Clearly, this letter *mattered*.

Moved as I was, Ishizuka's reaction to the letter did not come as a surprise. After all, it almost goes without saying that women have rarely been seen as vocal resisters in camp. If the wartime Nikkei community has been written as submissive and hyper-patriotic, women have been written even more so. If and when stories of Japanese American resistance have emerged out of the fog of the model minority myth and heroic tales of the 442nd Regimental Combat Team and the 100th Infantry Battalion, they tended to focus on men: Min Yasui, Gordon Hirabayashi, and Fred Korematsu's curfew resistance and subsequent legal battles; Harry Ueno, the heart of the Manzanar rebellion; outspoken critics like Joe Kurihara and Jimmie Omura; the No-No Boys' stand against the absurd loyalty oath; or the heartfelt conscience of the Heart Mountain Fair Play Committee and other draft resisters. One camp scholar even argues that male resistance often relied on discourses based in presumed patriarchal "rights," rights obviously curtailed by mass incarceration (Kurashige 2001). In contrast, women's protest has only been theorized through a lens similar to James C. Scott's (1990) "hidden transcripts," that of "everyday" or "covert" resistance (McKay 2001).

And if the resistant agency of incarcerated Nikkei women as a whole has been rhetorically unheard, the opposition of Issei women has been particularly silenced across history. Ishizuka herself misattributes the letter to *Nisei* women—in that it "defies stereotypes of . . . the supposedly . . . compliant Nisei woman" (Ishizuka 2006, 176). This misattribution may be because of the difficulty in imagining Issei verbalizing such protest. But Nikkei silence is a complex rhetorical activity, as discussed in chapter 4. While the silence of Issei women, in particular, was partially due to cultural beliefs shaped by the rhetorics of gaman and shikataganai, scholars in both comp/rhet and Asian American studies have argued that silence can be used strategically or rhetorically. And even if Issei women were outwardly silent in their opposition, many still used writing to "break into print," writing-to-redress in both public and private ways.

From the diaries and journals of Anonymous and Chica Sugino discussed in chapter 5 to the women of Heart Mountain who wrote-to-redress the unfulfilled promises for winter clothes and/or cash and the "Ladies of Hunt Relocation Center" (another name for Minidoka) writing-to-redress a lack of hot water, to women writing senryu and haiku in bluesy protest of camp life (De Cristoforo 1987, 1997a), Issei women continuously used literacy to redress the conditions of their incarceration.

While I did not know all of this at the time I read Ishizuka, I had begun to suspect that women were more rhetorically active than they are typically given credit for. So I tracked down the copy of the mothers' letter that Ishizuka cites. The document truly was amazing. What I did not know then, but would subsequently learn through more research, was that these mothers had not been the only ones.

Despite earlier suppositions that "women's acts of resistance [in camp] was unorganized and usually subtle in nature" (McKay 2001, 204), large numbers of women actively used writing to redress the draft. In Poston, Arizona, for example, over 100 women signed a resolution requesting that the induction of their brothers and sons be delayed. Right before Selective Service was reinstated for the Nisei, the WRA had announced that they would eventually be closing all of the relocation centers, and the Poston mothers argued that Nisei sons were needed to help transition families out of the camps (Poston Women's Club 1944). In Utah, a "Committee of Six for the Mothers of Topaz" penned a petition sent to President Roosevelt and five other officials to "humbly request that civil rights be restored to [their] children" so they could "courageously send forth [their sons] to fulfill their responsibility to their country without any fear whatsoever for their own or for their families' security" (Mothers of Topaz 1944). According to the *Topaz Times,* over 1,000 women signed this petition (Topaz Times 1944). Both of these rhetorical acts are powerful in their degree of amassing the authority of women. As explained in chapter 5, such amassed authority required that the women see each other as a collective, interdependent mass, out of which they could write-to-redress wrongs committed against them, have each other's back, and tend to their obligations to their families.

The same appeared to be true for the mothers of Minidoka. But since the text was just that—a text without a story—I simply asked for a copy and then filed it away with all the other textual samples of writing-to-redress I had started to gather, not thinking about the potential series of events that produced the letter. What I would find out later was that the mothers' letter-petition had an even more complex and significant backstory. Standing first "behind the podium" (Monberg 2008) yielded to a male citizen lawyer, these women grabbed the metaphorical mic for themselves and *rewrote*-to-redress not only the "reclassification of American citizens of Japanese ancestry" but also the "so-called 'military necessity'" of mass incarceration in general, including the "baseless and vague argument" used to deny the citizenship of their sons in the first place. Far from "submissive," "unorganized," or "hushed," the literacy activities performed by the mothers of Minidoka should not be relegated to simply "everyday" or "support." While their collective process was somewhat hidden, their final draft was, and is, fully public. To more fully understand what happened, though, let me further attend to the ways I came upon their story.

"IF YOU WANTED . . . REALITY": TRIANGULATING AN EVENT OF WOMEN WRITING-TO-REDRESS

Researching at UC Berkeley a few months after I read Ishizuka's book, I decided to see if I could find any reference to these women or their letter in the sprawling collection of the Japanese American Evacuation and Relocation Study (JERS), which is housed in the university's library. I had been hesitant to rely on JERS, recalling from personal memories of some redress events I had attended as a child some grumblings on the part of older activists about the collection and study. However, I also knew JERS contained a wealth of documents, notes, and reports. In addition, I recalled seeing in some secondary source a reference to a JERS field-worker based at Minidoka, so I decided to see if anything could help me understand what had led to the mothers' letter.

After learning that the name of the field-worker was James Sakoda, I began to look through his papers, now preserved entirely on microfilm. After turning the crank through pages and pages of his reports, I finally came upon a file labeled "Nisei Draft, Spr. 15, 1944." Slowing down, I could barely contain myself when my eyes reached a paragraph that started, "In the meantime, the mothers of the project were able to organize sufficiently to circulate a petition." The mothers' letter-petition.

As I continued reading, however, it became clear that *two* letter-petitions, or two drafts/versions had been written from the women in Minidoka. The final version—the text of which Sakoda reproduces in full—appeared to be the one that Ishizuka had seen. But according to Sakoda, this final version was actually a revision/revamping of an earlier one, the full text of which he also includes. And to my delight as a researcher, Sakoda also includes a narrative of what took place, what literacy theorists call the "literacy event." In other words, the missing story.

Well, *a* missing story. Attending to Sakoda's report means attending more closely to the politics of JERS. Summarized by Densho as a "a multi-disciplinary academic study on the migration, confinement, and resettlement of Japanese Americans during World War II," the "project" (as it is often called) was headed by UC Berkeley sociologist Dorothy Swaine Thomas (Densho 2013). The study was funded by the university and several foundations, and employed over two dozen graduate and undergraduate students as "fieldworkers," the majority of whom were Japanese Americans. In its description of the project, the *Encyclopedia of Japanese American History* makes explicit mention that it was "conducted with the cooperation of the WRA"; as such, several critics have argued that the project merely "exploit[ed] the experience of internees without actually doing anything to benefit them" (Niiya and JANM 2001, 221) and deserves scrutiny "due to the manner in which the data was collected and to admitted ethical lapses by its field workers" (Densho 2013).

Controversies surrounding both the written records of the study and the study itself have been discussed by a number of scholars in Asian American studies and anthropology (Ichioka 1989; Nishimoto 1995; L. Hirabayashi 1998, 1999; Suzuki 1981, 1986). Within these studies, JERS is shown to have been a complicated research endeavor, especially for the Nisei field-workers. After all, they were incarcerees themselves, "studying" other incarcerees for a white academic based far from the camps. But many of them—Sakoda included—also saw themselves as budding sociologists, anthropologists, and psychologists and were interested in the experience of conducting fieldwork. As such, they agreed to take part and generated an immense amount of notes, journals, and reports as "participant-observers." Today, even as most camp scholars understand the historical context and contemporary critiques of the study, it is difficult to deny the sheer volume of data within the JERS collection.

While I learned most of this after my initial discovery of Sakoda's report, these feelings had clearly trickled down to some of the redress activists with whom my father had worked in the 1980s. Hence, my initial felt sense that there was something suspect about JERS as a source. But my own personal memories aside, today even politically progressive camp researchers use JERS materials, but they do so carefully, heeding Asian American studies scholar Lane Ryo Hirabayashi's reminder to triangulate as much as possible. In addition, Hirabayashi argues that providing biographical information about the author of any given report, journal, or letter in the JERS collection can help contextualize the materials being referenced (L. Hirabayashi 1998, 169). As such, attending to a senior scholar's advice, let me offer a few words about Sakoda.

James Sakoda was one of the few Kibei—born in the United States, schooled in Japan—who worked on the project. Just a few years before the bombing of Pearl Harbor, he returned from attending high school and college in Japan. He spent one year at Pasadena City College before transferring to UC Berkeley, where he intended to major in psychology. A senior at the time mass incarceration began, he was recruited to JERS via some other Nisei social science students that Dorothy Swaine Thomas knew. Given his academic interests, Sakoda agreed to take part.

The challenges of fieldwork were many, especially at first. For one, there "was a perceived lack of direction from Thomas as to what exactly they [the researchers] should be taking note of." (Niiya and JANM 2001, 221). As Sakoda told Art Hansen in 1988, each field-worker had slightly different interests, and at first, they were only told to "observe what [they] could and see what was going on" (quoted in Hansen 1988, 373). Despite his lack of experience as a social science researcher, Sakoda had kept a diary for many years by the time of his incarceration, a literacy practice picked up while living in Japan. This transnational literacy practice ended up being good "training," he told Hansen, as he had already grown accustomed to regularly describing people and events. Since Thomas "wanted [them] not to hold back anything," Sakoda began to write as much as he could observe with little focus or direction except his own particular interest of the "psychological reactions of different [sub]groups" (quoted in Hansen 1988, 368, 376).

But it was also challenging for field-workers to conduct their research in such a volatile setting, "where group tensions ran so high" (Niiya and JANM 2001, 221). For Sakoda, this shaped how he took notes and wrote reports. By 1943 he grew increasingly aware that some of his notes and reports were not only potentially being shared with the WRA but could potentially be used against people. As he told Hansen,

> Usually, you had these two roles, right, the participant and the observer, and you could carry out the two roles without much conflict. So you were a teacher and you taught, and you said what you wanted to say. If you wanted to oppose the administration, you could oppose the administration or criticize the people if that was necessary. You could go on being a participant and also being an observer. But with the registration crisis [of 1943], there was a conflict between the two because you felt that what you had to record might be dangerous to the people you were observing . . . But if you wanted the reality of whatever it was that you were doing . . . That was the dilemma. So you remained acutely aware of the dilemma (quoted in Hansen 1988, 428).

As such, by spring 1943, during the registration period, Sakoda had developed coded ways to refer to people whose words and actions he quoted and described so they "couldn't be traced directly" (quoted in Hansen 1988, 428). These coded ways can be seen in any of Sakoda's materials written after spring 1943. There you find an abundance of initials, names in quotation marks, and even potentially purposeful misspelled names.

Sakoda's caution is understandable not just because of the politics of the mass incarceration generally, but because of the camp in which he was first placed: Tule Lake. In this camp there were both several strikes and large numbers of incarcerees who refused to answer the loyalty questionnaire. With such a high amount of political protest, anyone doing official-seeming work was often suspected of being a tool of the WRA, or an *inu* (dog). So Sakoda cautiously kept his distance from the administration in addition to ensuring the anonymity of his sources. He stayed at Tule Lake through the registration period and the reorganization of the camp as a "segregation center" for so-called disloyal families. But partially because he needed to maintain his cover as a relatively "loyal" incarceree and partially because he had recently gotten engaged to a woman whose family was being relocated to Minidoka, Sakoda convinced Thomas that his fieldwork could continue there.

When they arrived, Sakoda and the other "Tuleans" found a welcoming attitude from many Minidokans. But, as he explained to Hansen, this was not simply because Minidoka was the "model camp" the WRA claimed it be. While Sakoda agreed that Minidoka, in contrast to other camps, "was a mild place peopled by mild people" (quoted in Hansen 1988, 394), he also stated that a number of Minidokans had grown increasingly disillusioned with the camp administration by the time he and the others arrived from Tule Lake. As such, a kind of "reservoir . . . of discontent" (as Hansen put it) had grown within the camp, particularly in the wake of learning how the administration had lied to incarcerees about the implications of registration in order to yield the camp's high number of volunteers for military service (quoted in Hansen 1988, 395).[1] So when the Tuleans arrived from their former camp, known for its active and outspoken incarcerees, they were embraced as potential saviors by Minidokans eager to amass more rhetorical gumption to redress the wrongs of their collective experience. As such, Sakoda, as one of the Tuleans, and a rare Nisei fluent in Japanese, found it much easier to gain the trust of his fellow incarcerees.

This unearned reputation is, perhaps, one of the reasons Sakoda was privy to the secret meeting held by the Issei mothers who penned the final version of the letter-petition. As Lane Ryo Hirabayashi argues, "information gathered through a process of ethnographic fieldwork is predicated on a set of relationships" (L. Hirabayashi 1998, 170), and Sakoda may have been able to establish relationships of trust with incarcerees who may have been hesitant to publicly express their "discontent." While the final letter-petition written by the mothers of Minidoka became a public document, the literacy activities and rhetorical context that brought it forth are less so. As such, the story of its creation is difficult to track down. Sakoda's report on the "Nisei Draft" remains one of the few available tellings—however potentially distorted—of the letter's creation and its authors. As Hirabayashi argues, for all their limitations, reports by JERS field-workers remain some of the few places we can glimpse the nature of Issei "political participation" (168). And that includes the literacy activities of Issei women writing-to-redress.

Heeding Hirabayashi's call to contextualize reports like Sakoda's with biographic information and triangulate JERS materials with oral histories and interviews whenever possible, I returned to Densho. There I re-scoured the archive for interviews by word searching for "draft" and filtering for "Minidoka." At first, no clips emerged that I hadn't seen already, but when I searched for "writing" and "letter" and filtered for the camp, a video history popped up that had only recently been added: that of Sharon Tanagi Aburano.

In a segment labeled "Brother is drafted, mother writes letter to Eleanor Roosevelt," (Aburano 2008, segment 10), Aburano tells the Densho interviewers that her "mother wrote a letter to . . . Eleanor Roosevelt" after the draft was announced, and "it had everybody's signature." When asked if she can remember what was in it, Aburano replies, "Well, mainly that they were loyal, and they couldn't see their sons . . . going into the army." Hearing that, I became convinced it was the same letter, so I back-tracked and learned from Aburano's video history what I could about her mother, Fuyo Tanagi, and her literacy background, the details of which I weave through the following section.

But I also subsequently learned that my father and stepmother knew Aburano from their mutual work with the Japanese American community in the greater Seattle area. With their help, I met Aburano a couple of years later to share information and documents, including her own copy of the letter and the signatures and my copy of Sakoda's report, which she had never seen or known about.

In our personal meeting, Aburano told me that she had already left camp by the time the draft was announced in 1942. The year before, when she was seventeen, she was one of several young Nisei women recruited out of camp under the Bolton Act to become a cadet nurse.[2] As such, she never knew the letter had been written until she was much older, when a friend sent her a copy of the letter as well as the reply from the First Lady. She had presumed that it was written in her mother's English class and that her mother had been recruited because "her penmenship was better" (Aburano 2008, segment 10). However, when we met and I read Sakoda's comments to her, she did not dispute the report, saying that she had just always *thought* it was an English class since, she said, "*You* know, Mira. I was a teacher too. You always have to have a *project*" (S. T. Aburano, pers. comm.).

A project it was. In literacy terms, though, it was a *self*-sponsored project. At least, that's my current interpretation. As much as I would like to imagine a Freirian critical literacy teacher heading a camp English class, encouraging her or his students to "write the world" and protest the draft, I think Sakoda's story remains the most reliable blow-by-blow account we have of how the petition came about. And the information Aburano provides about her mother helped me see her as a wholly confident rewriter, in little need of a WRA-sponsored English class to sponsor her writing-to-redress. After all, Tanagi was both a former teacher and a former assistant editor for a Japanese-language vernacular in Seattle (Aburano 2008, segment 5). As someone who "refined" news stories before they ran, she would have been more than aware of the rhetorical dimensions of writing, the ways shifts in wording can change the meaning, and the ways a message is received. The story and texts of the mothers of Minidoka certainly suggest Tanagi and the other Issei women who rewrote the letter-petition thought this was so. As I started to put the story together with the changes in the actual text, I couldn't help but see the ways the mothers rewrote-to-redress not just the draft but a public perception of themselves.

A STRONGER PETITION: REWRITING-TO-REDRESS

While thirty-eight individual male resisters eventually emerged in Minidoka, draft-age citizen men (or Nisei) had not successfully organized as a whole by the time the mothers of Minidoka decided to write-to-redress (Muller 2001, 67–76). A few attempts had been made to take a collective stand, but such attempts fizzled out as the eligible incarcerees disagreed about the particulars of their written statement.[3]

According to Sakoda, while a few mothers had heard of the failed statement "indirectly" (Sakoda 1944, 65), others were "argu[ing] with their sons that they should put up some kind of protest" (78).[4] When nothing seemed to transpire within a couple of weeks of the draft's announcement, several women decided to "consult . . . a lawyer" to compose their own petition (71). This lawyer was most likely the infamous Nikkei lawyer, Min Yasui, given that the text of the actual draft of the letter explicitly says he drafted it. Yasui, a Nisei lawyer from Portland, Oregon, was well known and respected among many incarcerated Nikkei for both his early refusal to abide by the first round of discriminatory curfew laws handed down after Pearl Harbor and his legal challenge to end those laws. While he eventually lost his case and spent nine months in solitary confinement, by the time he was released to Minidoka he had already become a "folk hero" among many in the community (Muller 2001, 69).

Given his history, Yasui seemed to be the perfect person to organize a public stance against the draft. But despite his early commitment to civil disobedience, he publicly opposed all resistance to the draft. His March 11 editorial in the *Minidoka Irrigator*, for example, would eventually argue that Nisei "should welcome . . . an opportunity to get into the fight" and "demonstrate . . . willingness to assume fully and patriotically the obligations of citizenship before we are in any position to petition for a redress of our grievances" (Yasui 1944).

Given this opposition, it is not a surprise that Yasui's February 12 version of the mothers' petition never calls the draft itself into question (see appendix B). Instead, the letter-petition focuses on the news that the Nisei men were going to be placed in a segregated unit, and it made use of both emotional and subservient appeals common to the genre of petitions. "Plead[ing] with heartfelt earnestness" that the women's "sons be granted the dignity of serving . . . as free and equal citizens," Yasui constructs the women as both "mothers . . . tearfully consenting" to make "this ultimate sacrifice of [their] sons" and as "nationals of an alien enemy nation" who are "condemned and hated." Some of this rhetoric may have been the mothers' idea. Sakoda notes that the mothers had consciously decided to exploit the revered but silenced position of motherhood, since most believed that "neither the [camp] administration or the Government could arrest mothers for writing a petition on behalf of their sons" (Sakoda 1944, 71). But when the letter was circulated, Sakoda reports that many were unhappy with the petition's draft. Some women did not believe it would "be very effective," especially if it did not "state definitively that they would not allow their sons to be drafted unless they were given equal rights" (72). Others, however, had strong feelings about the tone, complaining that the "wording" in the lawyer's version was simply "too weak." Sakoda then implies that some of the women decided to take the rhetorical act into their own hands.

In the beginning of February, "women of a certain block" began to meet secretly and draft a "separate petition," admonishing each other not to "talk so loudly" so they wouldn't be "discovered" or reported to "the administration" (quoted in Sakoda 1944, 72). Sakoda writes,

> After reading the contents of the petition, the ladies decided that it was too weakly worded. They demanded a stronger petition stating that they refused to allow their sons to be drafted until they received an answer from the White House. Three members of the group . . . were assigned to work on the petition. Mrs. Miyata . . . was somewhat literary-minded and somewhat emotionally unstable. She prepared the first draft of the new petition. Mrs. Takagi had attended a girl's college in Japan, and was a devout Christian. She was

> stable emotionally and was willing to discuss both sides of the problem. Mrs. Washisu . . . also had a good educational background in Japan, and helped with the drafting of the petition.
>
> The three ladies put considerable time into drafting the petition. In writing it they seemed to have had in mind an emotional appeal from the standpoint of the mothers. (Sakoda 1944, 72–73)

Careful to note the mixed "credentials" of their collective authority—emotional "stability," religious affiliation and degree of higher education—Sakoda seems to genuinely respect the three women's efforts, even noting later in his report that the finalized letter "represented serious thinking of the most intelligent Issei mothers in the block" (Sakoda 1944, 73). In addition, he seems to have taken care to mask the women's identities. There is no Miyata, Takagi, or Washisu listed among the signatures on the final draft. Nor are there any women with these last names listed in the National Archives as having been at Minidoka (Department of Justice Civil Rights Division 1988). But in the National Archives database and among the signatures, there is a Ta*na*gi—Fuyo Tanagi, Aburano's mother—the exact name also used in the address of Eleanor Roosevelt's reply to the Mother's Society. Given Sakoda's attention to hiding the identities of his "informants," my suspicion is that the three women's names were altered for his report. And given the fact that Sakoda's description of the background of "Mrs. Takagi" matches that given by Aburano of her mother, I'm fairly confident the woman was indeed Tanagi.

Continuing his efforts to document "the attitude of the mothers [at Minidoka]" (Sakoda 1944, 72), Sakoda shares some of the detailed comments Mrs. Takagi makes "represent[ing] the disturbed state of mind of many of the mothers with sons of draft age," albeit in a "calm way":

> If Niseis are drafted now, it's <u>inu-jini</u> [dying for nothing]. They really have nothing to fight for. You can't blame the parents for not wanting them to go to war now . . . All their lives the Isseis have worked for their children, putting a great deal of hope in them. They gave up everything else in order to work for their children. They lost their business and everything except their children. Now they seem to take them away, too. And that's really the only thing they have left of their life effort. You can't blame them for not wanting them to go and die on the battlefield, especially when there's nothing for them to fight for. (quoted in Sakoda 1944, 72–73, notation in original)

If the words/sentiments of Mrs. Takagi were indeed representative, as Sakoda suggests, it is no wonder that the rhetorical differences between Yasui's version of the letter-petition and the one eventually signed by over 100 women are so vast (appendix C). The sons being called up for the draft were their children, the only "things" the women had left after mass incarceration. Of course, the women probably were feeling "great heartbreak and poignant suffering," as Yasui writes, but I suspect they did not want to come off as "emotionally unstable." After all, for many Nikkei women, emotional "masking" and/or the public restraint of emotions would have been seen as morally preferable (Yamamoto 1999).

So how to best rewrite their letter if they wanted to use "an emotional appeal from their standpoint of mothers?" How could they, as women, use emotion and still be seen as "stable," "serious," and worthy of being heard?

UNDERSTAND THE FEELING: CONSTRUCTING A STANDPOINT OF WISE MOTHERS

As Evelyn Nakano Glenn (1994, 24) has argued, while the "rhetorics of self-sacrificing motherhood" can "offer . . . a culturally sanctioned rationale for organizing," they can also "reinforce . . . patriarchal ideology and traditional gender hierarchy." As such, when women employ the rhetorics of motherhood, they always risk reinscribing a social order that suggests their words and ideas are less valuable. For women writing as "mothers" then, the trick becomes how to occupy that seemingly safe subject-position and not undercut the power of the collective voice at the same time. One strategy the mothers of Minidoka seem to have employed in their revision was to rely on a more transnational understanding of ideologies and discourses associated with motherhood.

While an act of revision always involves, as Morris Young writes, a reexamination of "existing material, ideas and arguments" in order to explore what they "can be" (Young 2004, 8), when we rewrite a text first penned by someone else, we often bring to the rhetorical task at hand even more ideas and arguments upon which we might draw. Such existing ideas and arguments, however, come from *all* of our lifeworlds, and for many immigrants, like the mothers of Minidoka, such preexisting rhetorics and ideologies have to be understood as transnational. That is, I would argue that to fully understand the letter-petition written by the mothers of Minidoka, one has to begin by considering the ways their rhetoric of motherhood may have been shaped by discourses from Japan, even as they knew their audience was located in the United States.

In the United States, discourses of motherhood during the two World Wars tended to argue that women were either good or bad mothers, in part depending how much they hindered their sons' involvement with war (Zeiger 1996; Michel 1987). But while this prevalent rhetoric may have indirectly impacted the consciousness of camp women, it would have mostly circulated in English. While many Issei women understood and could use English to function in daily life, their high literacy rates stemmed from the compulsory education laws in Japan, where they learned to read and write in their first language. According to Kyoko Fujisaka (2005, 126), over 80 percent of Issei women regularly read Japanese-language immigrant newspapers. In addition, as noted earlier, Tanagi herself was an assistant editor at one such newspaper (Aburano 2008). As such, the majority of women in the Mother's Society of Minidoka would have been more familiar with the discourses circulating in those papers, the most common arising from the gendered ideology of *ryosai-kenbo.*

Often translated as "good wife, wise mother," ryosai-kenbo has also been glossed as "dutiful wife, intelligent mother" (Ichioka 1980, 349). Both Fujisaka and Shiori Nomura argue that related discourses permeated the pages of Nikkei vernaculars read by Issei women before the war. As such, ryosai-kenbo, according to Nomura (2010, 260), "was one of the most influential gender discourses for Japanese immigrant women." Fujisaka emphasizes that this patriarchal ideology represented a slight shift in emphasis for Nikkei women, who, prior to the Meiji era (when most Issei women immigrated), tended to be encouraged to mainly focus on their domestic, wifely responsibilities or obligations to their *husbands*. During the Meiji era, this shifted to an emphasis on public, motherly duties or obligations to their *children*. With such concerted nation-unifying and empire-building efforts taking place in Japan, mothers were recruited by this discourse to become nurturers of "great" male citizens.[5] In other words, motherhood became central to the "public" work of building a strong nation (Fujisaka 2005, 222). Sharing some kinship with the discourse of Republican motherhood, then, ryosai-kenbo held that a mother's moral worth depended on her active role in rearing her child to be an effective public citizen of the nation-state, especially if that child was male. Such child rearing, however, depended not only on a mother's love but also on her intellect, or wisdom.

While it is, of course, impossible to fully determine to what degree the women in the Mother's Society were shaped by such discourses, or the degree to which the women adapted them to their own transnational circumstances, they remain important to keep in mind. If the women believed that writing (and rewriting) from a standpoint of mothers would, in fact, be effective, there is no reason to presume they would rely solely on one cultural set of motherhood rhetorics, especially if that set seemed limiting and weak. It is possible that the mothers of Minidoka, former journalist Tanagi included, were concerned about the prevalence of sentimental language in Yasui's "weakly worded" version of the letter-petition. After all, Yasui lays it on thick, outlining the women's "unaccustomed hardship" and the "great heartbreak and poignant sufferings of anxiety [they] have endured" even as they are "tearfully consenting to send [their] sons to war."

In contrast, instead of simply relying on rhetorics of wretched despair and appeals to abstract notions of "justice, democracy and freedom," the mothers' version—which, according to Sakoda, was first drafted in Japanese—uses reason and logic to make an "intelligent" case for both their children's and their own "feelings." Doing so, they hoped to prove their children's loyalty and explain their current feelings of disillusionment.

The women established their ethos as ryosai-kenbo early in the letter, as they begin to build a case for their request and feelings. Asserting that they "have brought [their children] up as splendid American citizens" who are "no less loyal than any other American," they then provide evidence for such "loyalty," citing easily verifiable, albeit proto–model minority, facts about Minidokan Nisei: a "lack of law-breakers among them" and "a considerable number of . . . volunteer[s] for the Armed Forces at the time conscription was [first] ordered [before Pearl Harbor]." Continuing, the women emphasize "the stand of Nisei citizens and their parents toward the war" by highlighting how even after "war broke out, unfortunately" between the United States and Japan, "each time a Nisei draftee or bolunteer [*sic*] left for the Army all of his relatives and friends encouraged and spurred him on and sent him off."

Highlighting the patriotism and enthusiasm of both "Nisei citizens" and their "relatives and friends," the women emphasize the ways both they and their sons have behaved in manners associated with good, public citizenship, regardless of their legal status in the country they called home. Doing so, they strengthen their transnational ethos of good and wise mothers loyal to their home republic/empire.

Having established a moral worth, the women then begin a restrained, but much more pointed and accusatory, outline of the ways mass incarceration has "completely overturned" their lives: "However, on the Pacific Coast with the so-called 'military necessity' as reason[,] the foundation of our life, the fruit of several decades of toil and suffering, was completely overturned; and first generation aliens and even Nisei—who are American citizens—were forced to lead a life within barbed-wire fences. This treatment that they received was far worse than that accorded to German and Italian enemy aliens." Using the adjective phrase *so-called* and putting *military necessity* in quotation marks, the mothers simultaneously demonstrate restraint and anger as they illustrate a critical "reading of the word and the world" (Freire and Macedo 1987) by rhetorically questioning the official rationale for their imprisonment. Then, reminding their readers that the Nisei are indeed "American citizens," they employ details of damage ("forced to lead a life within barbed-wire fences") to point to the first major wrong of incarceration. This is immediately followed by a second wrong: blatant racial discrimination. The damage heaped upon Nikkei "American *citizens*" was "far worse" than the damage faced by "German and Italian *enemy aliens*."

The mothers continue to build their case by recounting the damages their sons have faced: the psychological "blow to their spirit" of being reclassified as "enemy aliens"; General DeWitt's "baseless and vague argument" of " 'a Jap's a Jap' " that was used to "accuse Nisei of being spies and saboteurs"; and the rise of "anti-Nisei feeling on the Coast." Before continuing with the litany of wrongs, however, the mothers rhetorically pause to point out that even though their sons have been reclassified and accused of essentially being enemies and traitors, no Nisei has committed "a single case of sabotage."

These examples of broad-based racism impacting male Nisei as a whole are followed with a more pointed discussion of the ways "discrimination" has damaged those who have been, or would like to be, associated with the US military. Even World War I veterans, the mothers write, who "risked their lives for the United States," "are not allowed free travel through the Coast." And in regards to the sons who, in "desiring to improve the present discriminatory condition of citizens of Japanese ancestry," did "attempt to show their real spirits" by volunteering early (as many in Minidoka did), the women note that they faced "discriminatory treatment, even within the military camps." By discussing the damages faced by both veteran and enlisted Nisei, the women implicitly and tactfully question the public rhetoric of the Nisei draft—that it would be the first step toward public acceptance of Nikkei peoples, a way to "prove" loyalty to the (white) American public (quoted in Muller 2001, 68). How can this be, they seem to say, when there is discrimination "even within the military?"

Closing this ninth paragraph by writing that their sons have been left "in a state of constant anguish," the mothers also implicitly suggest a causal relationship between the damages and their sons' current emotional state. Significantly, aside from brief mentions of struggle ("against innumerable obstacles"; "the fruit of several decades of toil and suffering"), this is the first place the women employ any rhetorics of despair, and they do so not to describe themselves but their sons. This is in great contrast to the version put forth by Yasui. Yasui's version uses language to describe the emotional state of the women as early as the second paragraph, pointing to the "great heartbreak and poignant sufferings of anxiety" that the women have "endured," as precursor to "tearfully consenting" in the third paragraph to make this "ultimate sacrifice" from the "depths of their fundamental emotions" in the fourth paragraph. I highlight the difference in the use—both in terms of placement and of frequency—of such rhetoric because it points to a fundamental difference in approach: emphasizing a mother's feelings versus emphasizing *reasons* for those feelings, the list of damages that make up the larger injustice of the whole situation.

The mothers finish the main part of their letter by further explaining their sons', and thus their own, feelings. Highlighting the hypocrisy of the United States and its stated goal of World War II—"to establish 'freedom and equality' throughout the world"—the mothers write that their sons "consider this purpose" but "then think about the treatment they are receiving" and "discover a great paradox." By following this with a description of their sons as "dejected" and demoralized, now lacking their "firm, unshakeable faith and spirit," the women again suggest a logical cause-and-effect relationship between the paradox and their sons' feelings.

They follow this point with a closing statement about their *own* feelings, feelings they imply also have reasons: "To think of sending them in this condition to the front, we as mothers considering the past and future feel an extreme and unbearable anguish." This almost final mention of such "unbearable anguish" suggests that the women agreed with the rhetorical use of their own pathos in this "stronger version" of the letter. However, in contrast to Yasui's version, by the time we hear about "anguish," the mother's letter has already outlined a reasoned explanation of why—"considering the past"—they feel the way they do. In fact, aside from this final sentence of the main part of the letter, the mothers do not refer to their own feelings until they directly address the First Lady (who was one, but not the only, member of their targeted audience) in the final paragraph. "[F] rom the standpoint of love for humanity," they write, "*understand the feeling* of the small group of suffering mothers." By reserving this direct statement of "suffering," the women seem to assert that they are not the "tearfully consenting" women of their first draft. *We are in a state of despair* because *of all the damage we have faced, outlined in our letter.* Understand *us. Our feelings are* reasonable.

By first building a case for their feelings and reserving a rhetorics of despair, the women constructed a standpoint of mothers filled with emotion as well as reason. In doing so, they rewrote their "tearful" and "suffering" subject-position / ethos into one filled with both anguish *and* wisdom, all to make their letter-petition "stronger" and attend to the public rights of their citizen children.

FROM ENEMY ALIENS TO PARENTS OF CITIZENS

Aside from a more careful use of logos / reason and pathos / emotion in order to construct a more "stable" ethos, the mothers of Minidoka also seemed concerned with the ways they named another element of their ethos: their legal relationship to the United States. Yasui refers to the women, the supposed authors of his petition, as "national[s] of an alien enemy nation, condemned and hated." While the women knew that the subject-position of "mothers" could potentially bring forth sympathy, certainly the subject-position of "enemy alien" would not. They would need to find another way to name their legal position. And the mothers of Minidoka did so by using language to rhetorically reconstruct their relationship to the country that denied them citizenship.

"At its core," Susan Zaeske notes," a petition is a request for redress of grievances sent from a subordinate . . . to a superior." As such, it usually employs "a humble tone and acknowledgment of the superior status of the recipient" (Zaeske 2003, 3). But Gail Okawa (2011) notes that during the mass incarceration period, the right to petition "for a redress of grievances" was a right only afforded to US citizens (US Const. am. 1). Issei men and women, however, were legally barred from naturalization. As such, by making use of petitions, Okawa explains, any Issei writing-to-redress US officials "employ[ed] a genre and discourse categorically and purposefully outlawed to them" (Okawa 2011, 55). In other words, the power differences between the writer/s and the audience for Isseis writing-to-redress US officials were great. In cases like these, Okawa argues, the need for the writer to attend to their "situated ethos" becomes key. As scholars Sharon Crowley, Jacqueline Jones Royster, and Okawa have explained, a situated ethos is the way we construct a perception of ourselves when power imbalances exist between a writer and her audience. As Royster (2000, 64) notes, "The greater the disparity between [the] situated status of the writer and . . . audience, the greater the gap that must be traversed in order to communicate effectively." In order to "traverse" the "gap" between incarcerated Issei women and US government officials, both Yasui and the mothers who rewrote the letter-petition would have had to contend with their lower status as noncitizens. How that gap was negotiated, however, was quite different.

While Yasui uncritically embraces the women's identity as "nationals" of a "condemned and hated" nation that is both "alien" and the "enemy," the mothers of Minidoka simultaneously embrace *and* resist their legal status. From the second line of the letter, they introduce themselves not as enemy aliens but as "parents of citizens," rhetorically reconstructing their relationship to the United States very early in the text. Doing so, they implicitly ask their target audience of government officials to hear their petition not because officials should have pity on them as sacrificing, alien women, but because the women are legal guardians of legal citizens.

The women's version continues in this vein as the shift in focus is carried throughout the document. Relying heavily on a similar kind of Americanist rhetorics of citizenship employed by the Heart Mountain Fair Play Committee, the mothers of Minidoka focus on the injustices faced by "splendid American citizens," who happen to be the women's sons. This stands in marked contrast to the version put forth by Yasui who, as argued above, placed much more emphasis on the *feelings* of the mothers he constructs. That is, while Yasui's letter-petition seems to say *feel sorry for us because we have been wronged*, invoking the concept of "mother" at least five times across his letter, the mothers' own letter-petition seems to say *this is why this is wrong*, as the women invoke the concept of American citizenship repeatedly throughout the letter:

> Please allow us to present another earnest petition in regards to the reclassification of American *citizens* of Japanese ancestry. . .
>
> We, the parents of *citizens* of Japanese ancestry, longed for America, land of the free and equal . . .
>
> our children were born in this country, and we brought them up as splendid American *citizens*, who could not be pointed to with pride. They in turn did not disappoint us in hope and grew up to be American *citizens* no less loyal than any other American . . .
>
> Even Nisei—who are American *citizens*—were forced to lead a life within barbed-wire fence . . .
>
> . . . although they are American *citizens*, Niseis . . . are not allowed free travel through the Coast.
>
> Among them were some who, desiring to improve the present discriminatory condition of *citizens* of Japanese ancestry . . .
>
> please consider the suspension of the drafting of *citizens* of Japanese ancestry . . .

This is not to say that Yasui never mentions "American" citizenship. He does, but his letter hedges on the Nisei's status: "We *feel* that our sons are Americans"; "we *plead* . . . that our sons *be granted* the dignity of serving . . . *as* free and equal American citizens." In contrast, the mothers' version repeatedly states Nisei citizenship as a matter of fact. In other words, the mothers never ask for citizenship rights or offer a relative, subjective opinion ("We feel"). They simply assert an objective "fact": the Nisei were "born in this country" and thus, are "American citizens no less loyal than any other American."

For the mothers of Minidoka, then, revising the "weak" words of an earlier draft also meant resituating their ethos in relation to American citizenship, a legal birthright accorded to their sons. They were not simply "mothers" or "nationals of an enemy alien nation"; they were "parents of citizens," citizens who deserved the same treatment as any other "American."

CONCLUSION: WOMEN REWRITING-TO-REDRESS

> For writing is re-naming.
>
> —*Rich (1972)*

> [T]he re-visioning woman works to reconstruct those symbolic representations in a new and differently meaningful way. Both processes require a transformation in accustomed ways of thinking and involve not just a crossing out of old words, but the development of new concepts, new relational paradigms, new symbolic solutions that make meaning of our experience.
>
> —*Osborn (1991)*

> Though I am a woman who is regarded as weak,
> My real body is that of a mother.
> I live hard in this world.
>
> —*Yasuko Takahashi (cited in Nomura 2010, 1)*

A confession: Even though I barely included their work, I first learned of the Mother's Society of Minidoka long before my dissertation, the earlier version of this book, was written. Files and files of notes and ideas and false starts exist on my computer. For some reason, I was unable to finish a complete chapter focusing on the rhetorical significance of their literacy event. And I recognized it. I knew these women mattered. I knew the mothers were significant. And not just to the field of comp/rhet but to Asian American studies too. I just couldn't explain that significance with a depth the mothers deserved. So I simply included an anecdote about their writing in the section on collective authority and left their experience at that.

At the time, I was in my ninth year of attempting to get pregnant. Publicly refusing to give in to the idea that my body was incapable of developing new life, for some time I had privately begun to doubt whether or not I could conceive. Ardent feminist, I wanted to believe in the power of my body, believe in my own reproductive agency. But after years of acupuncture, diet changes, hormone shots, surgery, and bold-faced doctors telling me pregnancy was unlikely, my body felt out of my control. I wasn't sure I would ever achieve the status of a mother—biological or otherwise. Struggling with on-and-off depression those years, I couldn't even entertain the idea of a similar-but-different subject-position: that of a parent to someone who did not come from my body.

And then something odd happened. Two weeks after I finished my PhD, I found out I was pregnant.

I tend to scoff about an absolute need to fully identify with one's material. But honestly, it was not until I had my son, not until I assumed the subject-position of mother, that I was able to start writing about the mothers of Minidoka. Over the first two years of my son Mako's life, I began to cobble together short presentations for the Conference on College Composition and Communication, spending my first weekend away from him discussing the Mother's Society in Atlanta. And with the luxury of a short sabbatical and the beginning of preschool, I fleshed out the details, the context, the players, and the discourse.

In other words, this mother found a renewed energy in looking at those mothers' writing and their story. Before, I could only imagine their anguish in abstract terms, an idea of damage floating above my brain. Now, somehow, I *feel* it, understanding a feeling in my body, wrenching my gut as I try to find the right words to explain the letter's significance. And I think about the draft. I think about young men forced to fight in the face of such paradox, especially as the parent of a son in a time when wars not in our name are still fought and an "all-volunteer" military recruits children via more and more covert manners (see, for example, Mead 2013). My worst fear: Mako will choose to fight/die for a country and its corporations whose politics and history his father and I detest. But if he was forced to do so while we remained behind barbed wire, unaware of what awaited us, after years of racism, denied naturalization rights, forced "relocation" and indefinite imprisonment because we "looked like the enemy," I too would be in a state of "extreme and unbearable anguish."

And yet, they wrote. Out of that damage, amassing authority as they "organize[d] sufficiently to circulate a petition," to rewrite-to-redress. They disregarded the fact that petitioning the government was not a right afforded to them as noncitizens, and they addressed their letter-petition not only to the First Lady but to the president, the director of Minidoka, the director of all the WRA camps, and the Secretary of War. After first enlisting a male citizen lawyer, they seized their public presence for themselves as soon as they decided his words were "too weak."

Traversing the gap of their situated ethos, these enemy alien women rewrote those weak words and rewrote themselves as wise mothers and parents of citizens, filled with both emotion *and* reason. They demonstrated an acute understanding of Nikkei history and discrimination, pulling apart public rhetoric used to justify their mass incarceration. They outlined the feelings of both themselves and their sons, but not without listing everything that led to those feelings. And they highlighted the hypocrisy and paradox their sons faced. In doing so, they asked not for pity but for understanding.

In the end, only the First Lady replied to the women's letter. The curt note, dated March 4, 1944, was not even officially signed but "[d]ictated," since "Mrs. Roosevelt had to leave before signing." Her words? "The opportunity to serve through Selective Service may be the one thing which will make this nation see that Americans of Japanese decent should be treated in every way in the future like Americans after the was is over. Bitterness will pass and our sense of justice will make us treat our loyal citizens fairly, no matter what their origins" (Roosevelt 1944).

In most conventional ways of looking at rhetoric, then, the letter-petition had failed. However, as Royster and Kirsch argue, feminist rhetoricians have challenged how "success" is defined when it comes to rhetoric. Highlighting the work of Katrina Powell, who writes about Appalachian women writing to protest their removal from their homes, they agree that written rhetoric should not solely be defined as effective when it "succeeds with requests for action." Instead, they argue, the rhetorical significance lies in simply "engaging with those in positions of power," especially when a gap in power is so vast (Royster and Kirsch 2012, 896). As Powell (2007, 87) writes about the women on whom she focused, "[r]ather than view literacy and its power as achievement or success-based, the women's letters reflect their literacy's power lies in its interactive nature. The act of engaging those in positions of power is more salient than whether of not their requests were granted . . . Their literacy poignantly records their values, ethics, and critical awareness, all aspects not recognized by those who had power to determine their fates."

Just like the letters written by the women in Appalachia, the mothers' letter-petition "engaged those in positions of power" and "record[ed] values, ethics and critical awareness." Sakoda notes that the general reaction to the First Lady's response was "disappointment." Some had hoped for a "concrete result"; others were dismayed that while the letter seemed to admit that the Nisei had been denied their full rights, there was no promise of anything if the Nisei *did* serve (Sakoda 1944, 113). However, as the women were rewriting their letter-petition, Sakoda notes specifically that the women were "convinced," no matter what happened, that "a petition would be *useful in conveying the feelings of indignation* felt by the Japanese people *because of the injustice* heaped upon the Japanese in America" (73). In other words, while the women, of course, had hopes they could help stop the draft, they were also interested in breaking into print to convey their feelings and record their awareness of injustice.

And in revising to convey feelings and record injustice in a collaborative manner, the mothers also amassed authority. Writing out of a shared experience of damage, they revised their collective identity and claimed a unified voice. Oppressed but empowered, these "parents of citizens" gave each other authority to reject a handed-down subject-position of "tearful consent" and, instead, amassed permission to publicly question the unjust treatment of their children.

In all of these ways, the mothers of Minidoka *were* successful. Even though their letter-petition did not stop the draft, their literacy activity of rewriting-to-redress had been authorized not only by the damage of incarceration, the draft, and the weak subject-position composed for them but also by sponsoring ideologies and rhetorics like "American," "citizenship," and Japanese ryosai-kenbo and the amassed energy of all the Issei who, as Tanagi put it, "gave up everything" ***kodomo no tame ni*** (for the sake of their children). Out of this co-authorization, the women's wise indignation was recorded and conveyed in a unified voice through "another earnest petition," "stronger" in feeling and reason and words. In many ways, we can see these women as all of our mothers, biological or otherwise. If we let them, they can, regardless of status, parent our "citizenship"—our public participation in the political circumstances that govern our lives—as we all find ways, earnestly and wisely, to rewrite-to-redress and rewrite ourselves.

Notes

1. Sakoda told Hansen that during the registration crisis, Minidoka officials "persuaded" over 300 Nisei to volunteer for the military by telling them they "couldn't answer 'yes, yes' unless [they] volunteered" (Hansen 1988, 394–95)

2. Facing a shortage of nurses both at home and abroad, the federal government passed the Bolton Act of 1943. This act recruited and subsidized the education of several thousand women—including 350 Niseis—between the ages of seventeen and thirty-five to become "cadet nurses" during World War II, with the stipulation that they complete thirty months of training and then serve in a military or civilian capacity through the duration of the war (Frances Payne Bolton School of Nursing and Case Western Reserve University 2013).

3. During the first week of February, a petition from the young men was circulated, but many of the Nisei did not agree with the rhetorical choices made in the text, especially wording that suggested they were "willing and eager" to help win the war should their full citizenship rights be returned. Such language, Sakoda writes, "did not reflect the feeling of many of the boys at that moment. This petition, consequently, was not signed by a sizable number of Niseis, and died a natural death for lack of support" (Sakoda 1944, 65).

4. Sakoda (1944, 77–78): "They brought a newspaper article and later some literature of the Fair Play Committee in Heart Mountain to show that in other centers Niseis were organizing for protest. They claimed that protesting against an injustice was a just cause for which no one need be ashamed. It was a matter of life or death for their boys."

5. Fujisaka (2005, 222) cites a powerful example of this shift when she writes that during the Meiji era, the *mothers* of leaders were introduced to the country, not the wives.

7
RELOCATING AUTHORITY
Expanding the Significance of Writing-to-Redress

Where anyone is observed reading and writing something, it is well worth asking who else is getting something out of it; often that somebody will not be at the scene.

—*Brandt and Clinton (2002)*

[Neiji] Ozawa must have had a premonition of this prior to the evacuation. In 1941, as war seemed imminent, he emphasized at one of the last meetings of the Valley Ginsha his concern for the outlook of haiku in America; he stressed that members should try to preserve for future historians their wartime experiences.

—*De Cristoforo (1997b)*

Aki saku mono ni tsubomi ari kyo hito ni tayori kaku

[Buds on autumn flowering plants
today I am writing to someone]

—*Valley Ginsha Farewell Haiku Meeting, 1944, Tule Lake (translated by Violet Matsuda de Cristoforo)*

DOI: 10.5876/9781607324010.c007

Whether literacy is used to re-collect dissidence, Write-to-Gaman, collect authority, or revise identities, writing designed to survive + resist may seem to be limited in what it can effect when the forces of oppression remain strong. As I discussed in both chapters 5 and 6, much public writing-to-redress, for example, had to call upon sponsoring discourses, ideologies, and rhetorics that either implicitly or explicitly upheld systems of oppression. And while Writing-to-Gaman may have enabled incarcerees to simultaneously be able to sustain a degree of cultural competence while voicing their dissent in print, it may also have inadvertently helped give birth to, or perhaps simply sustain, passive stereotypes of not just the Nikkei but all people racialized as Asian. In other words, to cite Deborah Brandt and Katie Clinton (2002, 350) once again, "When we use literacy, we also get used." As disheartening as this point may be, in addition to remembering the historical context for any writing-to-redress, we must also remember that *history keeps going*.

UNKNOWN FLOWERS: GROWING A LEGACY OF NIKKEI ACTIVIST LITERACIES

> [W]ith encouragement from several haiku authorities both in America and Japan, I resolved to translate the poetry assembled in this anthology—I feel it is the legacy of wartime poets to future generations. Unfortunately, though, many of the verses have already been lost or discarded by these poets' descendents who, unable to read Japanese, did not appreciate the merit of this priceless literary heritage; it might have otherwise totally disappeared if someone had not acted at once.
>
> —*De Cristoforo (1997b)*

> The curatorial strategy of adopting and manifesting the inmates' perspective resulted in the discovery of extraordinary items that had been unknown and unseen for decades. Tucked away—sometimes neatly and sometimes haphazardly—for some fifty years, a cornucopia of photographs, documents, letters, and stories came tumbling out of people's garages and closets when it became known we were looking.
>
> —*Ishizuka (2006)*

Kobore dane mebuki nanibana ka chisana ha o mocha
[Spilled seeds
sprouting tiny leaves
of unknown flowers]

—*Incarcerated Issei poet Hekisamei Matsuda*
(translated by Violet Matsuda de Cristoforo)

As I argued in chapter 2, given the high status of text in industrialized societies, literacy can play a powerful recovery role in communities within those societies whose histories of resistance and other acts of agency have been rhetorically downplayed or denied. Literacy's role as a mediator of recovery becomes even more salient in contexts like that of the postwar Nikkei community, where multisourced collective silence has meant that even descendants of former incarcerees have had little personal or intimate access to the complex array of pain and struggle experienced by their parents and grandparents during World War II. For the Nikkei community, then, recovering writing-to-redress has often meant recovering truth rarely uttered out loud.

In the face of such realities, I would argue that Nikkei literacies of survivance both provided a means to redress mass incarceration during World War II and *continue* to provide a means to redress mass incarceration *during our own time.* That is, the activities and texts of writing-to-redress can become a powerful cultivator of contemporary redress or activism. By activism, I simply mean human actions or involvement, like those of survivance and resistance, which people deem necessary to effect social change and achieve social justice. While many mainstream accounts of camp history suggest that little Japanese American activism occurred behind the barbed wire (an assertion that is, as we have seen, false), it remains true that little incarceree activism, including that encoded in writing, achieved its stated and immediate goals. But as activity theorist Yrjö Engeström reminds us in his work on the ways activities can be "expanded" across time, "[e]very mediating artifact is polyvalent. A hammer, a word, a model—all may be put to a number of alternative uses depending on the total constellation of the activity system . . . In an otherwise analogous activity context in which the community is stronger, the decisive transforming actions may take a different form and content . . . In such cases the initial actions may expand into a new activity of organized resistance" (Engeström 1989, 40).

As I showed in chapters 3, 4, and 5, while both private and public forms of writing-to-redress should be understood as both active and rhetorical uses of literacy, the "initial actions" of such writing were often limited in the types of social change or justice they could effect during incarceration. As such, some might argue that the activist or rhetorical force of such literacy activities was ineffective. But following Engeström, I would argue that even when the rhetorical-activist effects of literacy employed in the interest of social justice are limited in the short term, they still retain the potential to relocate or "expand into a new activity."

Literacy holds this potential due to what Brandt and Clinton refer to as the "ontological relationship between people and things." Interested in the ways literacy can "travel, endure and integrate" "away from the immediate scene" (Brandt and Clinton 2002, 338), they argue that "literacy in use" can highlight the ways "elements of the human lifeworld" are "folded into" the "lives of things," so that those same "elements" may be "redistributed" in another place (353). While Brandt and Clinton apply this concept of what they call "folding in" to help point to the more sinister and oppressive "global" connections of "local" literacy practices across space, Engeström helps us see how resistant elements can be folded into literacy and thus, relocate or expand across *time*.

The expansion of Nikkei activism can be seen through a number of examples of writing first inscribed by incarcerees. As we have seen, behind the barbed wire of camp, literacy was used widely to redress the circumstances of incarceration. As such, the materiality of this literacy-in-action meant that elements of the Nikkei community's lifeworld, including the rhetorical-activist force of redress—the motivation to set right what was wrong or relieve suffering—could endure, travel, and integrate across time. And through examples of what Brandt and Clinton (2002) would call "transcontextualized" literacy, and what I would call *relocated* literacy, we can see such endurance, travel, and integration through what I consider the *reactivation* of that rhetorical-activist force by Japanese American activist-descendants operating in contexts in which the Nikkei community has grown stronger.

To Repose the Souls: Reactivating the Relief of Suffering

> It is also my earnest hope that the anthology will bring solace to the spirits of the former internees who died tragically in the camps, as well as to those who have passed on since.
>
> —*De Cristoforo*

One example of the reactivation of the rhetorical force of redress can be seen in the story of the Heart Mountain "mystery rocks." Recovered at the former site of the Heart Mountain internment camp in Wyoming, 656 "mystery rocks" were first discovered in a buried fifty-five-gallon oil drum unearthed during the late 1940s by white homesteaders Les and Nora Bovee. Years later, in the early 1990s, when Japanese American filmmaker Emiko Omori met the Bovees while shooting on location for her film about camp resistance, the homesteaders gave her some of the stones, each of which was inscribed with a different Japanese character. Taking advantage of what Japanese American National Museum Curator Karen Ishizuka would call "community as curator," Omori and the Bovees donated their inscribed stones to the museum's 1994 critically acclaimed exhibition, "America's Concentration Camps," in the hopes that the museum could help unravel the mystery. Once the mystery was mentioned in the museum newsletter, Shinjiro Kanazawa wrote to Ishizuka and explained, in Ishizuka's words,

> that when a child died, grieving parents would write passages from [Buddhist] sutras—and sometimes their children's names—on pebbles and build the stones into piles in order to help the deceased safely enter the other world. According to Kanazawa, the folk belief is that between this world and the next there is a "children's limbo"; when a deceased child succeeds at building a tower of pebbles in this limbo, Jizo, the guardian deity of children, appears to help the child across the river and safely onto the other shore. (Ishizuka 2006, 180)

With Buddhist practices often marking inmates as "pro-Japanese" and thus, aligned with the enemy in a time of war, Asian American studies historian Gary Okihiro has argued that "ethnic religions comprised a means to resist 'Americanization' and anti-Japanese racism, and formed the basis for a wider network of cultural resistance in camps" (Okihiro 1984, 224). When inscribed and recovered, these written rituals expanded the cultural resistance some fifty years later. Omori would eventually open her award-winning film, *Rabbit in the Moon* (1999) with ethereal images of the "small river stones" behind clear, translucent text that explained how they had been "buried by inmates" and now served as "fragments of memory"; Ishizuka would incorporate them into the exhibit designed for and with the community to "recover history and recover *from* history"; and Kanazawa, who maintained the Buddhist

FIGURE 7.1. Heart Mountain mystery rocks. Used by permission of the Japanese American National Museum (gift of Leslie and Nora Bovee. 94.158.1).

belief that the spirits of the children who had died in camp were still in limbo, would advise the Japanese American organizers (many of whom had little religious knowledge of their cultural heritages, since those heritages had been discouraged during the war) that they should "at least repose the souls of babies that the pebbles were gathered for, before you exhibit them" (Ishizuka 2006, 181). Without the inscriptions, even if they had been used in Buddhist rituals, the stones would most likely have been seen as something in need of disposal. Instead, incarcerees wrote to relieve suffering and, consciously or unconsciously, created the potential for future rhetorical action by folding cultural resistance into the rocks, so literacy could carry it across time and space and integrate it with other processes of recovery and renewal.

With the story of the Heart Mountain mystery rocks we can easily see how the redistribution of the collective practice of cultural resistance across time cannot be underestimated for a community's recovery. However, in the case of Japanese American writing from camp, cultural resistance is not the only activist or rhetorical force that has expanded across time. So has the more explicitly resistant, activist force first folded in by the Heart Mountain Fair Play Committee.

To Make Things Right: Reactivating Resistant Capital

> [T]these brave and resolute young men . . . faced the wrath of an oppressive government in the historic tradition of free men to repression. In some tomorrow, future scholars and historians will pay them honor. Even now the seeds are stirring.
>
> —*Omura*

Left dissatisfied with Bourdieu's (1991) concept of cultural capital, multicultural education scholar Tara Yosso (2005) has theorized that communities of color within the United States are continuously provided for by other forms of community "wealth." Included among these many forms is what Yosso calls "resistant capital," or the "knowledges and skills fostered through oppositional behavior that challenges inequality" (80). Developed out of studies of families where children were "consciously instruct[ed] . . . to engage in behaviors and maintain attitudes that challenge the status quo" (81), Yosso's concept helps give shape to the activist elements folded into literacy during initial actions of resistance. If resistant capital is something that can be passed down or inherited across generations, then so is an activist or rhetorical sensibility. And literacy is one means by which that inheritance might be recovered.

This inheritance can perhaps best be seen in the expansion of the activist force folded into the central manifesto of the Heart Mountain Fair Play Committee, discussed at length in chapter 5. For decades after camp, few people other than former incarcerees knew of the FPC's resistance, even within the community, as more conservative Japanese American leaders believed that images of self-sacrificing Nisei soldiers or well-behaved, assimilated Japanese American families were the best images to put forth in a country still struggling with white supremacy. But with the rise of the civil rights and liberation movements of the 1960s and 1970s, so came the rise of a new activity context: that of pan–Asian American activism committed to rewriting representations of people racialized as passive Orientals. At the cultural forefront of this movement was a Chinese American writer, actor, storyteller, and playwright who some people see as "the godfather of Asian American literature" (Partridge 2004, 96), Frank Chin.

Long concerned with public portrayals of "authentic" Asian American experience, in both his creative-critical and critical-creative writings, Chin has, throughout his career, railed against the perpetuation of passive and/or exoticized Asian stereotypes and the ways they feed the "racist love" that white America seems to have for Asian Americans (Chin 1991, 2). Since Chin's crusade has often been directed against other Asian American writers for their "fake" portrayals of Asian American life, his public persona remains a polarizing force within Asian America. But regardless of whether or not one agrees with Chin's polemics against texts that employ what David Palumbo-Liu (1999) calls "model minority discourse," the same crusade has also been instrumental in the recovery of early Asian American writing, including John Okada's novel about a former draft resister, *No-No Boy*.[1] And if it were not for Chin and his 1981 article on the Heart Mountain Fair Play Committee, an entire history of Japanese American resistance may have continued to be rhetorically forgotten.

After learning about the draft resistance from a former resister in Chicago, Chin told me he tried to convince the editor of the *Rafu Shimpo*, the nation's oldest vernacular serving the Nikkei community, to write an article about the FPC. But given the emphasis on Japanese American veterans by dominant community forces, the editor was too nervous to do so. Regardless, the editor told Chin he would publish an article if Chin wrote it. Like any good investigative journalist, Chin searched for anything and everything he could find, including the full transcripts of the FPC trial at which the leaders were convicted for conspiracy. Included in those transcripts was an index of evidence, including all the writing the government had collected by the FPC (Chin 2008), passages from which Chin included in his article "The Last Organized Resistance (Chin 1981b).

Never known to pretend objectivity in style, Chin does not merely include selections from the FPC's writings but, instead, rhetorically features and comments on the selections he includes, highlighting the resistant capital embedded in the prose. As Chin writes about the FPC's first bulletin, "[l]urking in the garble is the same patriotic and rhetorical embrace of the Constitution and the American way mouthed and written better by the JACL. What is new and different in the Fair Play Committee's Americanism is activism, and the re-invention of American civil disobedience" (Chin 1981b, 17). Distinguishing the FPC's use of Americanist discourse from that of the JACL, Chin inherits the resistant capital folded in to the FPC's writing and names it *activism*, as he attempts to discursively expand the FPC's rhetorical-activist force. After all, as Chin recently told me, he had hoped that by writing and publishing the article in a "community newspaper," he would "flush out" any additional former resisters who might be in the area (Chin 2008).

And flush out he did. After the article appeared, former FPC leader Frank Emi contacted Chin and began making more public appearances, receiving invitations to talk to college classes and emerging redress organizations like the National Coalition for Redress and Reparations. Emi told me that many of the young Sansei activists he met were eager to inherit the resistant capital he carried with him in body and in writing, eager to expand the activist force he and the rest of the FPC had folded in to their texts. After all, many were stunned by the story of the FPC, their own parents having said very little about camp or any Nikkei resistance (Emi 2008). As such, many of the young activists saw themselves as helping break the silence of the Quiet Americans their parents had been constructed to be by the Japanese American Citizens League chronicles available in print.

Such was the case for Frank Abe, Seattle-based journalist, filmmaker, and son of former incarcerees who, like many others, had read his "father's obligatory copy of 'Nisei: the Quiet Americans'" and learned that while "[w]e Japanese Americans weren't happy about incarceration," the community had gone "along in order to prove our loyalty, to protect our families and ensure good treatment, and to make a down payment on our hope for acceptance after the war" (Abe 1992). But like many Sanseis growing up in the activist era of the late 1960s and 1970s, Abe always wondered if there had ever been a resistance, and it was from Chin, and later from Emi himself, that Abe got his answer.

Sometime after learning about the Fair Play Committee, Abe (1992) wrote a moving personal essay that appeared as a column in both the *Northwest Nikkei* and the *Rafu Shimpo* titled "The Resistance in Me." He movingly describes what learning of the FPC has meant to him, a Sansei redress activist, proudly citing the FPC manifesto's second paragraph: "We, the members of the FPC are not afraid to go war—we are not afraid to risk our lives for our country. We would gladly sacrifice our lives to protect and uphold the principles and ideals of our country as set forth in the Constitution and the Bill of Rights, for on its inviolability depends the freedom, liberty, justice, and protection of all people including Japanese-Americans and all other minority groups. But have we been given such freedom, such liberty, such justice, such protection? NO!!" (quoted in Abe 1992). Abe's use of textual citation, his reactivation of a Nikkei activism "folded in" almost fifty years before the writing of his own essay, is important here because of what Abe writes next: that the passage "comes not from the overheated imagination of a Sansei but from a bulletin." Giving a specific genre name to signal an actual physical text ("bulletin") composed by actual "resisters" whose "actions were real," the intertextuality becomes Abe's proof in community vernaculars where readers have either rhetorically forgotten (Enoch 2008) or denied the existence of such activities.

Abe continued to spread his inheritance of resistance capital via the continued reactivation and refolding in of the Fair Play Committee's writing in his 2000 documentary about the FPC, *Conscience and the Constitution*, whose PBS-companion website contains images of the FPC bulletins. In addition, on Abe's personal website, resisters.com, viewers can download PDFs of those same bulletin images or Word documents of the text, suggesting that Abe is interested in the further expansion of not just the FPC story but the rhetorical force of its literate activities.

The bulletin has also started to make its way into classroom curriculums like that of Scott Kurashige at the University of Michigan, where he uses primary documents like the FPC manifesto to "let actors on all sides of historical debates and conflicts speak for themselves." Combining the FPC's writing with a statement from the JACL advocating cooperation, Kurashige asks his students how they would have acted under the same circumstances. In asking his students to debate the actions of the resisters, Kurashige explains that his goal is to have students see history as something "alive." And while he doesn't necessarily "expect that the students will become activists themselves," he parenthetically adds, "*some inevitably do*" (Kurashige 2007, 1180). It is with those students, the ones who "inevitably do" become activists, that we can see how people might inherit some resistance capital via a piece of literacy in which activists from long ago folded in their rhetorical actions only for those same actions to be expanded at a later date.

This expansion, which can be seen with Chin, Sansei redress activists, Abe, and Kurashige's students, is key to understanding the longitudinal potential of literacy to talk back not just to the authorities of the present, but also to the would-be authorities of the future. As Abe (1992) wrote toward the end of his essay, "I wish had known about their acts sooner. I can't undo the sting of those years of prison, those even longer years of isolation and ostracization. I can only try to make things right for them, and for us, now."

In Abe's final words—"I can only try to make things right for them, and for us, now"— we see the inheritance of resistant capital and the expansion of activism first begun some fifty years earlier. It is an inheritance and expansion made possible, in part, by the materiality of writing and its ability to travel, endure, and integrate across time and space where "stronger" communities, like a pan–Asian American movement, can facilitate "decisive transforming actions." And with such transforming actions like investigative journalism, published essays, critically acclaimed documentaries, and implemented curriculums, resistant capital, or the knowledges and skills necessary to challenge inequality, can be further inherited, further expanded, further passed on.

Out of the Mothballs: Reactivating Private Writing-to-Redress

> [T]hose paradigms that situate private writing tightly in particular contexts are the very ones that occlude its role as a link in more extensive networks of literate activity.
>
> —*Roozen (2009)*

Stronger communities would also prove vital for the decisive transforming reactivation of poetry first written in camp. For published poet and former incarceree Mitsuye Yamada, the activity of writing-to-redress began in Minidoka, where she was incarcerated with her family as a teenager. Before the war, both of her parents wrote Japanese-language poetry and her father founded one of the Seattle senryu clubs. While Yamada's mother preferred the "more metaphorical" and "elegant" observations embodied by haiku, as a child, Yamada herself was drawn to the "racy," "rough," and "down-to-earth poetry of daily living" composed by the mostly male senryu poets who regularly gathered in her dining room. As such, Yamada says she was raised around people regularly writing "right out of their experience," as the senryu poets often wrote "about the condition of . . . immigrant lives, and their pain and their difficulties of surviving in a world that doesn't seem to understand them" (Yamada 2002).

Whether Yamada was conscious of it at the time or not, the senryu poets seemed to have had a great effect on her, and she searched for circumstances that allowed her to write in camp. She found them at the camp hospital, where she worked evenings and eventually, graveyards. As Yamada (2002) explained to my stepmother, Alice, and Yamada's daughter, Jeni, in a video history available through Densho, the hospital was usually "very, very quiet" at night, and this enabled her to spend a lot of time writing.

At the time, though, Yamada did not think highly of her poems. In fact, she did not think of them as poems at all, just as "something [she] wrote that [she] was feeling and observing in camp." Yamada told Helen Jaskoski that when she left camp in 1943 to attend college, she threw out much of her writing because she did not have very much money to ship her belongings, but she saved quite a bit of her "camp things" since they seemed "sort of interesting" (Jaskoski and Yamada 1988, 101). Yamada's devaluing of her "personal writing" continued with the "strict training" she would eventually receive at the University of Chicago, training heavily influenced by New Criticism. As Yamada explained in her video history, it was "a period when the academic world thought of political poems as being something less than aesthetically correct . . . that poetry should not make a statement . . . [I]f you want to make a statement you'd write an essay or write a political pamphlet or something like that, you don't do that with poetry" (Yamada 2002). Despite Yamada's early love for the "down-to-earth" senryu, which could sometimes be direct statements made out of sociopolitical experience, it was not until she started to read some of the writing coming out of the predominately white women's movement of the late 1960s and early 1970s and met the "radical feminist" poet Alta, who was also the founder of a small feminist press, that she felt "awakened" to new ways to write (Yamada 2002). As she referenced Alta in her video history, "you know, she has a poem about . . . 'I'm not going to write any more metaphors, because if . . . you don't call a trump a trump, the men misunderstand it.' So it was quite a revelation for me" (Yamada 2002).

In this way the women's poetry movement provided the stronger community Yamada needed to retrieve her initial literacy actions "out of mothballs . . . and look at it and say, this is not bad" (Yamada 2002). As Yamada told her daughter and Alice, "[s]o I wrote it as a teenager but . . . I just thought, okay, and then Alta read it and she said, 'This is tremendous, do you have any more?' We were kind of dredging up all the poems out of the shoebox to publish it" (Yamada 2002).

In "dredging up" and preparing Yamada's poems for wider circulation, Yamada and Alta had begun to reactivate the rhetorical force of Yamada's initial writing-to-redress. But I would argue that more than the stronger community of women poets was necessary for the kind of rhetorical expansion to which I have been referring. As Yamada notes, during the same time that she was "awakened" by the women's poetry movement (and by extension, broader movements for women's rights), several struggles had begun across academia "over what constituted THE American culture" (Yamada 2001, 41). Such struggles provided more impetus to publish but also what I would call, following Engeström, an *analogous rhetorical activity context*. After all, during both incarceration in the 1940s and the struggles for multiculturalism in college curriculums in the 1970s and 1980s, a fundamental question of what ethnic backgrounds and histories are imagined as the United States of America were being struggled over in the public sphere. In this way, even though the two rhetorical activity contexts differed, they were analogous to one another. As such, the struggle of academic multiculturalism became a rhetorical activity context similar to the one in which Yamada's initial writing-to-redress actions had taken place.[2] But this time she was bolstered by a "stronger" "community" and activity context that allowed for her "decisive transforming action": publishing her poems. And in doing so, Yamada reactivated a rhetorical force she first folded in during camp.

Such rhetorical force can be seen in poems like "Desert Storm":

Near the mess hall
along the latrines
by the laundry
between the rows of
black tar papered barracks
the block captain galloped by.
Take cover everyone he said
here comes a twister.

Hundreds of windows
slammed shut.

Five pairs of hands
in our room
with mess hall
butter knives
stuffed
newspapers and rags
between cracks.
But the Idaho dust
persistent and seeping
found us crouched
under the covers.

This was not
im
prison
ment.
This was
re
location.

Here, Yamada records the details of a common occurrence in camp—a dust storm permeating barrack walls from which incarcerees could not escape—only to provide sarcastic commentary that resists one of the euphemisms the US government continued to use throughout the incarceration period. In this way, through her use of detailed counterevidence and a heightened attention to terminology created through unexpected line breaks, Yamada performed an initial action of writing-to-redress, as she wrote to set wrong terms right, even if only for herself at the time.

But Yamada also seems interested in recording the survivance strategies of incarcerees. As she writes in "The Watchtower":

The watchtower
With one uniformed
guard
in solitary
confined in the middle
of his land.

I walked towards the hospital
for the midnight shift.
From the rec hall the long body
of the centipede
with barracks for legs
came the sound of a
live band playing
Maria Elena
You're the answer to my dreams.
Tired teenagers
leaning on each other
swayed without struggle.

This is what we did with our days.
We loved and we lived
just like people.

If "Desert Storm" embodies an initial action of setting right what is wrong (in this case, terminology or language), "The Watchtower" embodies an initial action of relieving suffering, that a group of humans who, in the face of a denied humanity, find ways to "lean . . . on each other" and to "love" and "live" "just like people." By playing witness to the incarcerated community's humanity, Yamada codifies the idea for herself, as the closing line reiterates what should go without saying but is stated anyway in the interest of psychic survival. Without metaphor, Yamada reminds herself, and us, that like protesters today who yell at the cops beating them, "We're human, we're human, we're human," incarcerated Nikkei are/were like anyone else, *people*.

In these ways, Yamada's poems first served as initial actions of writing-to-redress, composed in private as a way to observe, document, and struggle with the meaning of mass incarceration for herself, only to be placed "in a shoebox" away from public sight for over thirty years. But with stronger communities of women poets, academic multicultural activists, and, by the time the book was published, a growing Japanese American redress movement, Yamada was able to take advantage of a public rhetorical activity context analogous to her previously private mind-struggle for justice and contribute her writing to the public struggles for justice being waged around her.

After all, Yamada's writing has since inspired a number of Sansei and Yonsei, including myself, cultivating further generations of Asian American women activist poets to write-to-redress the wrongs in our lives. As such, the rhetorical activist force of Yamada's literacy first privately folded in during camp continues to expand in widely public ways.

ALWAYS TOMORROW'S SEED: CULTIVATING LEGACIES OF WRITING-TO-REDRESS

Kiboo no nai mado kara satsukizora ashita mo aru
[From this window of despair
May sky
There is always tomorrow.]

—*Incarcerated Issei poet Neiji Ozawa*
(translated by Violet Kazue de Cristoforo)

Oh, guard the exposed roots against
Untimely sun and wind;
Some other soil may prove
More flower-wise and kind.

So let a richer earth restore
What once had died in need.
Strong roots will then respond
And bear tomorrow's seed.

—*Suyemoto*

Against all expectations, seed scientists . . . have germinated 200-year-old seeds discovered in The [British] National Archives—now growing into vigorous young plants.

Botanists . . . are used to planting seeds and letting them grow, but never before has the team been asked to use seeds that date back 200 years . . .

"This is a fantastic result," said seed ecologist Matt Daws. "The seed was so old and had been stored in some dubious conditions . . . We really did not expect to get anything."

—*Millenium Seed Project (2006)*

Given the limitations under which writing-to-redress first emerges, its legacy helps us understand that literacy in and of itself should never be understood as that grand emancipator that different "Literacy Myths" (Graff 1991) continue to insinuate. However, this same legacy shows us how under an experience of cultural and political oppression, literacy can provide a means by which culturally relevant rhetorics can be performed and public resistance can be amassed. And in using writing to encase such performances and amassing, participants can expand the longitudinal potential of their rhetorical-activist force. While there is no guarantee that any subsequent rhetorical acts will follow, such potential means that any written activity—private and public, silent and silenced, cultural and political—can be reactivated and regenerated into further rhetorical action. In this way, even if it did not take root under the dubious conditions of its own time, writing-to-redress, like the 200-year-old seeds scientists germinated, remains a fertile carrier of possibility.

In other words, writing-to-redress matters not just because of what it illuminates about the past but because of what it can generate anew. New activities can be generated out of old ones, with the material texts serving as mediators across time. As Jessica Enoch (2005, 7) argues, to truly understand the rhetorical significance of rhetorical acts performed by people with little recognized power, we must always look "beyond the immediate interaction" and ask "what else happened?" People can recover cultural and political activism that was folded into and accumulated through literacy. And through such recovery, they can regain "a clearer sense of their own *psychic wholeness*" (Royster 2000, 268). As Frank Abe (1992) writes, "There's a sense of liberation whenever we tell the story of the resisters." Literal or not, that felt sense of "liberation" is critical to relocating authority, critical to the development of a strong inward foundation that can, in turn, enable strong outward activism.

Which is why acts of reactivation are so important, why they too must be considered Asian American rhetoric. As examples of what LuMing Mao and Morris Young (2008, 3) define as the "systemic, effective use and development by Asian Americans of symbolic resources . . . to resist social and economic injustice and . . . bring about material and symbolic consequences that in turn destabilize the balance of power and privilege," these rhetorically expanded uses of Asian American literacy become not simply recoveries of material texts but recoveries of social-psychological selves. Recoveries of authority taken and denied.

And this is the experience I wish to redress here: Who cares what happened to a seven-year-old hapa girl whose blood relatives weren't even in camp? In the moment my father tells me we would have both had to go, I am silent, but only for a moment. In the next breath, I ask, *what about Mom*? My mother, a white woman, has recently moved out of the house, saying she needs *time*, shifting my life into something called "split custody." I spend a week in a house where we all once lived and a week in an apartment far across town. I'm still getting used to this arrangement, these continuous relocations that will soon become my life, when my father looks at the floor and says, *she would have to choose.*

Years I later I will learn from bell hooks that, by definition, "being oppressed means the *absence of choice*" (hooks 1984, 5,). In the moment I first learned about camp, I suddenly saw a line drawn between my white mother and my hapa self that has yet to disappear: the choice of going to camp, the choice of leaving, the choice of living wherever one wants to live. Of course, in a seven-year-old's mind, these choices blur together across time and elide others related to gender and class that my mother did not have. But in that moment I felt the symbolic damage of camp's legacy, felt the historical lack of choice weigh upon Nikkei bodies like my own, and felt the choice of my mother, a white person, to live where she wanted, which in some weeks was nowhere near me.

Fill in the gap.

This is ~~a text about~~ attendance.

This is ~~a text about~~ recovery.

This is ~~a text about~~ Writing-to-Gaman.

This is ~~a text about~~ collective authority.

This is ~~a text about~~ rewriting a subject-position.

This is ~~a text about~~ reactivation.

Fortunately, the story does not have to end with the damage, does not have to end with the pain. Out of damage inflicted, the possibility of transformation emerges. From negative-generic to positive-collective, I have, throughout this text, been collecting authority not only from the sponsors of my racial consciousness but from the sponsors of my literacy.

While I recall many people in my life reading, my memories are more full of people writing. Five years after my father joined the redress movement, he was offered a position as assistant editor of the *Pacific Citizen*, the JACL English-language vernacular based in Los Angeles. During my summer vacations, I would hang out with him at the office, fascinated with the giant layout table where stories were cut and shaped around the various-sized ads that kept the paper in business. A few years later his editorship of the *International Examiner*, a pan-ethnic Asian American vernacular in Seattle, meant visits included more than hanging out in the dark two-room office he shared with two other staff members. It also meant walking around the International District, Seattle's pan–Asian American 'hood, where we would inevitably bump into two or three longtime community activists and talk story or grab some food and, in the midst of it all, clarify facts. Sometimes the chance meeting ended with Dad telling whoever it was that they should write a story for the paper, that what they were doing was interesting and that it mattered. And sometimes they did, and Dad would then grumble to my stepmother or me about the passive voice or lifeless sentences even as he continued to encourage others to write. And after he left the paper to do more community organizing, he continued with his monthly columns, drafts of which he would often ask me to read, a pattern he later continued when he hired me in my twenties to help edit his book on the redress movement in Seattle.

But my father was not the only sponsor of my literacy. While my mother may not consider herself a writer, like most people growing in the twentieth-century United States, she has used writing both by choice and necessity. A longtime early child development worker—teacher, day-care director, curriculum specialist, federal reviewer—my mother has always used writing in her work life that, as is true for so many socially committed people working in education, often spilled over into what I saw her doing at home. Whether she was planning a lesson, classifying culturally relevant materials, writing an agenda, drafting a budget, or applying for a grant, my mother's work writing always started by hand, sometimes on loose sheets of construction paper or the backside of already used scraps she saved in giant piles. But my mother also used writing in her off-hours during my own early child development years, as an activist in the Portland Central America Solidarity Committee (PCASC), an organization she helped start, to join the broader US-based solidarity movement that was built on an ethos of *internationalismo*, as it linked its arms with leftist struggles in places like El Salvador and Nicaragua. Once in a while she would bring me along to PCASC's one-fluorescent-bulb office, where I could see the giant file cabinets, drafted flyers, donated typewriters, and stacks of scrap paper. Sometimes someone was writing on butcher paper taped to the wall while others took notes at a folding banquet table on what needed to be done, who was to do it, and when it needed to happen. Sometimes one of these people was my mother, but the tasks rotated; and when I think back, the individual bodies seem less important than the synergy first lighting up the dark room, later spilling into the streets: *el pueblo unido*. And in the midst of all of her commitments, my mother wrote poetry, not to publish but to give to other people. Perhaps implicitly understanding the advice I once read to "think of a poem as arms," for as long as I can remember, my mother has written me a poem for every one of my birthdays, ruminating on my development, on any emotional distance between us, on the political state of the world.

With these tacit literacy lessons, I know now that I must have internalized some guidelines still shaping my evolving ethos as a writer: use writing for work, activism, and emotional ties; share and reuse limited materials; collectivize the writing that needs to be done; draw upon the private qualities of writing to fill emotional gaps; check facts not just with books but with people; encourage other people to write and help them as you can; contend with the fact that what finally gets printed will partially be shaped by a sponsorship you can't always control.

These lessons were coupled with, or perhaps reinforced by, the intervention of two teachers who consciously embraced the critical literacy pedagogy of Paulo Freire. If my parents and their respective communities helped shape my attitude toward writing, Linda Christensen and Bill Bigelow helped me decide to become a writer. On my high school counselor's advice, I enrolled in their interdisciplinary class for juniors called Literature and American History. In it, we wrote and wrote and wrote: interior monologues, poems, "I-search" and response papers, dialogue journals, class and self-evaluations—all about, with, and through the history and literature of colonial conquest, reconstruction, labor struggles, American public education, and the Vietnam

War—as we attended to a "people's history of the United States" (Zinn 2001). I had written journals for years—*writing-to-gaman out of damage inflicted*—but Linda and Bill helped reinforce and codify my tacit awareness that writing could help us both name and extend beyond our individual selves. And years before Ratcliffe, my classmates and I learned to rhetorically listen, attending to our lives in each other's writing, as our entire class shared work in full-group read-arounds, praising particulars we might emulate on our own. And through it all, we came to know that this writing was not simply ourselves, it was history. It was our coming to know what it meant to resist colonization, fight for forty acres and a mule, organize against the exploitation of our labor, and struggle with the eugenicist origins of what was (for *all* of us, Bill and Linda insisted) a soon-to-come SAT. In all of these ways, my classmates and I learned to use literacy to see ourselves as connected to history and its struggles, that resistant capital we could inherit and expand and *reactivate*, should the moment arise.

Such is the ideological freight of my sponsors, ideas about writing pushing back on the pain. Of course, my literacy sponsorship began before and beyond my parents and teachers, all of whom collected authority from social movements that either took place during or stemmed directly from the politically committed energy of the 1960s. So even though I write relatively alone, I am fully aware of the multisources of my agency, fully aware of the authority I have collected across history, the authority I add to even now. After all, there is a synergy amassing with my own reactivation of writing-to-redress, the private voices that broke into print, the public petitions once downplayed or denied. All of them coalescing, collectively talking back to the absent presence of Asian America in the labyrinths of literacy and the rhetorical tradition, as they discursively fill in the gaps in that self-proclaimed friend-of-diversity, the field of comp/rhet. Out of damage inflicted, it's a reactivation of collective authority folded in to resistant capital accumulating across history. It's a reactivation of authority located in the seeds of writing-to-redress, seeds we can recover, seeds we can attend to, seeds we can grow.

But only if cultivated. And such cultivation—of rhetorical attendance, political dissidence, cultural rhetorics, collective authority, revised identities, and the reactivation of rhetorical activity—is at the heart of why I personally was drawn to writing as well as the teaching and study of writing. If Japanese American literature and culture enabled me to cultivate a culturally relevant methodology, then rhetorical attendance enabled me to cultivate my methods under the lifelong tutelage of Nikkei activists. If reCollecting Nikkei dissidence through research and writing enabled me to cultivate myself as both a Japanese American *and* a dissident, then theorizing the culturally relevant practice of Writing-to-Gaman enabled me to cultivate a dual sense of cultural competence *and* sociopolitical consciousness. And if recovering the range of public and private Writing-(and ReWriting-)to-Redress enables me to cultivate the cultural diversity of our field's rhetorical memory, then attending to the reactivation of public and private writing-to-redress enables me to cultivate our theoretical understanding of the relationship between literacy and social justice.

And if this study does indeed cultivate all of these things, as I sincerely hope it does, then I have been able to join the legacy I have named and to expand not simply the numerical but the *rhetorical* significance of literacy activities first performed in camp: that of an imprisoned people relocating authority away from the US government and back into their community body and ourselves.

This is ~~a text about~~ writing-to-redress.

Notes

1. First published in 1957, *No-No Boy* was, in many ways, rhetorically downplayed, forgotten, and subsequently unheard of until Chin and the other editors of Aiiieeeee! discovered the text in a used bookstore somewhere in San Francisco, tracked down Okada's widow, and arranged for its republication (Inada 1981; Chin 1981a; Partridge 2004).

2. Although Yamada does not mention it explicitly, I would argue that the national redress and reparations movement, which was also taking place during this time, provided another analogous rhetorical activity context for her decisive transforming action.

APPENDIX A

Heart Mountain Fair Play Committee's "Manifesto"

FAIR PLAY COMMITTEE
"One for all—all for one"

"No person shall be deprived of life, liberty, or property, without due process of law, nor private property be taken for public use without just compensation." Article V Bill of Rights.

"Neither slavery nor involuntary servitude, except as punishment for crime whereof the party shall have been duly convicted, shall exist within the United States, or any place subject to their jurisdiction." Article XIII Bill of Rights.

We, the Nisei have been complacent and too inarticulate to the unconstitutional acts that we were subjected to. If ever there was a time or cause for decisive action, IT IS NOW!

We, the members of the FPC are not afraid to go to war—we are not afraid to risk our lives for our country. We would gladly sacrifice our lives to protect and uphold the principles and ideals of our country as set forth in the Constitution and the Bill of Rights, for on its inviolability depends the freedom, liberty, justice, and protection of all people including Japanese-Americans and all other minority groups. But have we been given such freedom, such liberty, such justice, such protection? NO!! Without any hearings, without due process of law as guaranteed by the Constitution and Bill of Rights, without any charges filed against us, without any evidence of wrongdoing on our part, one hundred and ten thousand innocent people were kicked out of their homes, literally uprooted from where they have lived for the greater part of their life, and herded like dangerous criminals into concentration camps with barbed wire fences and military police guarding it, AND THEN, WITHOUT RECTIFICATION OF THE INJUSTICES COMMITTED AGAINST US NOR WITHOUT RESTORATION OF OUR RIGHTS AS GUARANTEED BY THE CONSTITUTION, WE ARE ORDERED TO JOIN THE ARMY THRU DISCRIMINATORY PROCEDURES INTO A SEGREGATED COMBAT UNIT! Is that the American way? NO! The FPC believes

DOI: 10.5876/9781607324010.c008

that unless such actions are opposed NOW, and steps taken to remedy such injustices and discriminations IMMEDIATELY, the future of all minorities and the future of this democratic nation is in danger.

Thus, the members of the FPC unanimously decided at their last open meeting that until we are restored all our rights, all discriminatory features of the Selective Service abolished, and measures are taken to remedy the past injustices thru Judicial pronouncement or Congressional act, we feel that the present program of drafting us from this concentration camp is unjust, unconstitutional, and against all principles of civilized usage. Therefore, WE MEMBERS OF THE FAIR PLAY COMMITTEE HEREBY REFUSE TO GO TO THE PHYSICAL EXAMINATION OR TO THE INDUCTION IF OR WHEN WE ARE CALLED IN ORDER TO CONTEST THE ISSUE.

We are not being disloyal. We are not evading the draft. We are all loyal Americans fighting for JUSTICE AND DEMOCRACY RIGHT HERE AT HOME. So, restore our rights as such, rectify the injustices of evacuation, of the concentration, of the detention, and of the pauperization as such. In short, treat us in accordance with the principles of the Constitution.

If what we are voicing is wrong, if what we ask is disloyal, if what we think is unpatriotic, then Abraham Lincoln, one of our greatest American President [*sic*] was also guilty as such, for he said, "If by the mere force of numbers a majority should deprive a minority on any Constitutional right, it might in a moral point of view justify a revolution."

Among the one thousand odd members of the Fair Play Committee, there are Nisei men over the draft age and Nisei girls who are not directly affected by the present Selective Service program, but who believe in the ideals and principles of our country, therefore are helping the FPC in our fight against injustice and discriminations.

We hope that all persons whose ideals and interests are with us will do all they can to help us. We may have to engage in court actions but as such actions require large sums of money, we do need financial support and when the time comes we hope that you will back us up to the limit.

ATTENTION MEMBERS! FAIR PLAY COMMITTEE MEETING SUNDAY, MARCH 5, 2:00 P.M. BLOCK 6-30 MESS. PARENTS, BROTHERS, SISTERS, AND FRIENDS INVITED

APPENDIX B

Letter drafted by Min Yasui for the Mother's Society of Minidoka

Drafted by Min Yasui
For Mothers of Block 35

Minidoka WRA
Hunt, Idaho

February 12, 1944

MOTHERS' PETITION

WE, the undersigned, a group of mothers of Japanese American sons now awaiting call under the selective service, at the Minidoka War Relocation Center, in Idaho, urgently desire to call attention to certain matters for consideration by the federal authorities, in connection with the impending draft of our sons.

We believe that the federal authorities are well aware of the tremendous unaccustomed hardships and bitter experiences that we, as mothers, and our families have had to undergo as a result of the forced evacuation from our homes on the West Coast; we are sure that the federal authorities are well aware of the great heartbreak and poignant sufferings of anxiety that we have endured, having been forcibly removed from our well loved comfortable homes and removed to the desert wastelands of an artificial frontier community surrounded by barbed wire fences.

Nevertheless, despite all these things, and a great deal more, we, as mothers, are tearfully consenting to send our sons to war, and in the true spirit of motherhood, urging our sons to serve faithfully and heroically in the service of the United States Army, even, if necessary, at the cost of their lives. We feel that our sons are Americans, a part of the good and great things of America, and that it is only fitting and proper that they respond patriotically to the call of their county.

For us, as mother, as national of an alien enemy nation, condemned and hated, this ultimate sacrifice of our sons to be laid on the altar of war moves us to the very bottom of our hearts, and to the depths of our most fundamental emotions, in a way that

DOI: 10.5876/9781607324010.c009

inexpressible; and yet, in making this sacrifice, we deeply feel that the lives of our sons are to be dedicated to the highest ideals and principles of justice, democracy, and freedom, for all peoples, regardless of race, color or creed.

In order that the future sacrifices of our sons shall have not been in vain, we prayerfully request and petition that the federal authorities give careful consideration to the granting of equal privileges as American soldiers to our sons when they are called into active service. We do not complain that our sons are being called, but we plead with heart-felt earnestness that our sons be granted the dignity of serving in the United States Army as free and equal American citizens, and that they do not be segregated in any special combat unit or in any other way be subjected to special rules and regulations on account of race and ancestry.

APPENDIX C

Revision of letter from the Mother's Society of Minidoka sent to authorities

Hunt, Idaho
February 20, 1944

President Franklin D. Roosevelt
Executive Mansion
Washington, D.C.

Dear President Roosevelt,

Please allow us to preset another earnest petition in regards to the reclassification of American citizens of Japanese ancestry.

We, the parents of citizens of Japanese ancestry, longed for America, land of the free and equal, left behind our familiar birthplace, and came a great distance to this country. And in this land of strange language and customs, struggling against innumerable obstacles, we attempted to gain a secure means of living. In time with grace of God out children were born in this country, and we brought them up as splendid American citizens, who could not be pointed to with pride. They in turn did not disappoint us in hope and grew up to be American citizens no less loyal than any other American, This, we believe, is demonstrated by the lack of law-breakers among them and the fact that a considerable number of them volunteered for the Armed Forces at the time conscription was ordered.

When [war] broke out, unfortunately, between America and Japan, each time a Nisei draftee or bolunteer [*sic*] left for the Army all of his relatives and friends encouraged and spurred him on and sent him off. This fact, we believe, shows the stand of Nisei citizens and their parents toward the war.

However, on the Pacific Coast with the so-called 'military necessity' as reason the foundation of our life, the fruit of several decades of toil and suffering, was completely overturned; and first

DOI: 10.5876/9781607324010.c010

generation aliens and even Nisei—who are American citizens—were forced to lead a life within barbed-wire fences. This treatment that they received was far worse than that accorded to German and Italian enemy aliens.

About the time of evacuation from the coast, their draft classification was changed to 4-C. They were considered enemy aliens. The blow to their spirit, they suffered at this time, was something that we could hardly bear to witness.

Again, Lr.-General DeWitt, Commanding Officer of the Western Defense Command, proclaimed in reference to them that "a Jap's a Jap": and, using a baseless and vague argument, accused Niseis of being spies and saboteurs, thus adding fuel to the anti-Nisei feeling among the people on the Coast. (1) However, to this day, two and half years since the outbreak of the war, not a single case of sabotage by a Nisei has occurred on the Pacific Coast or even in Hawaii.

But unfortunately the American public does not listen to the truth, and it seems that the discrimination against them is becoming even more intense.

Even today, although they are American citizens, Niseis—soldiers—are not allowed free travel through the Coast. Even Japanese war veterans who risked their lives for the United States and participated in World War I are interned in relocation centers. Since they have begun to feel deep down inside of them that these restrictions of freedom directed at American citizens of Japanese ancestry could not be understood as merely for the purpose of protection; we, their mothers, advised them that, this being war time, they should submit to military orders, and endure whatever place they are given.

Among them were some who, desiring to improve the present discriminatory condition of citizens of Japanese ancestry requested the modification of the Selective Service regulations, or took it upon themselves to volunteer for the Armed Forces and to attempt to show their real spirits. However, they took received discriminatory treatment, even within the military camps; and, contemplating the course to be followed by their juniors, they are in a state of constant anguish.

We understand that the purpose for which the United States is allowing tremendous sacrifices in fighting the war today is to establish 'freedom and equality' throughout the world. When they, the Nisei, consider the purpose of this war and then think about the treatment they are receiving at present, they discover the existence of a great paradox. They are dejected and now have lost their firm, unshakeable faith and spirit. To think of sending them in this condition to the front, we as mothers considering the past and the future feel an extreme and unbearable anguish.

Our loving and judicious Mrs. Roosevelt,

Please, from the standpoint of love for humanity, understand the feeling of the small number of suffering mothers, and advice us on the course that we should take. In this connection we would like to have you please consider the suspension of the drafting of citizens of Japanese ancestry until they regain the confidence that they can demonstrate their loyalty to the United States from the bottom of their hearts as formerly and we earnestly petition to be granted gracious words of advice and humbly await a reply from you.

Very respectfully yours,
Mother's Society

REFERENCES

Abe, Frank. 1944. "Our Cards on the Table." Accessed March 23. http://www.resisters.com/documents/HMS_OurCardsOnTheTable.htm.

Abe, Frank. 1992. "The Resistance in Me." *Rafu Shimpo*, September 1.

Abe, Frank. 2000. *Conscience and the Constitution*. Directed by Frank Abe. Hohokus, NJ: Transit Media. http://dx.doi.org/10.1037/e575452010-001.

Aburano, Sharon Tanagi. 2008. Interview by Tom Ikeda and Megan Asaka, July 1. Densho Visual History Collection, Densho.

Adler, Susan Matoba. 1998. *Mothering, Education, and Ethnicity: The Transformation of Japanese American Culture*. New York: Garland.

Akashi, Tom. 2004. Interview by Tom Ikeda and Chizu Omori, July 3. Densho Visual History Collection, Densho.

Akutsu, Gene. 1997. Interview by Larry Hashima and Stephen Fugita, July 25. Densho Visual History Collection, Densho.

Alexander, Michelle. 2011. *The New Jim Crow: Mass Incarceration in the Age of Colorblindness*. New York: The New Press.

Anderson, Benedict. 1991. *Imagined Communities: Reflections on the Origin and Spread of Nationalism*. Rev. and extended ed. New York: Verso.

Anderson, Perry. 1980. "Agency." In *Arguments within English Marxism*, 16–25. New York: Verso.

DOI: 10.5876/9781607324010.c011

Anonymous. 1942. Notebook/Journal. Japanese American National Museum, Los Angeles.

Apple, Michael W. 2000. *Official Knowledge: Democratic Education in a Conservative Age*. 2nd ed. New York: Routledge.

Apple, Michael W. 2004. *Ideology and Curriculum*. 3rd ed. New York: RoutledgeFalmer.

Apple, Michael, Wayne Au, and Luis Armando Gandin. 2009. Introduction to *The Routledge International Handbook of Critical Education*, edited by Michael W. Apple, Wayne Au, and Luis Armando Gandin, 3–20. New York: Routledge.

Apple, Michael W., and Lois Weis. 1983. "Ideology and Practice in Schooling: A Political and Conceptual Introduction." In *Ideology & Practice in Schooling*, edited by Michael W. Apple and Lois Weis, 3–33. Philadelphia: Temple University Press.

Arakawa, Suzanne. 2005. "Suffering Male Bodies: Representations of Dissent and Displacement in the Internment-Themed Narratives of John Okada and Toshio Mori." In *Recovered Legacies: Authority and Identity in Early Asian American Literature*, edited by Keith Lawrence and Floyd Cheung, 183–206. Philadelphia: Temple University Press.

Asakawa, Gil. 2004. *Being Japanese American: A J.A. Sourcebook For Nikkei, Happa—and Their Friends*. Berkeley, CA: Stone Bridge Press.

Asato, Noriko. 2006. *Teaching Mikadoism: The Attack on Japanese Language Schools in Hawaii, California, and Washington, 1919–1927*. Honolulu: University of Hawaii Press.

Azuma, Eiichiro. 2005. *Between Two Empires: Race, History, and Transnationalism in Japanese America*. New York: Oxford University Press.

Bahr, Diana Meyers. 2007. *The Unquiet Nisei: An Oral History of the Life of Sue Kunitomi Embrey*. London: Palgrave Macmillan.

Bankston, Russell. 1943. Registration at Topaz. NARA 6. H249. Bancroft Library, University of California, Berkeley.

Belanoff, Pat. 2001. "Silence: Reflection, Literacy, Learning and Teaching." *College Composition and Communication* 52 (3): 399–428. http://dx.doi.org/10.2307/358625.

Bizzell, Patricia, and Bruce Herzberg. 1996. *Negotiating Difference: Cultural Case Studies for Composition*. Boston: Bedford/St. Martin's.

Bizzell, Patricia, and Bruce Herzberg. 2001. *The Rhetorical Tradition: Readings from Classical Times to the Present*. 2nd ed. Boston: Bedford/St. Martin's.

Bloom, Lynn Z. 1976. "The Diary As Popular History." *Journal of Popular Culture* 9 (4): 794–807. http://dx.doi.org/10.1111/j.0022-3840.1976.00794.x.

Bourdieu, Pierre. 1991. *Language and Symbolic Power*. Translated by John B. Thompson. Cambridge, MA: Harvard University Press.

Brandt, Deborah. 1995. "Accumulating Literacy: Writing and Learning to Write in the Twentieth Century." *College English* 57 (6): 649–68. http://dx.doi.org/10.2307/378570.

Brandt, Deborah. 1998. "Sponsors of Literacy." *College Composition and Communication* 49 (2): 165–85. http://dx.doi.org/10.2307/358929.

Brandt, Deborah. 2001. *Literacy in American Lives*. New York: Cambridge University Press. http://dx.doi.org/10.1017/CBO9780511810237.

Brandt, Deborah, and Katie Clinton. 2002. "Limits of the Local: Expanding Perspectives on Literacy as a Social Practice." *Journal of Literacy Research* 34 (3): 337–56. http://dx.doi.org/10.1207/s15548430jlr3403_4.

Bruchac, Joseph. 1983. *Breaking Silence: An Anthology of Contemporary Asian American Poets*. 1st ed. Greenfield Center, NY: Greenfield Review Press.

Canagarajah, A. Suresh. 1999. *Resisting Linguistic Imperialism in English Teaching*. New York: Oxford University Press.

Card, Laura. 2005. " 'TREK' Magazine, 1942–1943: A Critical Rhetorical Analysis." PhD diss., University of Utah.

Chan, Jeffery Paul, Frank Chin, Lawson Fusao Inada, and Shawn Wong, eds. 1991. *The Big Aiiieeeee! An Anthology of Chinese American and Japanese American Literature*. New York: Meridian.

Chan, Sucheng. 1991. *Asian Americans: An Interpretive History*. Boston: Twayne.

Chang, Benji, and Wayne Au. 2008. "You're Asian, How Could You Fail Math? Unmasking the Myth of the Model Minority." *Rethinking Schools* 22 (2): 15–19.

Chang, Gordon H., ed. 1997. *Morning Glory, Evening Shadow: Yamato Ichihashi and His Internment Writings, 1942–1945*. Stanford, CA: Stanford University Press.

Chang, Juliana. 1996. *Quiet Fire: A Historical Anthology of Asian American Poetry, 1892–1970*. New York: Asian American Writers' Workshop.

Cheung, King-Kok. 1993. *Articulate Silences: Hisaye Yamamoto, Maxine Hong Kingston, Joy Kogawa*. Ithaca: Cornell University Press.

Chiang, Yuet-Sim. 1998. "Insider/Outsider/Other? Confronting the Centeredness of Race, Class, Color and Ethnicity in Composition Research." In *Under Construction: Working at the Intersections of Composition Theory, Research, and Practice*, edited by Christine Farris and Chris M. Anson, 150–65. Logan: Utah State University Press.

Chin, Frank. 1981a. Afterword to *No-No Boy*, by John Okada, 253–60. Seattle: University of Washington Press.

Chin, Frank. 1981b. "The Last Organized Resistance." *Rafu Shimpo*, December 19.

Chin, Frank. 1991. "Come All Ye Asian American Writers of the Real and the Fake." In *The Big Aiiieeeee! An Anthology of Chinese American and Japanese American Literature*, edited by Jeffrey Paul Chan, Frank Chin, Lawson Fusao Inada, and Shawn Wong, 1–93. New York: Meridian.

Chin, Frank. 2002. *Born in the USA: A Story of Japanese America, 1889–1947*. Lanham, MD: Rowman and Littlefield.

Chin, Frank. 2008. Interview with the author, July 9.

Chin, Frank, and Jeffery Paul Chan. 1971. "Racist Love." In *Seeing Through Shuck*, edited by Richard Kostelanetz, 65–79. New York: Ballantine.

Chin, Frank, Jeffrey Paul Chan, Lawson Fusao Inada, and Shawn Wong, eds. 1974. *Aiiieeeee! An Anthology of Asian-American Writers*. Washington, DC: Howard University Press.

Chuh, Kandace. 2001. "Imaginary Borders." In *Orientations: Mapping Studies in the Asian Diaspora*, edited by Kandace Chuh and Karen Shimakawa, 277–95. Durham, NC: Duke University Press.

Cintron, Ralph. 1997. *Angels' Town: Chero Ways, Gang Life, and Rhetorics of the Everyday*. Boston: Beacon.

Collins, James, and Richard K. Blot. 2003. *Literacy And Literacies: Texts, Power, and Identity*. New York: Cambridge University Press. http://dx.doi.org/10.1017/CBO9780511486661.

Conrat, Maisie, Richard Conrat, and Dorothea Lange. 1972. *Executive Order 9066: The Internment of 110,000 Japanese Americans*. Cambridge, MA: MIT Press for the California Historical Society.

Cooper, Frank. 2011. "Hyper-incarceration as a Multidimensional Attack: Replying to Angela Harris through *The Wire*." *Washington University Journal of Law and Policy* 37: 67–88.

Cornelius, Janet Duitsman. 1991. *"When I Can Read My Title Clear": Literacy, Slavery, and Religion in the Antebellum South*. Columbia: University of South Carolina Press.

Cushman, Ellen. 1998. *The Struggle and the Tools: Oral and Literate Strategies in an Inner City Community*. Albany, NY: State University of New York Press.

De Cristoforo, Violet Matsuda. 1987. *Poetic Reflections of the Tule Lake Internment Camp, 1944*. Salinas, California: Violet Matsuda de Cristoforo.

De Cristoforo, Violet Kazue. 1997a. *May Sky: There Is Always Tomorrow: An Anthology of Japanese American Concentration Camp Kaiko Haiku*. 1st ed. Los Angeles: Sun and Moon Press.

De Cristoforo, Violet Kazue. 1997b. "Preface." In *May Sky: There Is Always Tomorrow: An Anthology of Japanese American Concentration Camp Kaiko Haiku*, edited by Violet Kazue De Cristoforo, 287. Los Angeles: Sun and Moon Press.

Delegates of Manzanar Draft Age Citizens. 1944. Letter to Merritt. Japanese American National Museum, Los Angeles.

Densho. 1997a. "About Densho." Accessed July 1, 2008. http://www.densho.org/about/default.asp.

Densho. 1997b. "Densho: The Japanese American Legacy Project." Accessed July 1, 2008. http://www.densho.org/.

Densho. 2013. "Japanese American Evacuation and Resettlement Study." Accessed September 19, 2013. http://encyclopedia.densho.org/Japanese_American_Evacuation_and_Resettlement_Study/.

Department of Justice Civil Rights Division. 1988. "Records About Japanese Americans Relocated During World War II." Accessed October 3, 2013. http://aad.archives.gov/aad/series-description.jsp?s=623&cat=WR26&bc=,sl.

Dixon, John. 1975. *Growth through English*. London: Oxford University Press.

Duffy, John. 2004. "Letters from the Fair City: A Rhetorical Conception of Literacy." *College Composition and Communication* 56 (2): 223–50. http://dx.doi.org/10.2307/4140648.

Duffy, John. 2007. *Writing from These Roots: Literacy in a Hmong-American Community*. Honolulu: University of Hawaii Press.

Duncan, Patti. 2004. *Tell This Silence: Asian American Women Writers and the Politics of Speech*. Iowa City: University of Iowa Press.

Ede, Lisa, and Andrea Lunsford. 1984. "Audience Addressed/Audience Invoked: The Role of Audience in Composition Theory and Pedagogy." *College Composition and Communication* 35 (2): 155–71. http://dx.doi.org/10.2307/358093.

Editors. 1943. "Conditions at Camp Harmony." *New Republic*, 72.

Elbow, Peter. 2000. *Everyone Can Write: Essays Toward a Hopeful Theory of Writing and Teaching Writing*. New York: Oxford University Press.

Emi, Frank. 1944. "Letter to the Editor." *Heart Mountain Sentinel*, March 19, 4.

Emi, Frank. 1998. Interview by Frank Abe, March 12. Frank Abe Collection, Densho.

Emi, Frank. 2002. "Protest and Resistance: An American Tradition." In *A Matter of Conscience: Essays on the World War II Heart Mountain Draft Resistance Movement*, edited by Mike Mackey, 51–61. Powell, WY: Western History Publications.

Emi, Frank. 2008. Interview with the author, June 12.

Engeström, Yrjö. 1989. "The Cultural-Historical Theory of Activity and the Study of Political Repression." *International Journal of Mental Health* 17 (4): 29–41.

Enoch, Jessica. 2005. "Survival Stories: Feminist Historiographic Approaches to Chicana Rhetorics of Sterilization Abuse." *Rhetoric Society Quarterly* 35 (3): 5–30. http://dx.doi.org/10.1080/02773940509391314.

Enoch, Jessica. 2008. "Remembering and Forgetting: The Archive's Contests over Public Memory." Paper presented at Conference on College Composition and Communication, New Orleans, April 3.

Espiritu, Yen Le. 1992. *Asian American Panethnicity: Bridging Institutions and Identities*. Philadelphia: Temple University Press.

Fair Play Committee. 1944. "One for All—All for One." resisters.com. Accessed March 23, 2006. http://www.resisters.com/documents/FPC_Bulletin_3.htm.

Finders, Margaret J. 1997. *Just Girls: Hidden Literacies and Life in Junior High*. New York: Teachers College Press.

Fiset, Louis. 1997. *Imprisoned Apart: The World War II Correspondence of an Issei Couple*. Seattle: University of Washington Press.

Fiset, Louis. 2001. "Censored! U.S. Censors and Internment Camp Mail in World War II." In *Guilt By Association: Essays on Japanese Settlement, Internment, and Relocation in the Rocky Mountain West*, edited by Mike Mackey, 69–100. Powell, WY: Western History Publications.

Forman, James. 2012. "Racial Critiques of Mass Incarceration: Beyond the New Jim Crow." *NYU Law Review* 87: 21–69.

Frances Payne Bolton School of Nursing, Case Western Reserve University. 2013. "The Bolton Act: Making the Nursing Profession More Accessible to Everyone." Accessed October 10, 2013. http://fpb.case.edu/visitors/boltonact.shtm.

Freire, Paulo, and Donaldo Macedo. 1987. *Literacy: Reading the Word and the World*. South Hadley, MA: Bergin and Garvey.

Friedson, Anthony. 1984. "No More Farewells: An Interview with Jeanne and John Houston." *Biography* 7 (1): 50–73. http://dx.doi.org/10.1353/bio.2010.0703.

Fujino, Diane Carol. 2005. *Heartbeat of Struggle: The Revolutionary Life of Yuri Kochiyama*. Minneapolis: University of Minnesota Press.

Fujisaka, Kyoko Kakehashi. 2005. "Japanese Immigrant Women in Los Angeles, 1912–1942: A Transnational Perspective." PhD diss., University of Wisconsin–Madison.

Fujita, Gayle K. 1985. " 'To Attend the Sound of Stone': The Sensibility of Silence in Obasan." *MELUS* 12 (3): 33–42. http://dx.doi.org/10.2307/467119.

Fujitani, Takashi. 2002. "Cultures of Resistance: Japanese American Draft Resisters in Transnational Perspective." In *A Matter of Conscience: Essays on the World War II Heart Mountain Draft Resistance Movement*, edited by Mike Mackey, 21–37. Powell, WY: Western History Publications.

Fujita-Rony, Thomas. 2003. "'Destructive Force': Aiko Herzig-Yoshinaga's Gendered Labor in the Japanese American Redress Movement." *Frontiers* 24 (1): 38–60. http://dx.doi.org/10.1353/fro.2003.0017.

Gee, James Paul. 2008. *Social Linguistics and Literacies: Ideology in Discourses*. 3rd ed. New York: Routledge.

Gere, Anne Ruggles. 2001. "Revealing Silence: Rethinking Personal Writing." *College Composition and Communication* 53 (2): 203–23. http://dx.doi.org/10.2307/359076.

Gila News-Courier. 1944. "Draft Age Nisei Petition for Equal Opportunities." *Gila News-Courier*, March 9.

Glenn, Cheryl. 1997. *Rhetoric Retold: Regendering the Tradition from Antiquity through the Renaissance*. Carbondale: Southern Illinois University Press.

Glenn, Cheryl. 2004. *Unspoken: A Rhetoric of Silence*. Carbondale: Southern Illinois University Press.

Glenn, Evelyn Nakano. 1994. "Social Constructions of Mothering: A Thematic Overview." In *Mothering: Ideology, Experience, and Agency*, edited by Evelyn Nakano Glenn, Grace Chang, and Linda Rennie Forcey, 1–29. New York: Routledge.

Goldblatt, Eli C. 1995. *Round My Way: Authority and Double-Consciousness in Three Urban High School Writers*. Pittsburgh: University of Pittsburgh Press.

Gottheimer, Josh. 2003. *Ripples of Hope: Great American Civil Rights Speeches*. New York: Basic Civitas.

Gottschalk, Marie. 2015. *Caught: The Prison State and the Lockdown of American Politics*. Princeton, NJ: Princeton University Press.

Graff, Harvey J. 1987a. *The Legacies of Literacy: Continuities and Contradictions in Western Culture and Society*. Bloomington: Indiana University Press.

Graff, Harvey J. 1987b. "The Nineteenth-Century Origins of Our Times." In *The Legacies of Literacy: Continuities and Contradictions in Western Culture and Society*, x. Bloomington: Indiana University Press.

Graff, Harvey J. 1991. *The Literacy Myth: Cultural Integration and Social Structure in the Nineteenth Century*. New Brunswick, NJ: Transaction Publishers.

Greene, Jamie Candeleria. 1994. "Misperspectives on Literacy: A Critique of an Anglocentric Bias in Histories of American Literacy." *Written Communication* 11 (2): 251–69. http://dx.doi.org/10.1177/0741088394011002004.

Gregg, Richard B. 1971. "The Ego-Function of the Rhetoric of Protest." *Philosophy & Rhetoric* 4 (2): 71–91.

Groves, Fumiko Uyeda. 1998. Interview by Larry Hashima, June 16. Densho Visual History Collection, Densho.

Hansen, Arthur. 1988. "An Interview with James M. Sakoda." Japanese American Oral History Project Collection, California State University, Fullerton.

Hansen, Arthur A. 2002. "Protest-Resistance and the Heart Mountain Experience: The Revitalization of a Robust Nikkei Tradition." In *A Matter of Conscience: Essays on the World War II Heart Mountain Draft Resistance Movement*, edited by Mike Mackey, 81–117. Powell, WY: Western History Publications.

Hansen, Arthur A., and David A. Hacker. 1974. "The Manzanar Riot: An Ethnic Perspective." *Amerasia Journal* 2:112–57.

Harding, Sandra, ed. 2004. "Rethinking Standpoint Epistemology: What is 'Strong Objectivity'?" In *The Feminist Standpoint Theory Reader: Intellectual and Political Controversies*, 127–40. New York: Routledge.

Harrison, Kimberly. 2003. "Rhetorical Rehearsals: The Construction of Ethos in Confederate Women's Civil War Diaries." *Rhetoric Review* 22 (3): 243–63. http://dx.doi.org/10.1207/S15327981RR2203_02.

Harth, Erica. 2001. *Last Witnesses: Reflections on the Wartime Internment of Japanese Americans*. 1st ed. New York: Palgrave.

Hartsock, Nancy C. M. 1998. *The Feminist Standpoint Revisited & Other Essays*. Boulder, CO: Westview.

Hasegawa, Linnea. 2004. "Articulating Identities: Rhetorical Readings of Asian American Literacy Narratives." PhD diss., University of Maryland, College Park.

Hayami, Stanley. 1942–1943. Diary. Japanese American National Museum, Los Angeles.

Hayashi, Ann Koto. 1992. "Face of the Enemy, Heart of a Patriot: Japanese-American Internment Narratives." PhD diss., Ohio State University.

Hayashi, Brian Masaru. 2004. *Democratizing the Enemy: The Japanese American Internment*. Princeton, NJ: Princeton University Press.

Heart Mountain Sentinel. 1942. "Protest Petition Sent to W.R.A. Director. Removal of Barbed Wire Fence Asked." *Heart Mountain Sentinel*, November 21, 1, 3.

Heath, Shirley Brice. 1983. *Ways with Words: Language, Life, and Work in Communities and Classrooms*. New York: Cambridge University Press.

Herrington, Anne, and Marcia Smith Curtis. 2000. *Persons in Process: Four Stories of Writing and Personal Development in College*. Urbana, IL: National Council of Teachers of English.

Herzig-Yoshinaga, Aiko. 1997. Interview by Larry Hashima and Glen Kitayama, September 11. Densho Visual History Collection, Densho.

Herzig-Yoshinaga, Aiko. 2008. Interview with the author, July 10.

Herzig-Yoshinaga, Aiko. 2009. Interview with the author, March 31.

Hirabayashi, James. 1975. "Nisei: The Quiet American? A Re-Evaluation." *Amerasia Journal* 3:114–29.

Hirabayashi, James. 1992. Interview by Megan Asaka. Accessed February 10, 2008. Densho Visual History Collection, Densho.

Hirabayashi, Lane Ryo. 1998. "Re-Reading the Archives: Intersections of Ethnography, Biography, and Autobiography in Japanese American Evacuation and Resettlement." *Peace & Change* 23 (2): 167–82. http://dx.doi.org/10.1111/0149-0508.00079.

Hirabayashi, Lane Ryo. 1999. *The Politics of Fieldwork: Research in an American Concentration Camp*. Tucson: University of Arizona Press.

Hiramine, Ann Junko. 2004. "Resisting the Normativizing of Identity through Invisible Discursive Means: The Performance of Literacy in Asian America." PhD diss., University of Washington.

Hoang, Haivan Viet. 2004. "'To Come Together and Create a Movement': Solidarity Rhetoric in the Vietnamese American Coalition." PhD diss., Ohio State University.

Hoang, Haivan. 2015. *Writing against Racial Injury: The Politics of Asian American Student Rhetoric*. Pittsburgh: University of Pittsburgh Press.

Hoffman, Stuart D. 1999. "School Texts, the Written Word, and Political Indoctrination: A Review of Moral Education Curricula in Modern Japan (1886–1997)." *History of Education* 28 (1): 87–96. http://dx.doi.org/10.1080/004676099284816.

Hohri, William Minoru. 1988. *Repairing America: An Account of the Movement for Japanese-American Redress*. Pullman: Washington State University Press.

Honda, Sachiko. 1989. "Issei Senryu." In *Frontiers of Asian American Studies: Writing, Research, and Commentary*, edited by Gail M. Nomura, Russell Endo, Stephen H. Sumida, and Russell C. Leong, 169–78. Pullman: Washington State University Press.

hooks, bell. 1984. *Feminist Theory from Margin to Center*. Boston: South End.

Horio, Teruhisa. 1988. *Educational Thought and Ideology in Modern Japan: State Authority and Intellectual Freedom*. Translated by Steven Platzer. Tokyo: University of Tokyo Press.

Hosokawa, Bill. 1969. *Nisei: The Quiet Americans*. New York: W. Morrow.

Hosokawa, Bill. 1998. "The Sentinel Story." In *Remembering Heart Mountain: Essays of Japanese American Internment in Wyoming*, edited by Mike Mackey, 63–74. Cody, WY: Western History Publications.

Huggins, Nathan. 1991. "The Deforming Mirror of Truth: Slavery and the Master Narrative of American History." *Radical History Review* 49 (Winter): 25–48.

Ichikawa, Yasashi. 1999. Interview II by Tomoyo Yamada, November 20. Densho Visual History Collection, Densho.

Ichioka, Yuji. 1980. "*Amerika Nadeshiko*: Japanese Immigrant Women in the United States, 1900–1924." *Pacific Historical Review* 49 (2): 339–57. http://dx.doi.org/10.2307/3638905.

Ichioka, Yuji. 1988. *The Issei: The World of the First Generation Japanese Immigrants, 1885–1924*. New York: Free Press.

Ichioka, Yuji. 1989. *Views from Within: The Japanese American Evacuation and Resettlement Study*. Los Angeles: Resource Development and Publications, Asian American Studies Center, University of California at Los Angeles.

Ichioka, Yuji. 2006. *Before Internment: Essays in Prewar Japanese American History*. Edited by Gordon H. Chang and Eiichiro Azuma. Stanford, CA: Stanford University Press.

Ina, Satsuki. 1998. "Tule Lake Reunion Symposium." Symposium Comments. Accessed January 21. http://www.pbs.org/childofcamp/project/remarks.html.

Ina, Satsuki. 2015. "I Know an American 'Internment' Camp When I See One." Accessed on June 1. https://www.aclu.org/blog/speak-freely/i-know-american-internment-camp-when-i-see-one.

Inada, Lawson Fusao. 1981. Preface to *No-No Boy*, by John Okada, vii–xi. Seattle: University of Washington Press.

Inada, Lawson Fusao. 2000. *Only What We Could Carry: The Japanese American Internment Experience*. Berkeley, CA: Heyday Books.

Inouye, Frank. 1943. Letter to the editor. *Heart Mountain Sentinel*, February 11, 4.

Inouye, Frank T. 1998. "Immediate Origins of the Heart Mountain Draft Resistance Movement." In *Remembering Heart Mountain: Essays on Japanese American Internment in Wyoming*, edited by Mike Mackey, 121–39. Powell, WY: Western History Publishing.

Ishizuka, Karen L. 2006. *Lost and Found: Reclaiming the Japanese American Incarceration*. Urbana: University of Illinois Press.

Ito, Kazuo. 1973. *Issei: A History of Japanese Immigrants in North America*. Seattle: Japanese Community Service.

James, Thomas. 1987. *Exile Within: The Schooling of Japanese Americans, 1942–1945*. Cambridge, MA: Harvard University Press. http://dx.doi.org/10.4159/harvard.9780674184749.

JanMohamed, Abdul R., and David Lloyd. 1990. "Introduction: Toward a Theory of Minority Discourse: What Is To Be Done?" In *The Nature and Context of Minority Discourse*, edited by Abdul R. JanMohamed and David Lloyd, 1–16. New York: Oxford University Press.

Japanese American National Museum. n.d. "Hirasaki National Resource Center." Accessed July 1. http://www.janm.org/nrc.

Jaskoski, Helen, and Mitsuye Yamada. 1988. "A MELUS Interview: Mitsuye Yamada." *MELUS* 15 (1): 97–108. http://dx.doi.org/10.2307/467043.

Kanemoto, Marion Tsutakawa. 2003. Interview by Alice Ito. Accessed February 5, 2008. Densho Visual History Collection, Densho.

Kashima, Tetsuden. 1980. "Japanese American Internees Return, 1945 to 1955: Readjustment and Social Amnesia." *Phylon* 41 (2): 107–15. http://dx.doi.org/10.2307/274964.

Kashima, Tetsuden. 1997. Foreword to *Personal Justice Denied: Report of the Commission on Wartime Relocation and Internment of Civilians*, edited by Commission on Wartime Relocation and Internment of Civilians, xxx. Seattle: Civil Liberties Public Education Fund/University of Washington Press.

Kashima, Tetsuden. 2003. *Judgment without Trial: Japanese American Imprisonment during World War II*. Seattle: University of Washington Press.

Kessler, Lauren. 1988. "Fettered Freedoms: The Journalism of World War II Japanese Internment Camps." *Journalism History* 15 (2–3): 70–8.

Kikuchi, Charles, and John Modell. 1973. *The Kikuchi Diary: Chronicle from an American Concentration Camp*. Urbana: University of Illinois Press.

Kikumura, Akemi, and Michiko Tanaka. 1981. *Through Harsh Winters: The Life of a Japanese Immigrant Woman*. Novato, CA: Chandler & Sharp.

Kim, Elaine. 1990. "Defining Asian American Realities through Literature." In *The Nature and Context of Minority Discourse*, edited by Abdul R. JanMohamed and David Lloyd, 146–70. New York: Oxford University Press.

Kinoshita, Cherry. 1997. Interview by Becky Fukuda and Tracy Lai, September 26. Densho Digital Visual Archive, Densho.

Kinoshita, Lisa M. 2001. "The Japanese Internment During World War II and the Second Generation Nisei: An Examination of Their Past and Present Coping and Adjustment." PhD diss., Pacific Graduate School of Psychology.

Kirsch, Gesa E., and Jacqueline J. Royster. 2010. "Feminist Rhetorical Practices: In Search of Excellence." *College Composition and Communication* 61 (4): 640–72.

Kitano, Harry H. L. 1976. *Japanese Americans: The Evolution of a Subculture*. 2nd ed. Englewood Cliffs, NJ: Prentice-Hall.

Kitasako, John. 1944. "Faith in American Democracy Keeps Nisei Going." *Heart Mountain Sentinel*, February 12, 1, 5.

Kobayashi, Audrey. 1995. "Birds of Passage or Squawking Ducks? Writing Across Generations of Japanese-Canadian Literature." In *Writing Across Worlds: Literature and Migration*, edited by Russell King, John Connell, and Paul White, 216–28. New York: Routledge. http://dx.doi.org/10.4324/9780203426128_chapter_14.

Kobayashi, Junko. 2005. "Bitter Sweet Home: Celebration of Biculturalism in Japanese Language Japanese American Literature, 1936–1962." PhD diss., University of Iowa.

Kochiyama, Yuri. 1981. C.W.R.I.C. statement. Collection of Aiko Herzig-Yoshinaga.

Kogawa, Joy. 1981. *Obasan*. Boston: D. R. Godine.

Koshiyama, Mits. 2001. Interview by Alice Ito. Densho Visual History Collection, Densho.

Kubota, Gloria. 1993. Interview by Frank Abe and Frank Chin. Densho Digital Visual Archive, Densho.

Kunitsugu, Kats. 1995. Interview by Paul Tsuneishi, August 22. Densho Digital Visual Archive, Densho.

Kurashige, Lon. 2001. "Resistance, Collaboration, and Manzanar Protest." *Pacific Historical Review* 70 (3): 387–417. http://dx.doi.org/10.1525/phr.2001.70.3.387.

Kurashige, Scott. 2007. "Exposing the Price of Ignorance: Teaching Asian American History in Michigan." *Journal of American History* 93 (4): 1178–85. http://dx.doi.org/10.2307/25094608.

Kurihara, Joe. 1943a. Letter. *Saturday Evening Post*, November 2. Japanese American National Museum, Los Angeles.

Kurihara, Joseph Y. 1943b. "Niseis and the Government of the United States." Japanese American National Museum, Los Angeles.

Ladies of Hunt Relocation Center. 1944. Letter to Dillon Myer, January 6. NARA 85, Folder 4. Bancroft Library, University of California, Berkeley.

Ladson-Billings, Gloria. 1995a. "But That's Just Good Teaching! The Case for Culturally Relevant Pedagogy." *Theory Into Practice* 34 (3): 159–65. http://dx.doi.org/10.1080/00405849509543675.

Ladson-Billings, Gloria. 1995b. "Toward a Theory of Culturally Relevant Pedagogy." *American Educational Research Journal* 32 (3): 465–91. http://dx.doi.org/10.3102/00028312032003465.

Lain, Brian Anderson. 2005. "Remembering Internment: The Function of Japanese American Rhetorics in Multicultural America." PhD diss., University of Iowa.

Lanham, Betty B. 1979. "Ethics and Moral Precepts Taught in Schools of Japan and the United States." *Ethos* 7 (1): 1–18. http://dx.doi.org/10.1525/eth.1979.7.1.02a00010.

Lawrence, Keith. 2005. "Toshio Mori, Richard Kim and the Masculine Ideal." In *Recovered Legacies: Authority and Identity in Early Asian American Literature*, edited by Keith Lawrence and Floyd Cheung, 207–28. Philadelphia: Temple University Press.

Lawrence, Keith, and Floyd Cheung. 2005. *Recovered Legacies: Authority and Identity in Early Asian American Literature*. Philadelphia: Temple University Press.

Lee, Josephine, Imogene L. Lim, and Yuko Matsukawa, eds. 2002. *Re/collecting Early Asian America: Essays in Cultural History*. Philadelphia: Temple University Press.

Lee, Stacey J. 1996. *Unraveling the "Model Minority" Stereotype: Listening to Asian American Youth*. New York: Teachers College Press.

Lim, Deborah K. 1990. *The Lim Report: A Research Report of Japanese Americans in American Concentration Camps during World War II*. Kearney, NE: Morris.

Lu, Min-Zhan. 1987. "From Silence to Words: Writing as Struggle." *College English* 49 (4): 437–48. http://dx.doi.org/10.2307/377860.

Lu, Min-Zhan. 2004. "An Essay on the Work of Composition: Composing English against the Order of Fast Capitalism." *College Composition and Communication* 56 (1): 16–50. http://dx.doi.org/10.2307/4140679.

Lu, Min-Zhan, and Bruce Horner. 2013. "Translingual Literacy, Language Difference, and Matters of Agency." *College English* 75 (6): 582–607.

Mackey, Mike. 2002. *A Matter of Conscience: Essays on the World War II Heart Mountain Draft Resistance Movement*. Powell, WY: Western History Publications.

Maeda, Robert J. 2001. "Isamu Noguchi: 5–7-A, Poston, Arizona." In *Last Witnesses: Reflections on the Wartime Internment of Japanese Americans*, edited by Erica Harth, 153–66. New York: Palgrave Macmillan.

Maki, Mitchell T., Harry H. L. Kitano, and S. Megan Berthold. 1999. *Achieving the Impossible Dream: How Japanese Americans Obtained Redress*. Urbana: University of Illinois Press.

Mao, LuMing. 2006. *Reading Chinese Fortune Cookie: The Making of Chinese American Rhetoric*. Logan: Utah State University Press.

Mao, LuMing, and Morris Young. 2008. Introduction to *Representations: Doing Asian American Rhetoric*, edited by LuMing Mao and Morris Young, 1–22. Logan: Utah State University Press.

Masaoka, Mike, and Bill Hosokawa. 1987. *They Call Me Moses Masaoka: An American Saga*. 1st ed. New York: William Morrow.

Mass, Amy Iwasaki. 2002. "Psychological Effects of Internment." In *A Matter of Conscience: Essays on the World War II Heart Mountain Draft Resistance Movement*, edited by Mike Mackey, 145–52. Powell, WY: Western History Publications.

Matsumoto, Valerie. 1984. "Japanese American Women during World War II." *Frontiers* 8 (1): 6–14. http://dx.doi.org/10.2307/3346082.

McKay, Susan. 2001. "Young Women's Everyday Resistance: Heart Mountain, Wyoming." In *Guilt by Association: Essays on Japanese Settlement, Internment, and Relocation in the Rocky Mountain West*, edited by Mike Mackey, 203–16. Powell, WY: Western History Publications.

Mead, Corey. 2013. "Military Recruiters Have Gone Too Far." Time Magazine, September 17. http://ideas.time.com/2013/09/17/military-recruiters-have-gone-too-far/.

Michel, Sonya. 1987. "American Women and the Discourse of the Democratic Family in World War II." In *Behind the Lines: Gender and the Two World Wars*, edited by Margaret R. Higonnet, Jane Jensen, Sonya Michel, and Margaret Collins Weitz, 154–67. New Haven, CT: Yale University Press.

Mignolo, Walter D. 1992. "On the Colonization of Amerindian Languages and Memories: Renaissance Theories of Writing and the Discontinuity of the Classical Tradition." *Comparative Studies in Society and History* 34 (2): 301–30. http://dx.doi.org/10.1017/S0010417500017709.

Millenium Seed Project. 2006. "Germinating History: 200 Year Old Seeds Spring to Life." Accessed August 11, 2015. http://www.kew.org/about/press-media/press-releases/germinating-history-200-year-old-seeds-spring-life.

Miller, Laura. 2004. "Consuming Japanese Print Media in Chicago." In *Ethnolinguistic Chicago: Language and Literacy in the City's Neighborhoods*, edited by Marcia Farr, 357–80. Mahwah, NJ: Lawrence Erlbaum.

Miller, Susan. 2002. "Writing Studies as a Mode of Inquiry." In *Rhetoric and Composition as Intellectual Work*, edited by Gary Olson, 41–54. Carbondale: Southern Illinois University Press.

Mirikitani, Janice. 1987. *Shedding Silence*. Berkeley, CA: Celestial Arts.

Miyamoto, Nobuko. 1983. *Best of Both Worlds*. Great Leap, 33 1/3 rpm.

Miyatake, Henry. 1998. Interview II by Tom Ikeda, May 4. Densho Visual History Collection, Densho.

Mizuno, Takeya. 2001. "The Creation of the 'Free' Press in Japanese-American Camps: The War Relocation Authority's Planning and Making of the Camp Newspaper Policy." *Journalism & Mass Communication Quarterly* 78 (3): 503–18. http://dx.doi.org/10.1177/107769900107800307.

Mizuno, Takeya. 2003. "Journalism under Military Guards and Searchlights: Newspaper Censorship at Japanese American Assembly Camps during World War II." *Journalism History* 29 (3): 98–106.

Molden, Danny Toshio. 1998. "Seven Miles from Independence: The War, Internee Identity and the 'Manzanar Free Press.'" PhD diss., University of Minnesota.

Moll, Luis C., and Norma González. 1994. "Lessons from Research with Language Minority Children." *Journal of Reading Behavior* 26 (4): 439–56.

Monberg, Terese Guinsatao. 2002. "Re-Positioning Ethos: Rhetorics of Hybridity and the Filipino American National Historical Society." PhD diss., Rensselaer Polytechnic Institute.

Monberg, Terese Guinsatao. 2008. "Listening for Legacies; or, How I Began to Hear Dorothy Laigo Cordova, the Pinay behind the Podium Known as FANHS" In *Representations: Doing Asian American Rhetoric*, edited by LuMing Mao and Morris Young, 83–105. Logan: Utah State University Press.

Mortensen, Peter, and Gesa E. Kirsch. 1993. "On Authority in the Study of Writing." *College Composition and Communication* 44 (4): 556–72. http://dx.doi.org/10.2307/358390.

Mothers of Topaz. 1944. The Mothers of American Citizens of Japanese Descent Request that Civil Rights Be Restored to Their Children, March 11. NARA 9, H466. Bancroft Library, University of California, Berkeley.

Mother's Society of Minidoka. 1944. Letter to the President and Mrs. Roosevelt, February 20. Japanese American National Museum, Los Angeles.

Muller, Eric L. 2001. *Free to Die for Their Country: The Story of the Japanese American Draft Resisters in World War II*. Chicago: University of Chicago Press.

Murray, Alice Yang. 2008. *Historical Memories of the Japanese American Internment and the Struggle for Redress*. Stanford, CA: Stanford University Press.

Myer, Dillon S. 1971. *Uprooted Americans: The Japanese Americans and the War Relocation Authority during World War II*. Tucson: University of Arizona Press.

Nagata, Donna K. 1993. *Legacy of Injustice: Exploring the Cross-Generational Impact of the Japanese American Internment*. New York: Plenum.

Nagata, Donna K. 1994. "Coping with Internment: A Nisei Woman's Perspective." In *Women Creating Lives: Identities, Resilience, and Resistance*, edited by Carol F. Franz and Abigail J. Stewart, 115–26. Boulder, CO: Westview.

Nagata, Donna K. 2000. "World War II Internment and the Relationships of Nisei Women." In *Relationships among Asian American Women*, edited by Jean Lau Chin, 49–70. Washington, DC: American Psychological Association. http://dx.doi.org/10.1037/10349-004.

Nakadate, Paul. 1944. Letter to the editor. *Heart Mountain Sentinel*, March 18, 4.

Nakahara, Mary. 1942a. "The Bordered World." Vol. 1. April 3–June 30. Japanese American National Museum, Los Angeles.

Nakahara, Mary. 1942b. "The Bordered World." Vol. 2. July 2–November 26. Japanese American National Museum, Los Angeles.

Nakano, Mei. 1990. *Japanese American Women: Three Generations, 1890–1990*. Berkeley, CA: Mina Press.

Nakashima, Ted. 1942. "Concentration Camp: US Style." *New Republic* 106 (24): 822–23.

Nam, Victoria. 2001. *Yell-Oh Girls!: Emerging Voices Explore Culture, Identity, and Growing Up Asian American*. 1st ed. New York: Quill.

Nash, Phil Tajitsu. 1999. "In Memoriam: Michi Nishiura Weglyn." *Amerasia Journal* 25 (1): iv–viii.

Nelson, Douglas W. 1976. *Heart Mountain: The History of an American Concentration Camp*. Madison: State Historical Society of Wisconsin for the Dept. of History, University of Wisconsin.

Nishimoto, Richard S. 1995. *Inside An American Concentration Camp: Japanese American Resistance at Poston, Arizona*. Edited by Lane Ryo Hirabayashi. Tucson: University of Arizona Press.

Niiya, Brian, and JANM. 2001. *Encyclopedia of Japanese American History: An A-to-Z Reference from 1868 to the Present*. Updated ed. New York: Facts on File.

Nomura, Gail. 2001. "*Tsugiki*, a Grafting: A History of a Japanese Pioneer Woman in Washington State." In *Women in Pacific Northwest History*, edited by Karen J. Blair, 284–307. Seattle: University of Washington Press.

Nomura, Shiori. 2010. "The Voices of Women on Birth Control and Childcare: A Japanese Immigrant Newspaper in the Early Twentieth-Century USA." *Japan Forum* 21 (2): 255–76. http://dx.doi.org/10.1080/09555801003679165.

Northwest Nikkei. 1996. "What Is Nikkei Culture? Panelists Define and Discuss Japanese American Culture and Its Preservation." *Northwest Nikkei*. April 15, 1.

Nunley, Vorris L. 2004. "From the Harbor to Da Academic Hood: Hush Harbors and an African American Rhetorical Tradition." In *African American Rhetoric(s): Interdisciplinary Perspectives*, edited by Elaine B. Richardson and Ronald L. Jackson II, 221–41. Carbondale: Southern Illinois University Press.

O'Brien, David J., and Stephen Fugita. 1991. *The Japanese American Experience*. Bloomington: Indiana University Press.

Odo, Franklin. 2002. *The Columbia Documentary History of the Asian American Experience*. New York: Columbia University Press.
Okabe, Roichi. 2007. "The Concept of Rhetorical Competence and Sensitivity Revisited: From Western and Eastern Perspectives." *China Media Research* 3 (4): 74–81.
Okawa, Gail. 1998. "Coming (in)to Consciousness: One Asian American Teacher's Journey into Activist Teaching and Research." In *Under Construction: Working at the Intersections of Composition Theory, Research, and Practice*, edited by Christine Farris and Chris M. Anson, 282–301. Logan: Utah State University Press.
Okawa, Gail Y. 2003. "Letters to Our Forebears: Reconnecting Generations through Writing." *English Journal* 92 (6): 47–51. http://dx.doi.org/10.2307/3650534.
Okawa, Gail Y. 2008. "Unbundling: Archival Research and Japanese American Communal Memory of U.S. Justice Department Internment, 1941–45." In *Beyond the Archives: Research as a Lived Process*, edited by Gesa E. Kirsch and Liz Rohan, 93–106. Carbondale: Southern Illinois University.
Okawa, Gail Y. 2011. "Putting Their Lives on the Line: Personal Narrative as Political Discourse among Japanese Petitioners in American World War II Internment." *College English* 74 (1): 50–68.
Okihiro, Gary Y. 1973. "Japanese Resistance in America's Concentration Camps: A Re-evaluation." *Amerasia Journal* 2:20–34.
Okihiro, Gary. 1977a. "Review of 'Years of Infamy.'" *Amerasia Journal* 4 (1): 167–71.
Okihiro, Gary Y. 1977b. "Tule Lake under Martial Law: A Study in Japanese Resistance." *Journal of Ethnic Studies* 5 (3): 71–85.
Okihiro, Gary Y. 1984. "Religion and Resistance in America's Concentration Camps." *Phylon* 45 (3): 220–33. http://dx.doi.org/10.2307/274406.
Okihiro, Gary Y. 2001. "Japanese American Resistance." In *The Columbia Guide to Asian American History*, 164–74. New York: Columbia Press.
Olneck, Michael R. 1989. "Americanization and the Education of Immigrants, 1900–1925: An Analysis of Symbolic Action." *American Journal of Education* 97 (4): 398–423. http://dx.doi.org/10.1086/443935.
Omatsu, Glenn. 1986–1987. "Always a Rebel: An Interview with Kazu Iijima." *Amerasia Journal* 13 (2): 83–98.
Omori, Emiko. 1999. *Rabbit in the Moon*. Directed by Emiko Omori. San Francisco, CA: Wabi-Sabi Productions.
Omura, James. 1944a. "Gila Nisei Send Petition to President." *Rocky Shimpo*, May 22.
Omura, James. 1944b. "Heart Mtn. Mothers Ask Nisei Ruling." *Rocky Shimpo*, March 13.
Omura, James. 1989. "Japanese American Journalism during World War II." In *Frontiers of Asian American Studies: Writing, Research, and Commentary*, edited by Gail M. Nomura, Russell Endo, Stephen H. Sumida, and Russell C. Leong, 71–80. Pullman: Washington State University Press.
Ono, Kent Alan. 1992. "Representations of Resistance and Subjectivity in Japanese American Discourse." PhD diss., University of Iowa.

Osajima, Keith. 1988. "Asian Americans as the Model Minority: An Analysis of the Popular Press Image in the 1960s and 1980s." In *Reflections on Shattered Windows: Promises and Prospects for Asian American Studies*, edited by Gary Y. Okihiro, Shirley Hune, Arthur A. Hansen, and John M. Liu, 165–74. Pullman: Washington State University Press.

Osborn, Susan. 1991. "Revision/Re-Vision: A Feminist Writing Class." *Rhetoric Review* 9 (2): 258–73. http://dx.doi.org/10.1080/07350199109388932.

Oye, Mari Michener. 2008. "Redress." *Pacific Citizen*, December, 53.

Palumbo-Liu, David. 1999. "Appendix: Model Minority Discourse and the Course of Healing." In *Asian/American: Historical Crossings of a Racial Frontier*, 395–466. Stanford, CA: Stanford University Press.

Partridge, Jeffrey F. L. 2004. "Aiiieeeee! and the Asian American Literary Movement: A Conversation with Shawn Wong." *MELUS* 29 (3/4): 91–102. http://dx.doi.org/10.2307/4141844.

Pittman, Coretta. 2006. "Black Women Writers and the Trouble with *Ethos*: Harriet Jacobs, Billie Holiday, and Sister Souljah." *Rhetoric Society Quarterly* 37 (1): 43–70. http://dx.doi.org/10.1080/02773940600860074.

Poston Women's Club. 1944. "Draft Resolution in Response to the Draft w/ Signatures, January 28, 1944." Chica Sugino Papers. Japanese American National Museum, Los Angeles.

Powell, Katrina M. 2007. "Virginia Mountain Women Writing to Government Officials: Letters of Request as Social Participation." In *Women and Literacy: Local and Global Inquiries for a New Century*, edited by Beth Daniell and Peter Mortensen, 71–90. New York: Lawrence Erlbaum.

Powell, Malea. 2002. "Rhetorics of Survivance: How American Indians Use Writing." *College Composition and Communication* 53 (3): 396–434. http://dx.doi.org/10.2307/1512132.

Pratt, Mary Louise. 1987. "Linguistic Utopias." In *The Linguistics of Writing: Arguments between Language and Literature*, edited by Nigel Fabb, Derek Attridge, Alan Durant, and Colin MacCabe, 48–66. Manchester: Manchester University Press.

Prendergast, Catherine. 1998. "Race: The Absent Presence in Composition Studies." *College Composition and Communication* 50 (1): 36–53. http://dx.doi.org/10.2307/358351.

Ratcliffe, Krista. 2005. *Rhetorical Listening: Identification, Gender, Whiteness*. Carbondale: Southern Illinois University Press.

Reynolds, Nedra. 1993. "*Ethos* as Location: New Sites for Understanding Discursive Authority." *Rhetoric Review* 11 (2): 325–38. http://dx.doi.org/10.1080/07350199309389009.

Rich, Adrienne. 1972. "When We Dead Awaken: Writing as Re-Vision." *College English* 34 (1): 18–30. http://dx.doi.org/10.2307/375215.

Richardson, Elaine. 2003. *African American Literacies*. New York: Routledge. http://dx.doi.org/10.4324/9780203166550.

Roosevelt, Eleanor. 1944. "Reply to Mrs. Tanagi and The Mothers' Society of Minidoka, March 4, 1944." Collection of Sharon Tanagi Aburano.

Roozen, Kevin. 2009. "From Journals to Journalism: Tracing Trajectories of Literate Development." *College Composition and Communication* 60 (3): 541–72.

Royster, Jacqueline Jones. 2000. *Traces of a Stream: Literacy and Social Change among African American Women*. Pittsburgh: University of Pittsburgh Press.

Royster, Jacqueline Jones, and Gesa E. Kirsch. 2012. *Feminist Rhetorical Practices: New Horizons for Rhetoric, Composition and Literacy Studies*. Carbondale: Southern Illinois University Press.

Rubinger, Richard. 2007. *Popular Literacy in Early Modern Japan*. Honolulu: University of Hawai'i Press.

Sakoda, James. 1944. "Nisei Draft." BANC MSS67/14 c. Bancroft Library, University of California, Berkeley.

Schweik, Susan. 1989. "The 'Pre-Poetics' of Internment: The Example of Toyo Suyemoto." *American Literary History* 1 (1): 89–109. http://dx.doi.org/10.1093/alh/1.1.89.

Schweik, Susan M. 1991. *A Gulf So Deeply Cut: American Women Poets and the Second World War*. Madison: University of Wisconsin Press.

Scott, James C. 1990. *Domination and the Arts of Resistance: Hidden Transcripts*. New Haven: Yale University Press.

Several, Michael. 1997. "Ninomiya Kinjiro: Background Information." http://www.publicartinla.com/Downtown/Little_Tokyo/kinjiro.html.

Shafer, Harry M. 1925. "Tendencies in Immigrant Education." *Los Angeles School Journal* 9 (5): 9–11, 46.

Shibata, Masako. 2004. "Controlling National Identity and Reshaping the Role of Education: The Vision of State Formation in Meiji Japan and the German *Kaiserreich*." *History of Education* 33 (1): 75–85. http://dx.doi.org/10.1080/00467600410001648788.

Shimabukuro, Robert Sadamu. 2001. *Born in Seattle: The Campaign for Japanese American Redress*. Seattle: University of Washington Press.

Shimabukuro, Robert. 2008. "Re: Ch 2 and 3." Email to author, November 20.

Shimbori, Michiya. 1960. "A Historical and Social Note on Moral Education in Japan." *Comparative Education Review* 4 (2): 97–101. http://dx.doi.org/10.1086/444837.

Shimomura, Roger. 2003. Interview by Alice Ito and Mayumi Tsutakawa, March 18 and 20. Densho Visual History Collection, Densho.

Silva, Noenoe K. 2004. *Aloha Betrayed: Native Hawaiian Resistance to American Colonialism*. Durham, NC: Duke University Press. http://dx.doi.org/10.1215/9780822386223.

Smitherman, Geneva. 1977. *Talkin and Testifyin: The Language of Black America*. Boston: Houghton Mifflin.

Soga, Keiho, Taisanboku Mori, Sojin Takei, and Muin Pzaki. 1983. *Poets behind Barbed Wire*. Translated by Jiro Nakano and Kay Nakano. Honolulu: Bamboo Ridge.

Spivak, Gayatri Chakravorty. 1987. *In Other Worlds: Essays in Cultural Politics*. New York: Methuen.

Streamas, John. 2005. "Toyo Suyemoto, Ansel Adams, and the Landscape of Justice." In *Recovered Legacies: Authority and Identity in Early Asian American Literature*, edited by Keith Lawrence and Floyd Cheung, 141–57. Philadelphia: Temple University Press.

Sugino, Chica. 1942. Daily planner. Chica Sugino Papers. Japanese American National Museum, Los Angeles.

Sugino, Chica. 1943a. "EVACUEE, MY EVACUEE." Chica Sugino Papers. Japanese American National Museum, Los Angeles.

Sugino, Chica. 1943b. Letter to Gale Seaman, October 4. Chica Sugino Papers. Japanese American National Museum, Los Angeles.

Sugino, Chica. 1943c. Letter to Mabelle Shelp, March 20. Chica Sugino Papers. Japanese American National Museum, Los Angeles.

Sugino, Chica. n.d. "The Barbed Wires." Chica Sugino Papers. Japanese American National Museum, Los Angeles.

Sumida, Stephen H. 1988. "Hawaii, the Northwest, and Asia: Localism and Local Literary Developments in the Creation of an Asian Immigrants' Sensibility." *Seattle Review* 11:9–18.

Sumida, Stephen H. 1998. "East of California: Points of Origin in Asian American Studies." *Journal of Asian American Studies* 1 (1): 83–100. http://dx.doi.org/10.1353/jaas.1998.0012.

Suyemoto, Toyo. 1942. "Gain." *Trek* 1: 6.

Suyemoto, Toyo. 2007. *I Call To Remembrance: Toyo Suyemoto's Years of Internment*. Edited by Susan B. Richardson. New Brunswick, NJ: Rutgers University Press.

Suzuki, Peter T. 1976. "The Ethnolingustics of Japanese Americans in the Wartime Camps." *Anthropological Linguistics* 18 (9): 416–27.

Suzuki, Peter T. 1981. "Anthropologists in the Wartime Camps for Japanese Americans: A Documentary Study." *Dialectical Anthropology* 6 (1): 23–60. http://dx.doi.org/10.1007/BF02068210.

Suzuki, Peter T. 1986. "The University of California Japanese Evacuation and Resettlement Study: A Prolegomenon." *Dialectical Anthropology* 10 (3-4): 189–213. http://dx.doi.org/10.1007/BF02343105.

Takahashi, Jere. 1997. *Nisei/Sansei: Shifting Japanese American Identities and Politics*. Philadelphia: Temple University Press.

Takahashi Cates, Rita. 1980. "Comparative Administration and Management of Five War Relocation Authority Camps: America's Incarceration of Persons of Japanese Descent during World War II." PhD diss., University of Pittsburgh.

Takaki, Ronald T. 1998. *Strangers from a Different Shore: A History of Asian Americans*. Updated and rev. ed. Boston: Little, Brown.

Takezawa, Yasuko I. 1995. *Breaking the Silence: Redress and Japanese American Ethnicity*. Ithaca: Cornell University Press.

Tamura, Eileen. 1994. *Americanization, Acculturation, and Ethnic Identity: The Nisei Generation in Hawaii*. Urbana: University of Illinois Press.

Tateishi, Carol. 2007–2008. "Taking a Chance with Words: Why Are the Asian American Kids Silent in Class?" *Rethinking Schools* 22 (2): 20–5.

Tirrell, Lynne. 1993. "Definition and Power: Toward Authority without Privilege." *Hypatia* 8 (4): 1–34. http://dx.doi.org/10.1111/j.1527-2001.1993.tb00273.x.

Topaz Citizens for the Principles of American Democracy. 1944. "Recommendations of Topaz Citizens for the Principles of American Democracy." BANC MSS 67/14 c, Reel 333, Bancroft Library, University of California, Berkeley.

Topaz Times. 1943. "Text of Resolution." *Topaz Times*, February 15.

Topaz Times. 1944. "1141 Mothers Sign Petition." *Topaz Times*, March 15.

Trimbur, John. 1989. "Consensus and Difference in Collaborative Learning." *College English* 51 (6): 602–16. http://dx.doi.org/10.2307/377955.

US Commission on Wartime Relocation and Internment of Civilians. 1997. *Personal Justice Denied*. Washington, DC: Civil Liberties Public Education Fund/Seattle: University of Washington Press.

Uchida, Yoshiko. 1943. Diary. Bancroft Library, University of California, Berkeley.

Uchida, Yoshiko. 1976. *The Rooster Who Understood Japanese*. New York: Scribner.

Uchida, Yoshiko. 1982. *Desert Exile: The Uprooting of a Japanese American Family*. Seattle: University of Washington Press.

Ueno, Harry Y., Sue Kunitomi Embrey, Arthur A. Hansen, and Betty Kulberg Mitson. 1986. *Manzanar Martyr: An Interview with Harry Y. Ueno*. 1st ed. Fullerton: Oral History Program, California State University.

Villanueva, Victor. 2004. "'Memoria' Is a Friend of Ours: On the Discourse of Color." *College English* 67 (1): 9–19. http://dx.doi.org/10.2307/4140722.

Wacquant, Loïc. 2010. "Class, Race, and Hyperincarceration in Revanchist America." *Daedulus* (Summer): 75–90.

War Relocation Authority. 1944. WRA Memo: Emergency Instruction, February 21. Japanese American National Museum, Los Angeles.

Weglyn, Michi. 1976. *Years of Infamy: The Untold Story of America's Concentration Camps*. New York: Morrow.

Wells, Susan. 1996. "Rogue Cops and Health Care: What Do We Want from Public Writing?" *College Composition and Communication* 47 (3): 325–41. http://dx.doi.org/10.2307/358292.

Wu, Hui. 2007. "Writing and Teaching behind Barbed Wire: An Exiled Composition Class in a Japanese-American Internment Camp." *College Composition and Communication* 59 (2): 237–62.

Yamada, Mitsuye. 1976. *Camp Notes and Other Poems*. San Lorenzo, CA: Shameless Hussy Press.

Yamada, Mitsuye. 1983. "Invisibility Is an Unnatural Disaster: Reflections of an Asian American Woman." In *This Bridge Called My Back: Writings By Radical*

Women of Color, edited by Cherríe Moraga and Gloria Anzaldùa, 35–40. New York: Kitchen Table, Women of Color Press.

Yamada, Mitsuye. 2001. "Legacy of Silence (1)." In *Last Witnesses: Reflections on the Wartime Internment of Japanese Americans*, edited by Erica Harth, 35–44. New York: Palgrave Macmillan.

Yamada, Mitsuye. 2002. Interview by Alice Ito, October 9 and 10. Densho Visual History Collection, Densho.

Yamada, Mitsuye, Joe Yasutake, and Tosh Yasutake. 2002. Interview by Alice Ito and Jeni Yamada, October 8 and 9. Densho Visual History Collection, Densho.

Yamamoto, Traise. 1999. *Masking Selves, Making Subjects: Japanese American Women, Identity, and the Body*. Berkeley: University of California Press.

Yamasaki, James. 2003. Camp journal. Japanese American National Museum, Los Angeles.

Yasui, Min. 1944. "Nisei and the Selective Service." *Minidoka Irrigator*, March 11.

Yogi, Stan. 1997. "Japanese American Literature." In *An Interethnic Companion to Asian American Literature*, edited by King-Kok Cheung, 125–55. Cambridge: Cambridge University Press.

Yoo, David. 2000. *Growing Up Nisei: Race, Generation, and Culture among Japanese Americans of California, 1924–49*. Urbana: University of Illinois Press.

Yoon, K. Hyoejin. 2003. "The Subjects of Critical Pedagogy and Composition: The Asian American Teacher-Intellectual and the Problem of Affect." PhD diss., State University of New York at Albany.

Yosso, Tara J. 2005. "Whose Culture Has Capital? A Critical Race Theory Discussion of Community Cultural Wealth." *Race, Ethnicity and Education* 8 (1): 69–91. http://dx.doi.org/10.1080/1361332052000341006.

Young, Morris. 2004. *Minor Re/Visions: Asian American Literacy Narratives as a Rhetoric of Citizenship*. Carbondale: Southern Illinois University Press.

Young, Vershawn Ashanti. 2007. *Your Average Nigga: Performing Race, Literacy, and Masculinity*. Detroit: Wayne State University Press.

Zaeske, Susan. 2002. "Signatures of Citizenship: The Rhetoric of Women's Antislavery Petitions." *Quarterly Journal of Speech* 88 (2): 147–68. http://dx.doi.org/10.1080/00335630209384368.

Zaeske, Susan. 2003. *Signatures of Citizenship: Petitioning, Antislavery, and Women's Political Identity*. Chapel Hill: University of North Carolina Press.

Zeiger, Susan. 1996. "She Didn't Raise Her Boy to Be a Slacker: Motherhood, Conscription, and the Culture of the First World War." *Feminist Studies* 22 (1): 6–39. http://dx.doi.org/10.2307/3178245.

Zinn, Howard. 2001. *A People's History of the United States, 1492–Present*. New York: Perennial Classics.

INDEX